A MODERN METHOD FOR GUITAR

WILLIAM LEAVITT

VOLUMES **1** **2** **3** COMPLETE

MW00852706

To access the accompanying audio and video files, go to www.halleonard.com/mylibrary and enter the code found on the first page of this book. This will grant you instant access to every example. Examples with accompanying media are marked with these two icons:

Video   Audio

Editor in Chief: Jonathan Feist
Senior Vice President of Online Learning and Continuing Education/CEO of Berklee Online: Debbie Cavalier
Vice President of Enrollment Marketing and Management: Mike King
Vice President of Academic Strategy: Carin Nuernberg
Editorial Consultants: Larry Baione and Charles Chapman

RECORDINGS

Video, Vol. 1: Larry Baione, Guitar; Produced by Craig Reed

Audio, Vols. 1 and 2: Charles Chapman

Audio, Vol. 3: Larry Baione, Guitar; Engineered by Andy Edelstein

ISBN 978-0-87639-199-0

Berklee
Press

1140 Boylston Street
Boston, MA 02215-3693 USA
(617) 747-2146

Visit Berklee Press Online at
www.berkleepress.com

Berklee Online

Study music online at
online.berklee.edu

DISTRIBUTED BY

HAL•LEONARD®
7777 W. BLUEMOUND RD. P.O. BOX 13819
MILWAUKEE, WISCONSIN 53213

Visit Hal Leonard Online
www.halleonard.com

Berklee Press, a publishing activity of Berklee College of Music, is a not-for-profit educational publisher.
Available proceeds from the sales of our products are contributed to the scholarship funds of the college.

A MODERN
METHOD
FOR GUITAR

william leavitt

volume

Introduction

This book has been specifically designed to accomplish two things:

1. To teach the student to *read* music.

Reading "crutches" have been eliminated as much as possible. Fingering and counting indications have been kept at what I consider a sensible minimum.

2. For the gradual development of dexterity in *both* hands.

This is the physical part of learning to play the guitar and as such cannot be rushed. Practice all material slowly enough to maintain an even tempo. Do not skip or "slight" anything, and also do not attempt to "completely perfect" any one lesson before going on. Playing technique is an accumulative process and you will find that each time you review material already studied it will seem easier to play. (Slow, steady practice and constant review will eventually lead to speed and accuracy.)

I should like to mention at this point that all music presented for study on these pages is original and has been created especially for the guitar. *Each* composition has been designed to advance the student's musical knowledge and playing ability, and yet be as musical as possible. There is no student/teacher division in the duets; both guitar parts are written to be studied by the pupil, and almost all parts will musically stand alone.

I have not included any "old favorites," as guitar arrangements of these songs are available in many existing publications. (Also, you do not learn to *read* music by playing melodies that are familiar to you.)

I have not tried to make this book into a music dictionary by cramming it with pages filled with nothing but musical terms and markings, as it is considerably more important to give the student as much music to play as possible. (The most common and necessary terms and markings are, of course, used and explained. If further information is desired, some very excellent music dictionaries in soft cover editions can be obtained at a small cost.)

I do feel, however, that with this method (as with all others), you must search out additional material to practice, as your ultimate ability depends entirely on how much reading and playing you do.

So good luck, and have fun.

Wm. G. Leavitt

Contents

It is important that the following material be covered in consecutive order. The index on page 126 is for reference purposes only and will prove valuable for review or concentration on specific techniques.

About The Author

William Leavitt was a long-time chair of Berklee's Guitar Department, serving from 1965 to 1990. He had a profound influence on Berklee's guitar curriculum, as well as jazz guitar education worldwide, and he mentored thousands of musicians. As a performer and/or arranger, he worked with many renowned artists, such as Ella Fitzgerald, Andy Williams, and Patti Page.

SECTION ONE

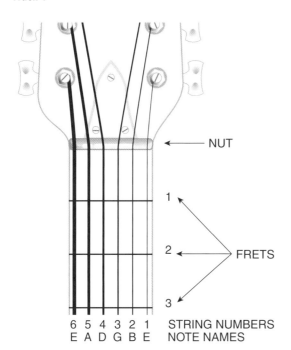

NUT

1
2 → FRETS
3

6 5 4 3 2 1   STRING NUMBERS
E A D G B E   NOTE NAMES

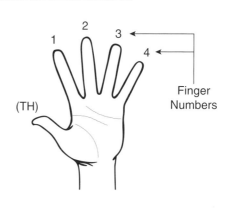

1 2 3 4
(TH)   Finger Numbers

TO TUNE THE GUITAR: (using piano or pitch pipe)

1. Tune the open 1st string to the first E above middle C.
2. Press the 2nd string down at the fifth fret and tune (2nd string) until it sounds exactly the same as the open 1st string.
3. Press the 3rd string down at the fourth fret and tune (3rd string) until it sounds exactly the same as the open 2nd string.
4. Press the 4th string at the fifth fret and tune to the open 3rd string.
5. Press the 5th string at the fifth fret and tune to the open 4th string
6. Press the 6th string at the fifth fret and tune to the open 5th string

THE STAFF: consists of five lines and four spaces, and is divided into *measures* by *bar lines*.

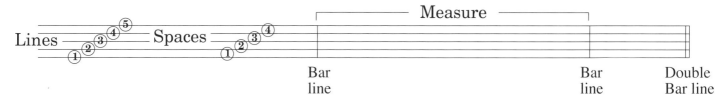

Measure

Lines   Spaces

Bar line   Bar line   Double Bar line

CLEF SIGN: Guitar music is written in the *treble* (or "G") *clef.* The number of sharps (♯) or flats (♭) found next to the clef sign indicate the key signature (to be explained more fully later).

"G" clef shows the position of the note G

COMMON TIME VALUE OF THE NOTES:

Whole note   Half notes   Quarter notes   Eighth notes (in groups) (or singly)

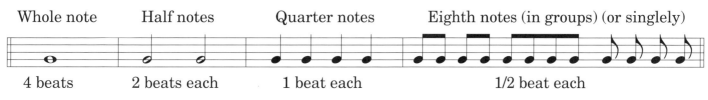

4 beats   2 beats each   1 beat each   1/2 beat each

(Continued on next page)

TIME SIGNATURES: Next to the clef sign (at the beginning of a composition), locate the two numbers (like a fraction) or a symbol that represents these numbers. The top number tells how many beats (or counts) in a measure, and the bottom number indicates what kind of note gets one beat.

EXAMPLE: $\frac{4}{4}$ means four quarters, or four beats per measure, with a quarter note receiving one beat or *count*. The symbol is **C** .

Notes in the First Position
No sharps or flats—Key of C major.

Order of the notes going up the scale:
A B C D E F G, A B C D E F G, A B...
Start at any point and read left to right.

■ **EXERCISE 1**

Track 2

4

❚ Read the *notes*, not the fingering. Fingering numbers will eventually be omitted.

■ **EXERCISE 2**
Track 3

hold notes down

■ **EXERCISE 3**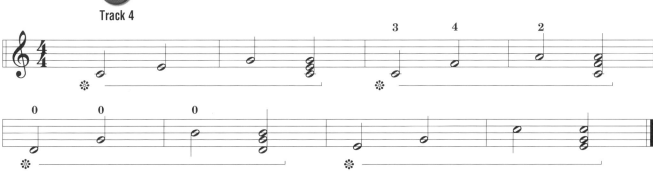
Track 4

■ **EXERCISE 4**
Track 5

count 1 2 3 4   1 2 3 4 etc.

Sea to Sea (duet)

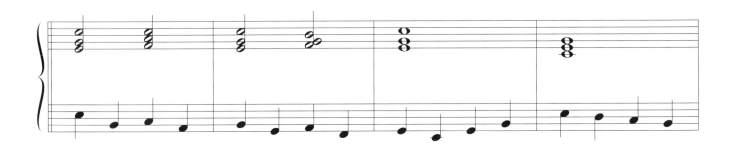

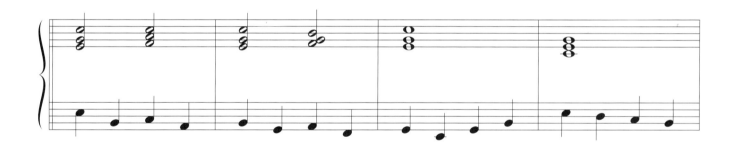

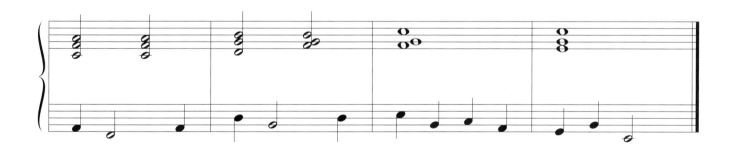

Starting on C one *octave* higher than C found on the 5th string, we complete the *upper register* of the first position.

7

■ **EXERCISE 5**

Track 7

■ **EXERCISE 6**

Track 8

Note and Chord Review

■ **EXERCISE 7**

Track 9

■ **EXERCISE 8**

Track 10

Regular review of all material is a must!

9–11 Track 11

One, Two, Three, Four (duet)

Tempo (Speed): Moderate 4

12 **Track 12**

Rhythm Accompaniment

(Chord symbol
or name)

strum again for each diagonal line

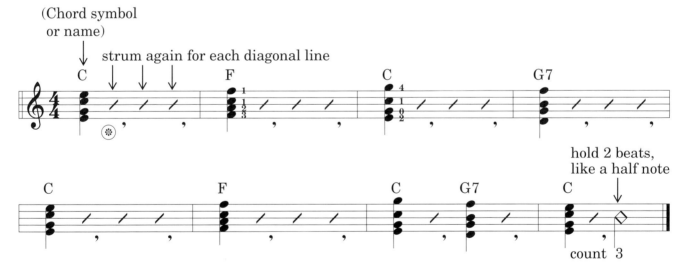

✳ A better rhythmic pulse is produced if you relax left-hand pressure at these points (').

However, do not remove fingers from strings. Also, if open strings are involved, mute them with the side of the right hand at the same instant that you relax left-hand pressure.

■ *Ledger lines* are added below or above the staff for notes too low or too high to appear on the staff.

13   Track 13

■ **EXERCISE 9**

Review

Complete first position—Key of C major.

■ EXERCISE 10

Imitation Duet

(1st Guitar)

(2nd Guitar)

Sharps and Flats

A note that is not altered by a sharp or flat is called *natural*.

■ A *sharp* (♯) raises the note a half tone (one fret). A *flat* (♭) lowers the note a half tone (one fret).

❙ When a sharp or flat appears in the *key signature* (between the clef sign and the time signature), it is used throughout the entire piece.

❙ When a sharp or flat that is not in the key signature appears in the piece, it is called an *accidental* and is used only for the remainder of that measure. The next bar line cancels it out.

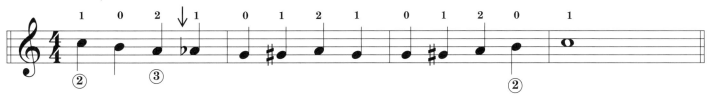

❙ The natural sign (♮) is used to cancel out accidentals within the same measure. It is also used as a reminder that the bar line has cancelled the accidental.

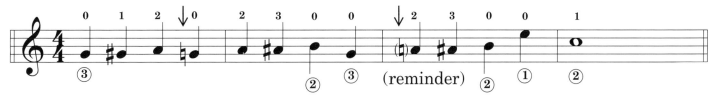

❙ When the natural sign is used to cancel a sharp or flat found in the key signature, cancellation is good only for the remainder of the measure.

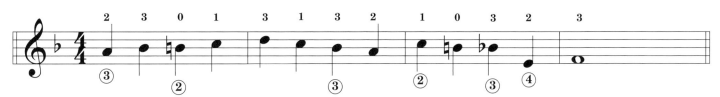

■ **EXERCISE**

15

Here We Go Again (duet)

❋ *Mute,* or deaden, the 5th string by lightly touching it with the side of the third finger so it will not sound.

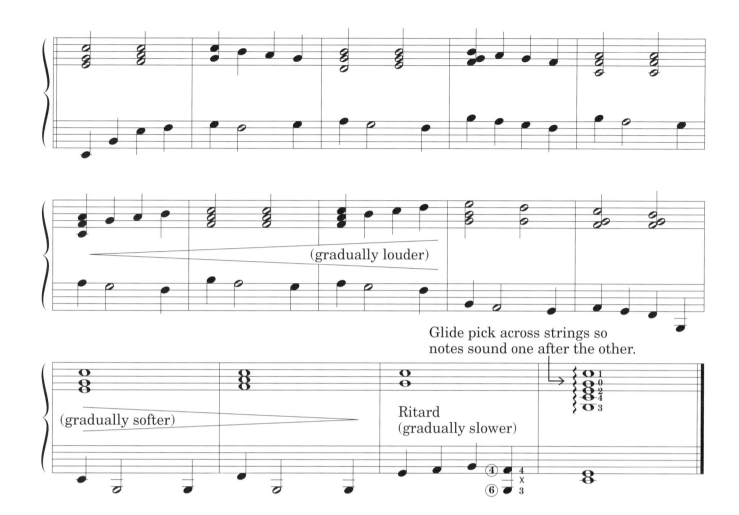

(gradually louder)

Glide pick across strings so
notes sound one after the other.

(gradually softer)

Ritard
(gradually slower)

23   Track 17

Rhythm Accompaniment
Bass Notes and Chords

All chord symbols (names) appearing as only a letter are assumed to be *major* chords. A letter followed by the number "7" represents *dominant 7* chords. A letter followed by a small "m" indicates *minor*.

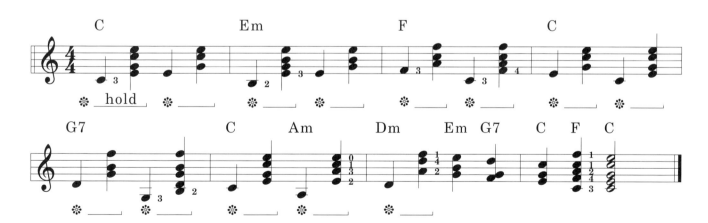

Do not skip or "slight" any lesson material.

Eighth Notes—Counting and Picking

■ **EXERCISE 1**

■ **EXERCISE 2**

❋ *Fermata* means "hold."

⌢ is a fermata. It indicates to hold the note.

Review of all material is a must.

EXERCISE 3

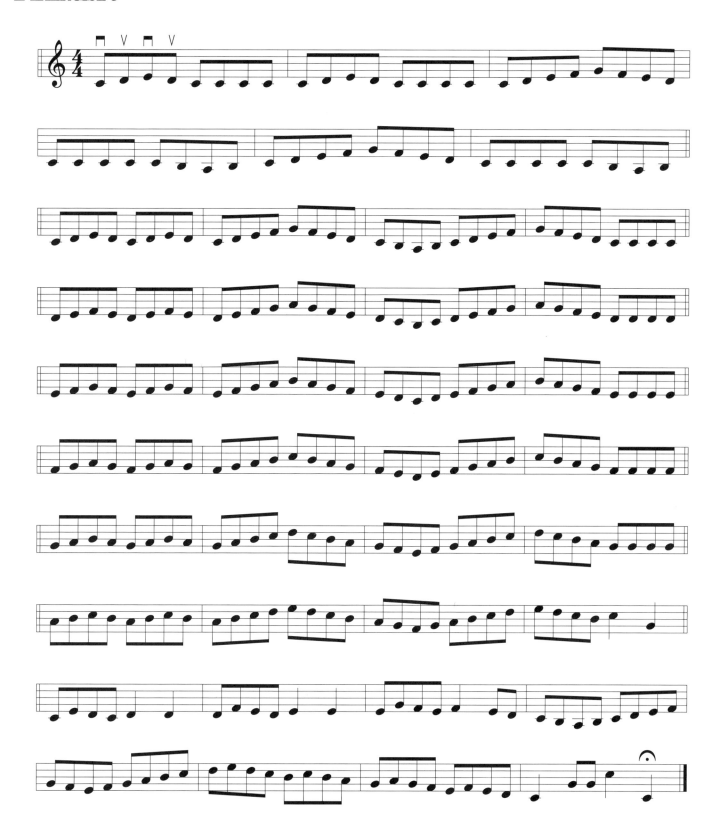

Etude No. 1 (duet)

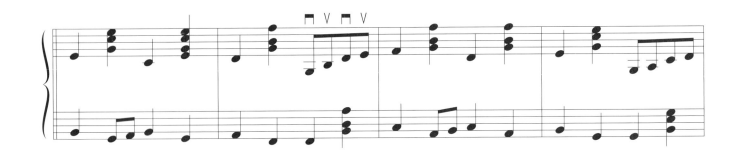

Fine
(the end)

Rests, Tied Notes, Dotted Notes

COMMON TIME VALUES OF RESTS (periods of silence):

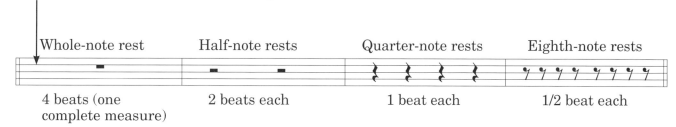

Whole-note rest	Half-note rests	Quarter-note rests	Eighth-note rests
4 beats (one complete measure)	2 beats each	1 beat each	1/2 beat each

TIED NOTES: When two notes are "tied" together with a curved line, only the first note is picked. The second note is merely held and counted.

DOTTED NOTES: A "dot" placed after any note increases the time value of the note by one-half. Or you may say a "dot" found next to any note receives half the time value of the note itself.

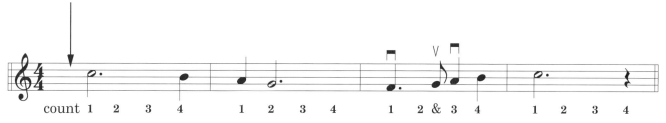

This is the same example as shown above but using "tied" notes. . . .

■ **EXERCISE**

❚ Count aloud as you play.

21

Etude No. 2 (duet)

(1st Guitar)

(2nd Guitar) "Tacet" (remain silent)

Fine

32

First Solo

Solo arrangement: with melody and accompaniment.

Accompaniment chord is
played on the 2nd beat

Melody note is picked on the 1st beat
and held while chord is played

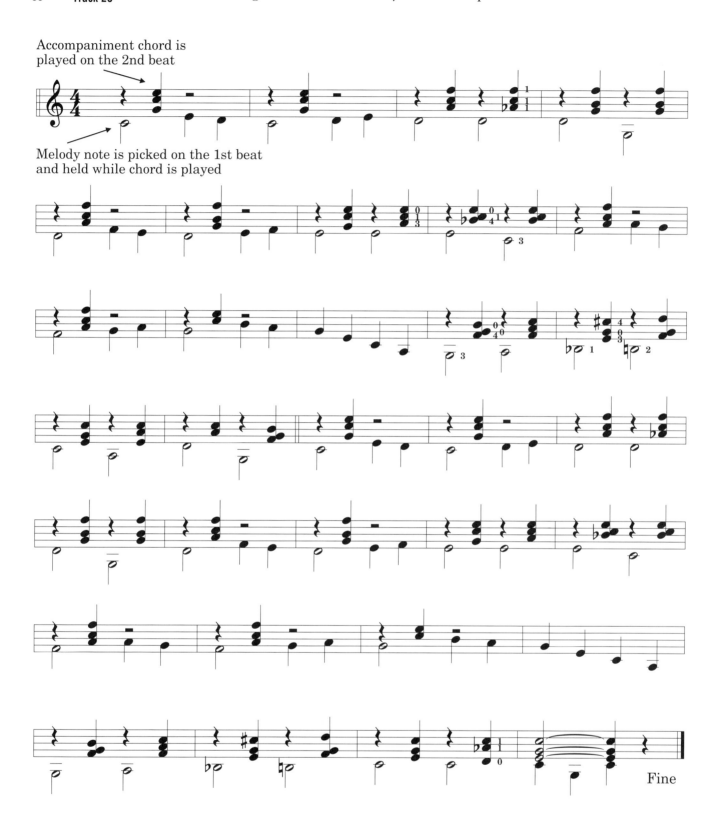

Fine

Be sure to hold all notes for their full time values.

Rhythm Accompaniment

CHORD DIAGRAMS

1. Vertical lines represent strings.
2. Horizontal lines represent frets.
   (See illustration, pg. 3.)
3. Dots represent finger placement.
4. Numbers indicate fingers to be used.
5. Zero means open string.
6. × means muted string.

NUT → C(Major) ← CHORD NAME
→ FRETS (1-2-3)
(optional open or muted string)
× 3 2 0 1 0
(×)

C7(Dominant 7)   F(Major)   Fm(Minor)   G7(Dominant 7)

■ EXERCISE 1

Use only the chord forms shown above.

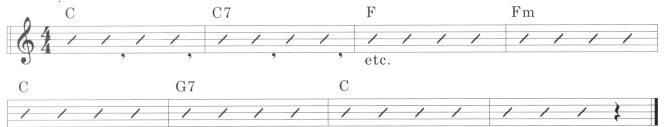

If no number, zero, or × is found below the diagram, do not allow the pick to strike the string

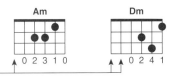

Am   Dm
0 2 3 1 0   0 2 4 1

Optional fingered note or open string

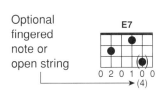

E7
0 2 0 1 0 0
(4)

■ EXERCISE 2

■ EXERCISE 3

This exercise combines all forms shown above, and should not be attempted until the preceding chord sequences are mastered at least partially.

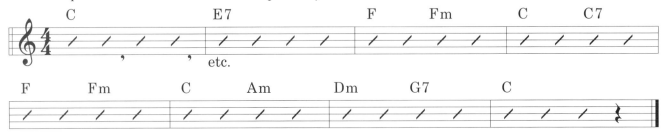

All chord forms must be memorized.

24

Second Solo

Solo arrangement with melody *above* (and *below*) the chord accompaniment.

Hold all notes for their full value.

25

Etude No. 3 (duet)

count   1   2   3   4   &

count   1   2   3   &   4   &

1   2   &   3   4

Ritard   Fine

Review everything regularly.

Picking Etude No. 1

For development of the right hand.

PREPARATION

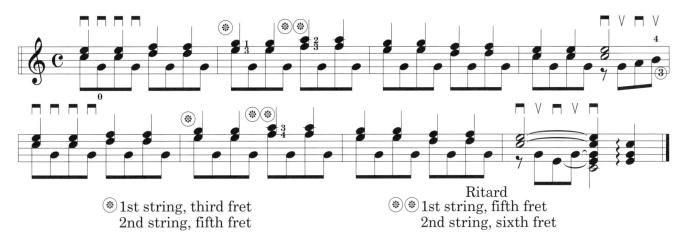

⊛ 1st string, third fret
2nd string, fifth fret

⊛⊛ 1st string, fifth fret
2nd string, sixth fret

40 Track 24

Etude

Tempo: Moderately Slow 4

A tempo (back to original tempo)

Two, Two (duet)

₵ is often misused to represent 4/4 in popular music.

Play again from the ($\mathbf{\%}$) sign to the al coda. Then skip to the coda ($\mathbf{\oplus}$).

Fine

Key of G Major (First Position)

(All Fs are sharped.)

Rhythm Accompaniment

G

G°7 (Diminished 7)
× 1 3 2 4

This chord structure is also indicated by the abbreviation "dim." Even though the numeral 7 is often omitted from the symbol, diminished 7 is intended.

D7
0 2 1 3

■ **EXERCISE 1**

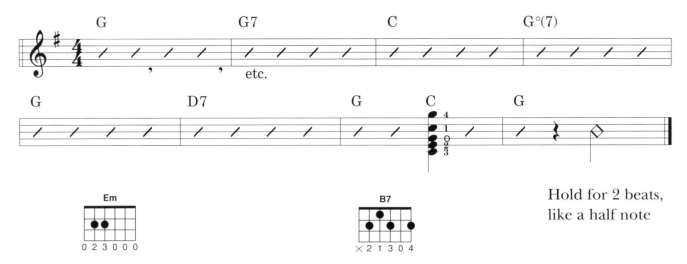

Em
0 2 3 0 0 0

B7
× 2 1 3 0 4

Hold for 2 beats, like a half note

■ **EXERCISE 2**

30

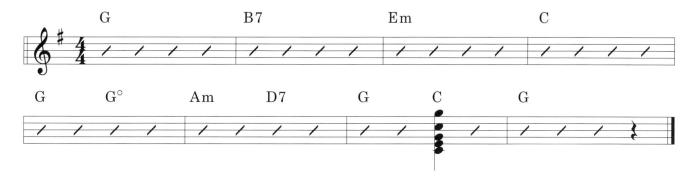

Sixteenth Notes

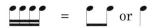

Slowly and Evenly

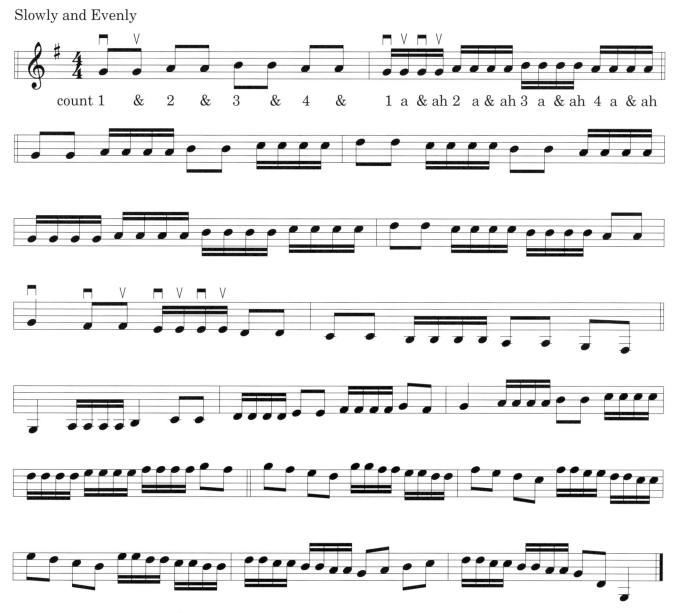

count 1 & 2 & 3 & 4 &   1 a & ah 2 a & ah 3 a & ah 4 a & ah

Duet in G

Picking Etude No. 2

For alternate picking while skipping strings.

■ Pay very strict attention to "down" and "up" pickings on all eighth-note passages.

Fine

Another Duet in G

count   1 & 2 & 3 & 4 &

Ritard

Fine

55

Key of F Major (First Position)

(All Bs are flatted.)

57

Rhythm Accompaniment

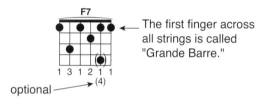

The first finger across all strings is called "Grande Barre."

optional → (4)

Bb

C9 (Dominant 9)

This C9 chord has the same function as C7 and is often substituted for it.

■ EXERCISE

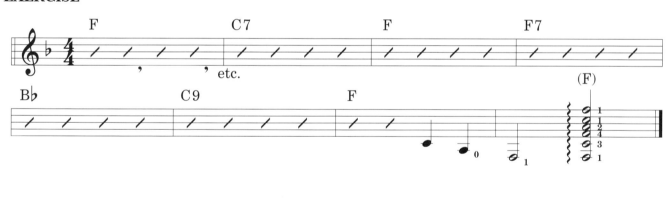

', etc.

(F)

Note the slight difference between this D minor fingering and the one on pg. 24.

Dm
× 3 2 4 1

Gm
2 × 0 3 3 3

A7
× 0 1 1 1 2

■ EXERCISE

Dm   Gm   A7   Dm

■ Several of the forms presented above will take some time to play clearly. Be patient and keep at them.

Duet in F

58–60 Track 30

The Triplet

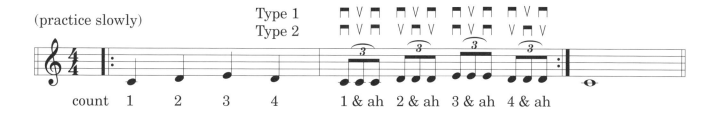

There are two ways to pick consecutive sets of triplets. Practice the entire exercise thoroughly, using first the picking marked Type 1. Then practice using Type 2.

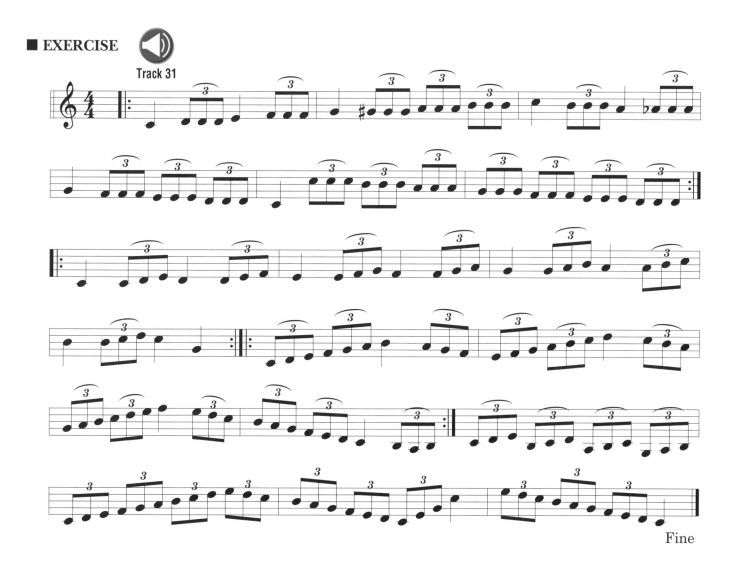

Review all material.

Waltz in F (solo)

A waltz has three beats per measure.

Notes appearing
before the beginning
measure are called
pick-ups

count   2   3   1   2   3 etc.

Rall. ("Rallentando," or slow down)   A tempo
(back in tempo)

Ritard poco a poco (little by little)

Fine

Key of A Minor (First Position)

Relative to C major.

The sixth degree (note) of any major scale is the tonic (first note) of its *relative minor key*. The major and relative minor key signatures are the same. There are three different scales in each minor key.

A Natural Minor: All notes exactly the same as its relative major, C major.

A Harmonic Minor: The 7th degree, counting up from A, is raised a half step.

A Melodic Minor: The 6th and 7th degrees are raised *ascending* but return to normal descending.

Rhythm Accompaniment

We now begin to observe that many chords have more than one fingering. The choice of which one to use generally depends upon the chord fingerings that immediately precede and/or follow. In the following exercise use the large diagrams *or* the smaller optional fingerings in sequence. Do not mix them!

■ EXERCISE

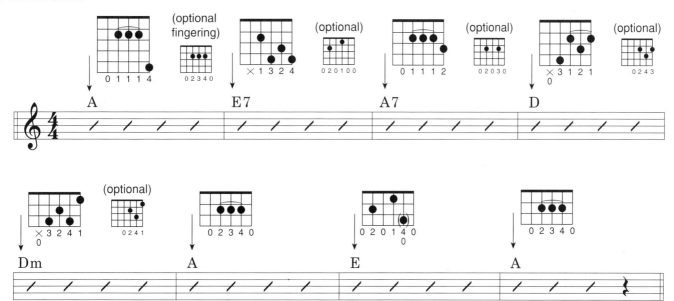

Smooth, melodic accompaniment depends
on the number of chord forms mastered.

39

Pretty Pickin' (duet)

For alternate picking while skipping strings.

CHORD PREPARATION

Fine

Duet

Moderate Waltz Tempo

(All notes under the curved line must be kept ringing.)

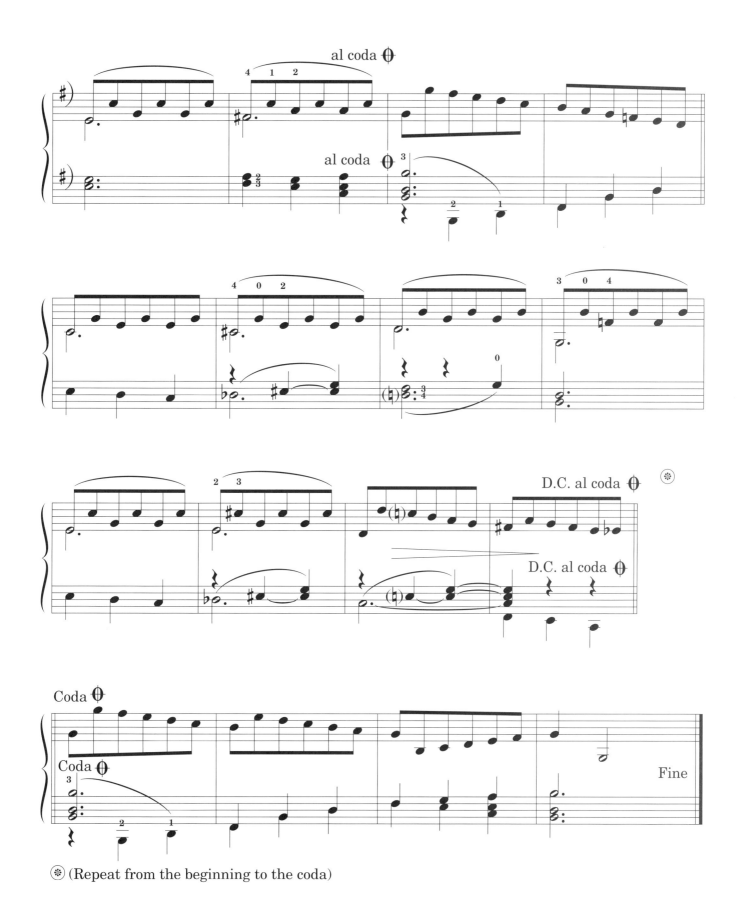

※ (Repeat from the beginning to the coda)

Dotted Eighth and Sixteenth Notes

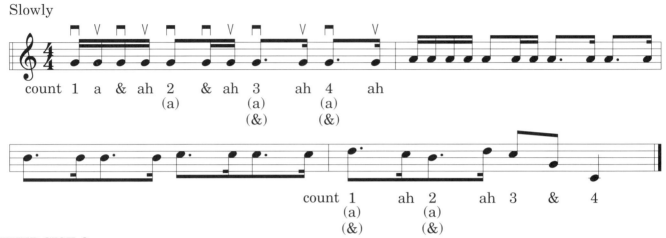

■ **EXERCISE 1**

Slowly

```
count 1   a   &   ah   2   &   ah   3   ah   4   ah
         (a)           (a)           (a)
         (&)           (&)
```

```
count 1      ah   2   ah   3   &   4
         (a)           (a)
         (&)           (&)
```

■ **EXERCISE 2**

Slowly

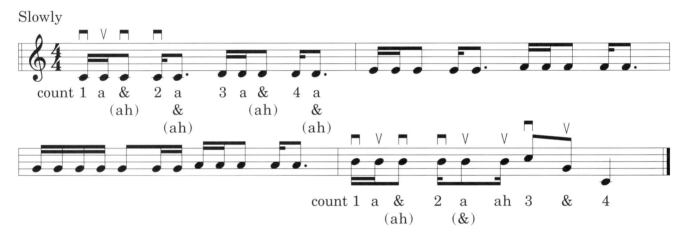

```
count 1   a   &   2   a   3   a   &   4   a
        (ah)      &        (ah)      &
        (ah)               (ah)
```

```
count 1   a   &   2   a   ah   3   &   4
        (ah)     (&)
```

Note that the above "strict" (or "legitimate") interpretation of dotted eighth and sixteenth notes produces a rather jerky rhythm. In pop music and jazz they are played more *legato* (smoothly, in a flowing manner). This is done by treating them as triplets.

Example:

■ **EXERCISE 3**

Slowly

```
count 1   &   ah   2   &   ah   3   ah   4   ah
              (&)           (&)
```

(Keep the "3" feeling)

Key of E Minor (Scales in First Position)

Relative to G major.

E Natural Minor

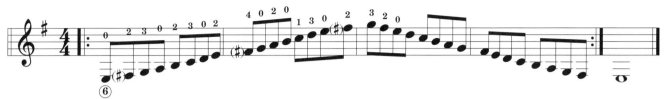

E Harmonic Minor

E Melodic Minor

Rhythm Accompaniment

■ **EXERCISE 1**

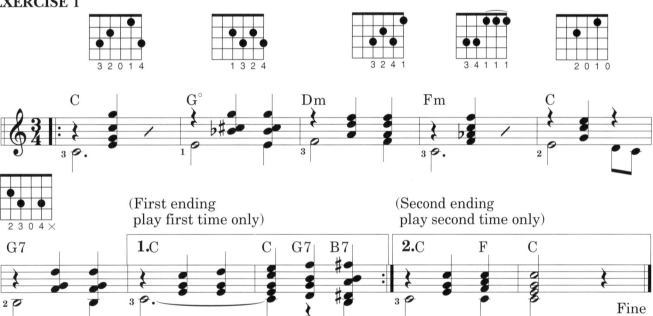

(First ending
play first time only)

(Second ending
play second time only)

Fine

■ **EXERCISE 2**

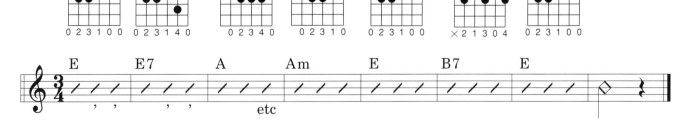

In waltz time, chords are muted immediately after the second and third beats.

Take Your Pick (duet)

For alternate picking while skipping strings.

CHORD PREPARATION

Duet

Rhythm Accompaniment

The principle of movable chord forms.

Moving up the fingerboard in pitch, *natural* notes are two frets apart, except E to F, and B to C. They are one fret apart.

EXAMPLE (1st or 6th string)

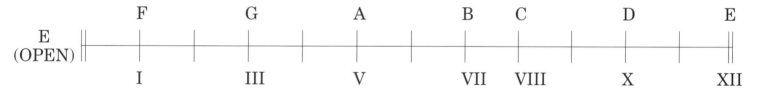

This fact applies to chord playing as follows:

1. If you play F major, F minor, and F7 on the first fret, then (using the same fingering) G major, G minor, and G7 will be on the third fret (two frets above F). Moving still higher, A major, A minor, and A7 will be on the fifth fret, B major, B minor, and B7 on the seventh fret, and C major, C minor, and C7 will be on the eighth—one fret up from B.

2. All *movable* forms will have *no open strings*.

3. Sharps and flats alter chord positions by one fret, the same as single notes.

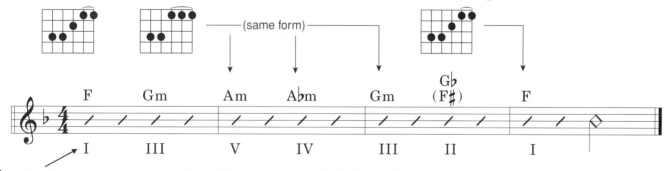

■ The Roman numerals (called "Position Marks") indicate the frets on which the first finger plays.

■ On the following pages, all new chord forms will be movable.

Chromatic Scale (First Position)

76

■ The *chromatic scale* is made up of semi-tones (half steps).

Speed Studies

77

Play the following eighth-note patterns at an even speed, slowly at first. Very gradually (over a period of time), increase the tempo. *Memorize the patterns*, and practice each one in all keys. Always start on the *tonic* (first note) of each scale and *transpose* the rest of the notes by the following pattern. (Write them out if necessary.)

PATTERN 1

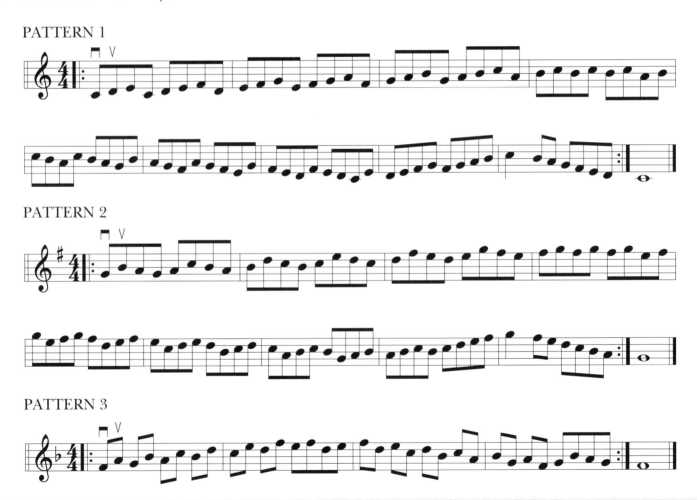

PATTERN 2

PATTERN 3

First-position F and G scales can be played in two octaves. Play all patterns in *both* octaves.

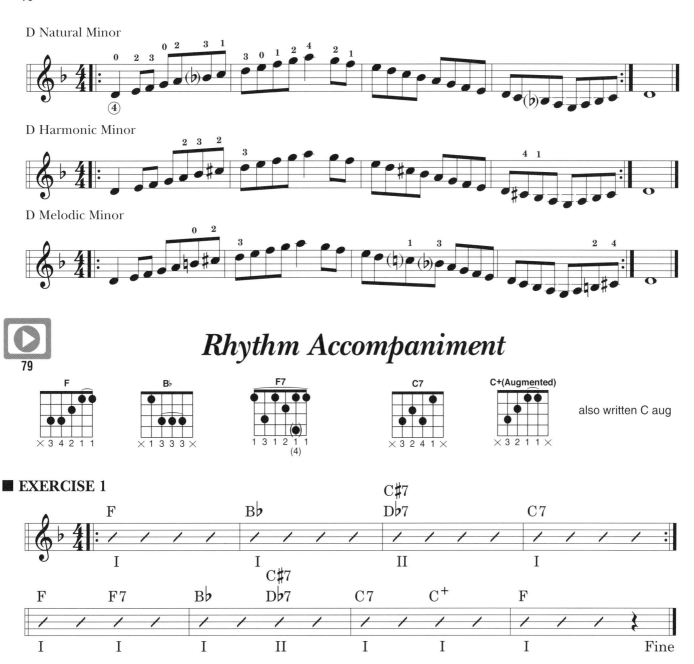

Key of D Minor (Scales in First Position)

Relative to F major.

D Natural Minor

D Harmonic Minor

D Melodic Minor

Rhythm Accompaniment

also written C aug

■ **EXERCISE 1**

■ This is the same chord sequence but *transposed* to a different key. Watch the position marks.

■ **EXERCISE 2**

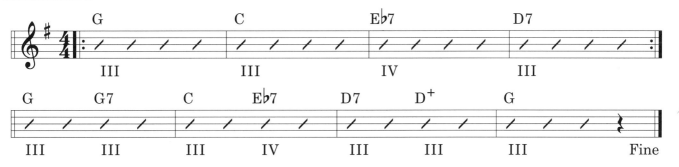

The augmented chord can actually be named from any note within the form (C+ = E+ = G♯+ or A♭+).
Augmented chords repeat themselves every fifth fret.

Endurance Etude
Picking Etude #3

Hold fourth finger down throughout.

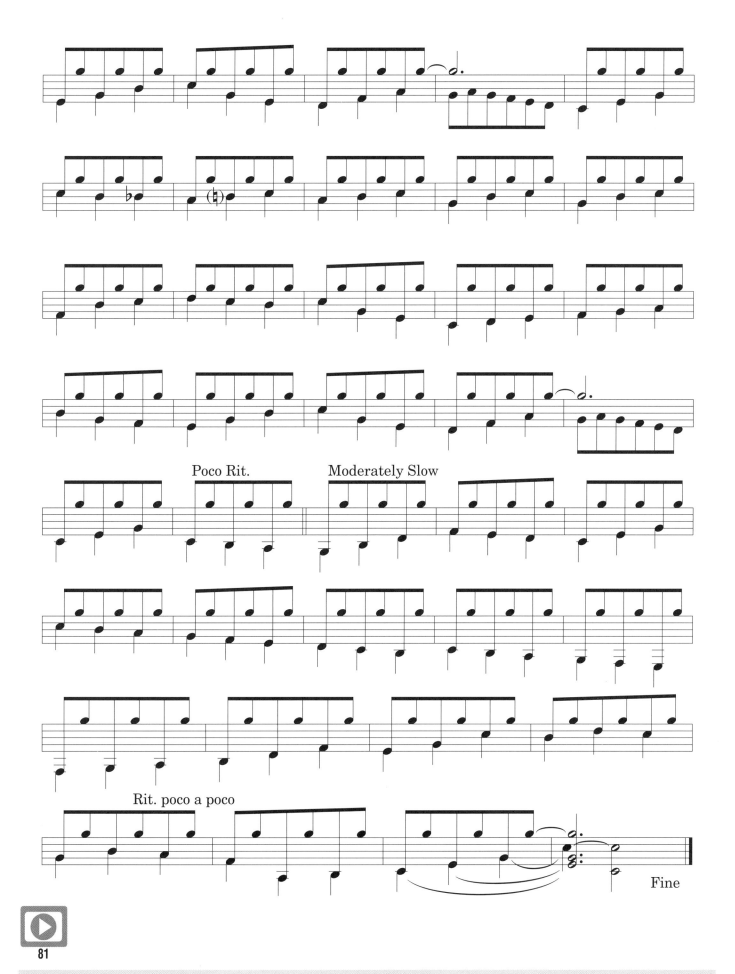

Be sure to observe tempo changes. Also, vary the *dynamics* (degrees of volume, loud and soft) to make the music more interesting to listen to.

49

Key of B♭ Major (Scales in First Position)

(All Bs and Es are flatted.)

When a key signature has two or more flats, the name of the next-to-last flat is the name of the key.

Rhythm Accompaniment

 Fm

 B♭m

Mute the 5th string with the tip of your first finger. Mute the 6th by touching it with your thumb. →

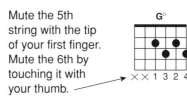 G°

also written as G dim (see p.30)

■ **EXERCISE 1**

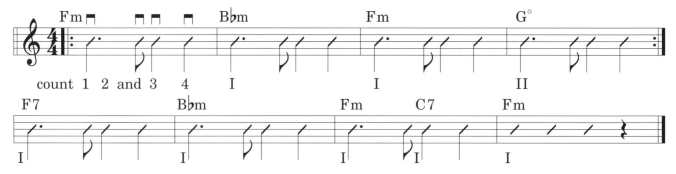

■ **EXERCISE 2**

■ This is the same chord sequence but transposed to a different key. Watch the position marks.

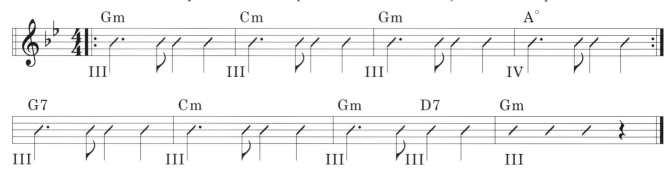

The diminished chord can actually be named from any note in the form (G° = B♭° = C♯° or D♭° = E°).
Diminished chords repeat themselves every fourth fret.

Duet in B♭

(Finger complete chord form.
Do not strum top string.)

51

Reverse Alternate Picking Study

■ Pay very strict attention to picking as indicated.

(hold down bottom note)

Review all material.

Key of D Major (Scale in First Position)

(All Fs and Cs are sharped.)

In any sharp signature, the first note above
the last sharp is the name of the key.

Duet in D

Track 38

count (1   2) 3 4 &   1 & 2 & 3 (4   1)& 2 & 3 (4)

Dot over a note
means staccato

Play like this.   II Fine

53

Dynamic Etude (duet)

Etude #4

▌ Be sure to hold all notes for their full value.

Moderato

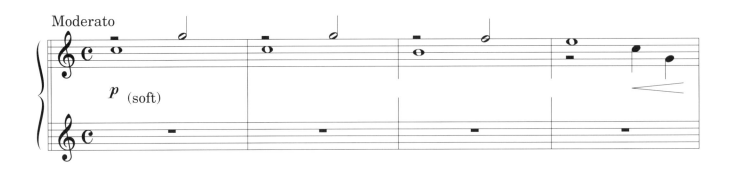

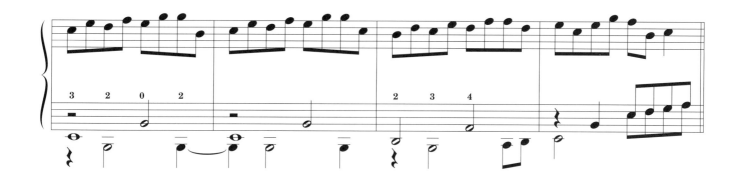

(soft)

(Repeat previous measure)

(loud)

count 1 2 3 4

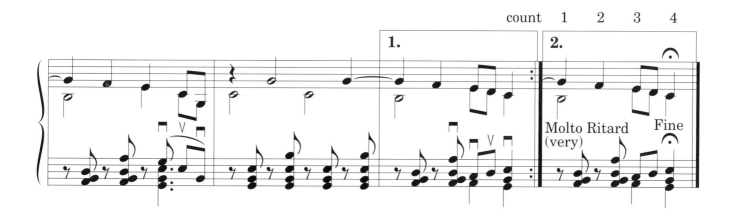

1.

2.

Molto Ritard (very)

Fine

95–97   Track 40

Key of A Major (First Position)
Duet in A

(All Fs, Cs, and Gs are sharped.)

Rhythm Accompaniment

■ EXERCISE 1

■ EXERCISE 2

56

99

Key of E♭ Major (Scale in First Position)

(All Bs, Es, and As are flatted.)

100–102 **Track 41**

Duet in E♭

▌ Remember the flats. Count time carefully.

57

103

Movable Chord Forms

A compilation of movable forms presented in Section I.

Related Fingerings

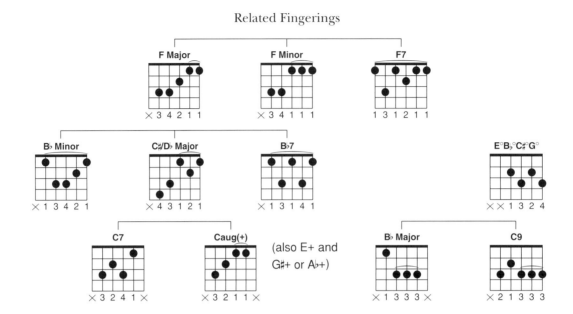

■ With these eleven forms, you can play the accompaniment to any song in any key, providing:
1. That you understand the principle of movable chord forms discussed on pg. 45, and
2. That you observe the following chart.

Chord Simplification and Substitution Chart

TYPE	WRITTEN					SIMPLIFIED SUBSTITUTION	
Major	C6	Cmaj7	Cmaj9	C_6^9	$Cmaj_7^9$	Use:	C major
Dominant 7th	C9	C13	C9(11+)	C11+	———	Use:–	C7
Dom 7-Altered 9th	C7(-9)	C7(♭9)	C13(-9)	C13(♭9)	———	—	C7 or G dim { build dim chord
	C7(+9)	C7(◦9)	C13(+9)	etc.	———	—	C7 (or G°) { on 5th note above C
Dom 7-Altered 5th	C7+	C7(+5)	Caug7	C9+	C9(+5) C+9	Use:	C+ { build substitute
	C7(-5)	C7(♭5)	C9(-5)	etc. . .	$C7_{+5}^{-5}$ ——	—	C+ or G♭+ { chord on flatted
Dom 7-Altered 5, 9	$C7_{+5}^{-9}$	$C7_{+5}^{+9}$	$C7_{-5}^{+9}$	$C7_{-5}^{-9}$	———	—	C+ or G♭7 { 5th above C
Dom 7-Sus 4	C7(sus4)	C7(susF)	C9(sus4)	C9(susF)	C11	Use:	G minor 5th note above C
Minor	Cm6	Cm_6^9				Use:	C minor
Minor 7th	Cm7	Cm9	Cm11			Use:	Cm
Min-with Maj7	Cm(♮7)	Cm(◦7)	Cm(maj7)			Use:	G+(5th above C) or Cm
Min 7-Altered 5th	Cm7(-5)	Cm7(♭5)				Use:	E♭m { built on minor, (or
							lowered) 3rd above C }

■ Of course, having only eleven chord forms at your command will cause you to move up and down the fingerboard much more than is desired for good rhythm playing. The more forms you know, the less distance you have to travel and the more melodic your rhythm playing can become.

Picking—A Different Technique

The principle is to attack each new string with a downstroke.

This technique is older than alternate picking, and less emphasis is placed on it today. However it is one more step in right-hand control and, when mastered, it is very fast in ascending passages.

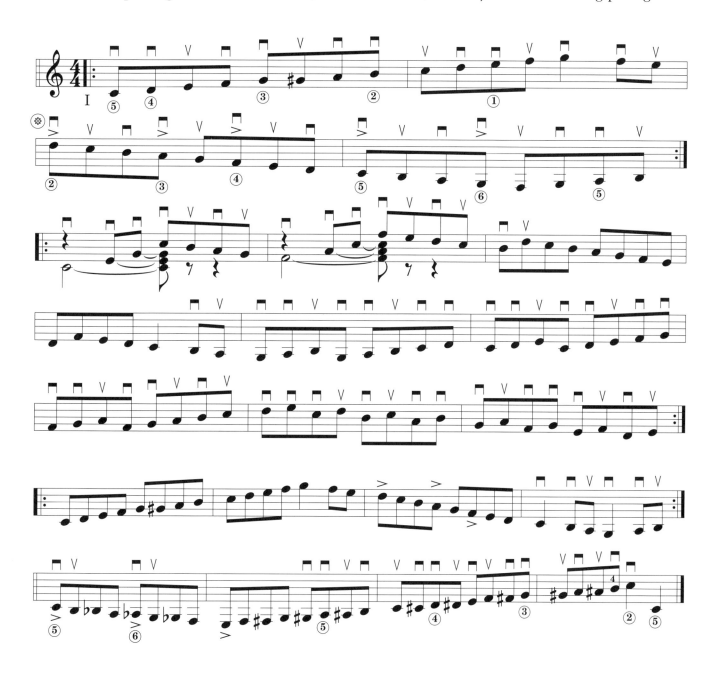

An example of this technique in use can be found on pg. 48, measure 20 of the "Endurance Etude." This type of picking will be suggested on the following pages from time to time *but only in certain situations* (arpeggios, whole tone scales, etc.) and only in addition to alternate picking. It will be up to you to gradually master and (whenever practical) add this style to your overall right-hand technique. However: the most concentrated effort must still be placed on alternate picking.

✳ (>) Accent mark: strike more sharply

SECTION TWO
Position Playing

Position is determined by the fret on which the first finger plays. It is indicated by a Roman numeral. Strictly speaking, a position on the fingerboard occupies four adjacent frets. Some scales have one or more notes that fall outside this four-fret area, and these notes are to be played by reaching out with the first or fourth finger without shifting the entire hand, i.e. finger stretch or "FS." When the out-of-position note is a scale tone, the finger stretch is determined by the *fingering type* (Type I = first finger stretch, Type IV = fourth finger stretch). When the out-of-position note is not a scale tone and moving upward, use finger stretch 1, and moving downward finger stretch 4—regardless of fingering type. (All scale fingerings introduced from this point on will not use any open strings, and therefore they are movable in the same manner as the chord forms presented earlier. See pg. 45.)

107

Major Scales
C Major (Fingering Type 1)
Second Position

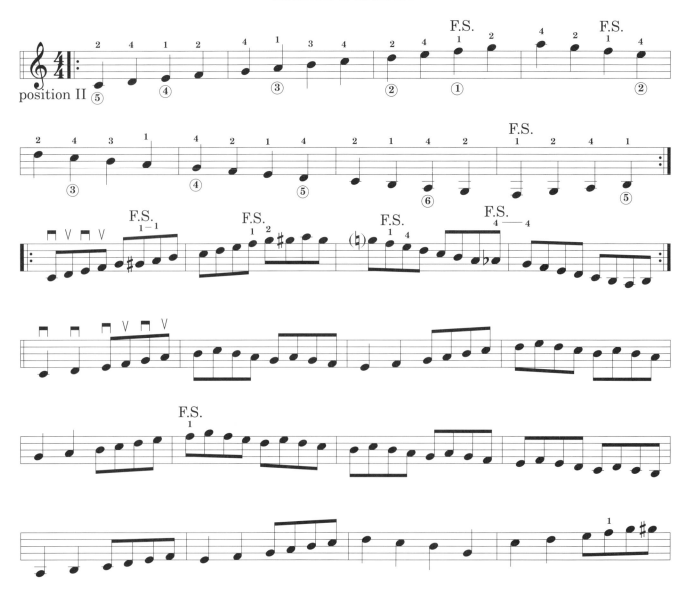

✹ When an out-of-position note is immediately preceded or followed by a note played with the same finger that would normally make the stretch, reverse the usual finger-stretch procedure. Always move back into a position from a finger stretch, never away from it.

EIGHTH-NOTE STUDY

ARPEGGIO STUDY: BROKEN CHORDS

▌ Practice picking as indicated and also with alternate ⊓ V picking.

✹ ✹ When two consecutive notes are played with the same finger on adjacent strings, "roll" the finger tip from one string to the next. Do not lift the finger from the string.

Chord Etude No. 1

Practice slowly and evenly, connecting the chords so they flow from one to the next with no silences between them. Observe fingering and position marks!

62

Etude No. 5 (duet)

Remember, all natural notes on the guitar are two frets apart except E to F and B to C.

Reading Studies

Do not *practice* these two pages. Just read them, but not more than twice through during any single practice session. Do not play them on two consecutive days. Do not go back over any particular section because of a wrong note. Do keep an even tempo and play the proper time values.

By obeying these rules, you will never memorize the reading studies, so they will always be good reading practice. A little later on, it is recommended that you use this procedure with a variety of material, as this is the only way for a guitarist to achieve and maintain any proficiency in reading. (Even when working steadily, we are not reading every day, so "scare yourself" in the privacy of your practice sessions.)

C MAJOR 1 (FINGERING TYPE 1)

C MAJOR 2 (FINGERING TYPE 1)

Fine

If you encounter unusual difficulty reading these pages, go back to pg. 60 and start again.

Ballad (duet)

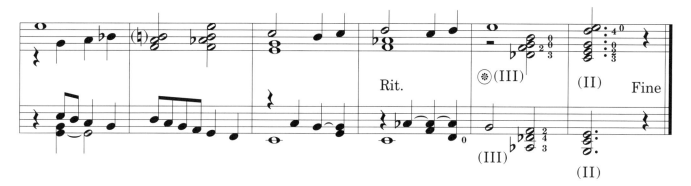

✿ A position mark in parentheses represents placement of second finger, as first finger is not used.

116

Movable Chord Forms
Rhythm Accompaniment, Part Two

The most difficult part of learning to play chords on the guitar is getting the fingers to fall instantly and without conscious effort in the proper arrangement on the fingerboard. This is mainly a physical problem, and a certain amount of practice time seems to be the only solution.

However, I have found that learning new chord forms in a certain order (a sequence of related fingerings) seems to lessen the time normally required to perform them.

Therefore, the following chord forms are presented in a particular order. We will use three of the previously learned fingerings as basic forms. We will alter these forms by moving, or removing, one or more fingers. In this way each new fingering is directly related to the one(s) preceding it.

So, each of the basic forms and each derivative is a preparation for another new chord form.

No specific letter names are given—only the chord type and the string on which the root is found.

Memorize the fingerings for all chord structures in their order of appearance. Do not skip around. Do not change the fingering of any form, even if you already play it in a different way. It will appear later on with "your" fingering, but related to a new set of forms. Practice all chord forms chromatically up and down the fingerboard, observing root (chord) names.

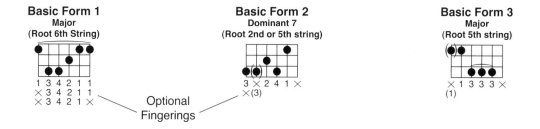

A dot in parentheses (•) means that although the note belongs to the chord, it need not sound and, in many cases, sounds better without it.

67

Chord Forms

Shown below is Basic Form 1 and seven derivative fingerings. When the basic form has been mastered, the performance of the derivatives is relatively easy to accomplish. Memorize the type of chord (major, minor, etc.) each form produces and the string on which the root (or name) is found. All optional fingerings should eventually be learned, but first concentrate on the one appearing directly below the diagram. It is the preferred one.

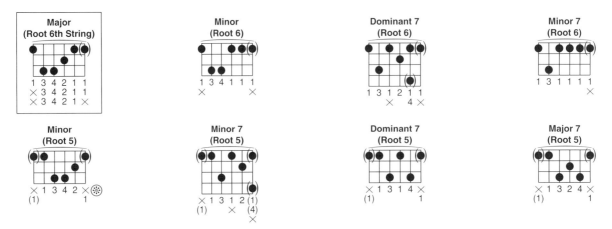

A word about notation:

1. When a chord is indicated by just a letter, it is major.
2. When it is a letter followed by a 7, it is a dominant 7 chord.
3. Minor is indicated by min, m, or a dash(–).
4. Major 7 is indicated by maj7, ma7, or sometimes M7.

■ **EXERCISE**

Use only the forms shown above. Watch the position marks!

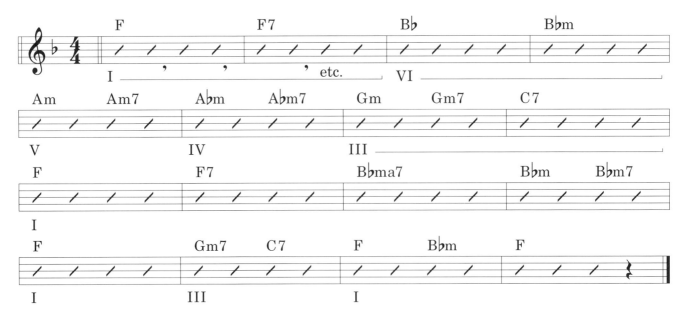

✸ The first string is not very effective in rhythm playing, and even when it is pressed down with a "barre" it is usually best to omit it by making the pick travel in an arc across the strings, passing above it. (⌢......)

Rhythm Accompaniment—Right-Hand Technique

To most beginners, strumming chords (pushing the pick across the strings so they sound one after the other) is easy and natural.

However, striking the chords so that the sound fits with a modern rhythm section is quite another thing, and requires considerable practice and know-how.

First, by using a combination rotary forearm and loose-wrist motion (snap the wrist as if flicking something from the back of your hand), you produce an explosive attack in which all notes seem to sound simultaneously.

Secondly, the placement of "pressure release points" ( ) and accents determines the types of beat produced. (Much more about all this later.)

Picking Etude No. 4

Observe fingering.

118   Track 46

Hold third finger down throughout.

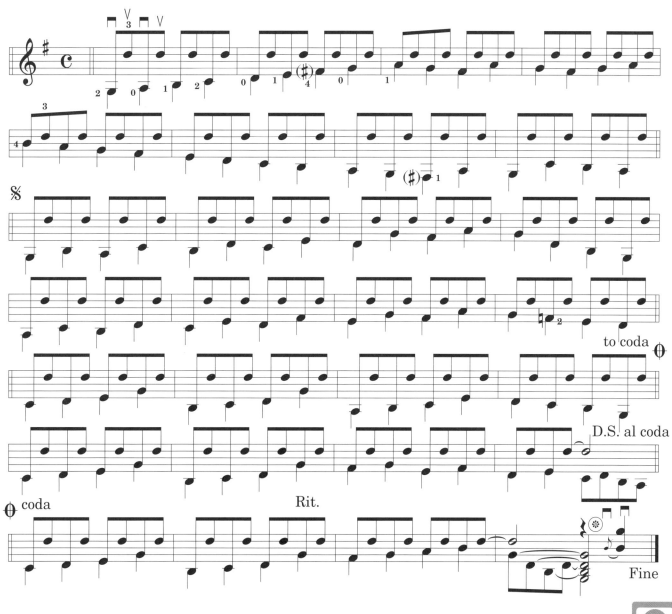

119

Grace note to played slightly before the top note G on the fourth beat.

F Major Scale
(Fingering Type 1A, Second Position)

The F major scale shown above is in the second position even though the first finger plays the first fret on three strings. This is because the three scale tones require stretches by the first finger. The basic four-fret position is never numbered from a stretch.

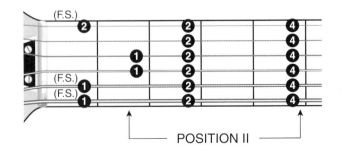

POSITION II

70

EIGHTH-NOTE STUDY

ARPEGGIO STUDY

Also practice arpeggios with alternate ⊓ V picking, which is generally the most practical.

121

Chord Forms

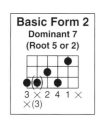

Basic Form 2
Dominant 7
(Root 5 or 2)

3 × 2 4 1 ×
×(3)

Augmented (+)
(Root any string)

× 3 2 1 1 ×

Augmented (add 9)
(Root 5)

× 3 2 1 4 ×

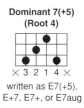

Dominant 7(+5)
(Root 4)

× 3 2 1 4 ×

written as E7(+5),
E+7, E7+, or E7aug

■ EXERCISE

Use the above forms plus some of the preceding ones.

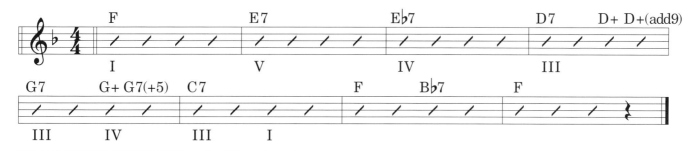

Transpose, write out, and practice all rhythm exercises in one or more higher keys.

Chord Etude No. 2

Rubato: Freedom of tempo. Accelerate and ritard as you wish.

These chord exercises are very important and should be reviewed *regularly,* as they serve many purposes, such as physical development of the left hand, fingering relationship between chord structures, and eventual "chord picture" recognition.

Another Duet in F

Regular review is a must!

Reading Studies

Just play these Reading Studies: Do not *practice* them, and do not play them on two consecutive days (See pg. 64.)

F MAJOR 1 (FINGERING TYPE 1A)

F MAJOR 2 (FINGERING TYPE 1A)

F.S.

FS: Finger Stretch. Stretch the finger; do not move the entire hand.

Play It Pretty (duet)

✻ A temporary change to position III at this point will simplify the fingering this passage, and eliminate the necessity of the open E (preceding the high B♭).

Chord Forms

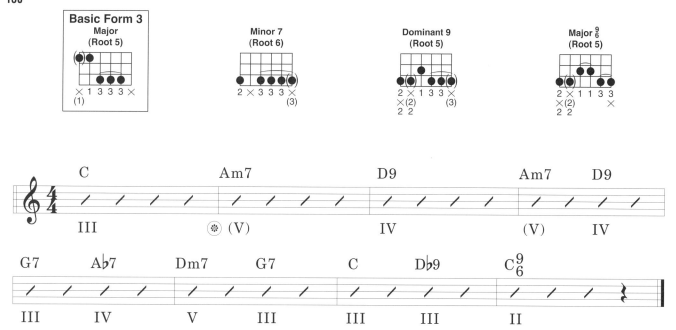

131

❀ A position mark in parentheses means that the first finger is omitted from the form. The position number is determined by the lowest fret used.

Triplet Study

Practice using both patterns of picking. See pg. 37.

Speed Study—Fingering Type 1

Maintain an even tempo. Play no faster than perfect coordination in both hands will allow. An increase in speed will come gradually.

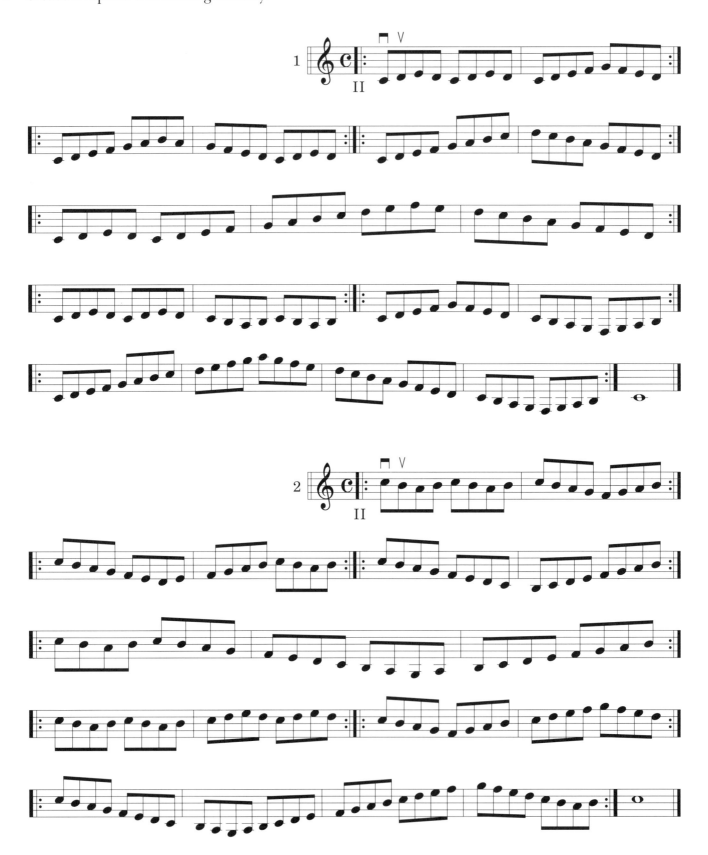

Speed Study—Fingering Type 1A

■ Practice all speed studies as written and with a ♩♪ rhythm. Also play with and without repeats.

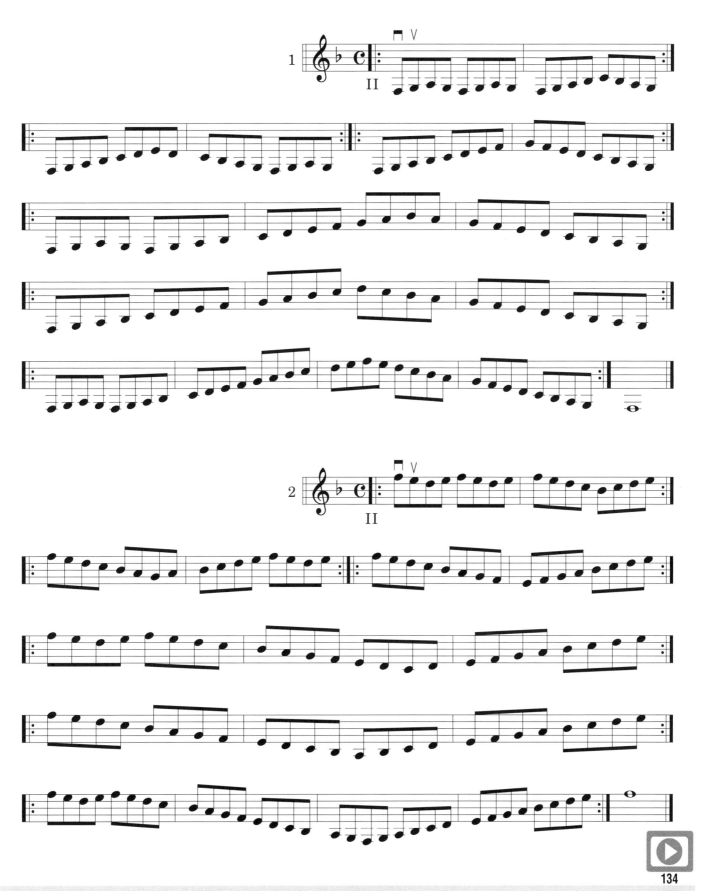

For additional technique-building patterns, see pg. 46.

G Major Scale
(Fingering Type 2, Second Position)

135

EIGHTH-NOTE STUDY

ARPEGGIO STUDY

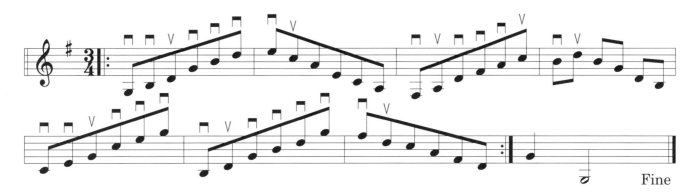

Also practice arpeggios with an alternate ⊓ ∨ picking.

136

Dotted Eighth and Sixteenth Study

Practice as legitimate ♪♪ and as ♩♪ rhythms. See pg. 42.

When two consecutive notes on adjacent strings require the same finger, roll your finger; don't lift it.

Waltz for Two (duet)

Harmonic. Lay the third finger lightly on the strings directly over the twelfth fret. Sharply strike the strings indicated, removing the third finger at almost the same instant. The resulting sound is in the same octave as notated (one octave above what you would expect to hear, as the guitar sounds one octave below the written note). These "natural" harmonics (from open strings) are also possible on other frets—the most practical being on the seventh and fifth frets.

Chord Forms

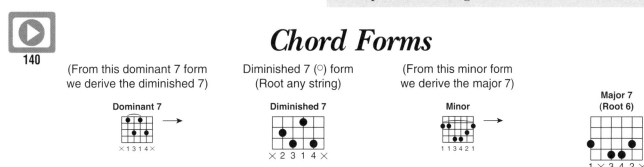

140

(From this dominant 7 form we derive the diminished 7)

Diminished 7 (°) form (Root any string)

(From this minor form we derive the major 7)

Major 7 (Root 6)

▌ Diminished 7 chords are indicated by Gdim or G°. (The 7th is assumed.)

■ EXERCISE 1

Gmaj7	G7	Cma7	Cm

III

Gma7	A7	D7	F♯°	G

III   V _____ III

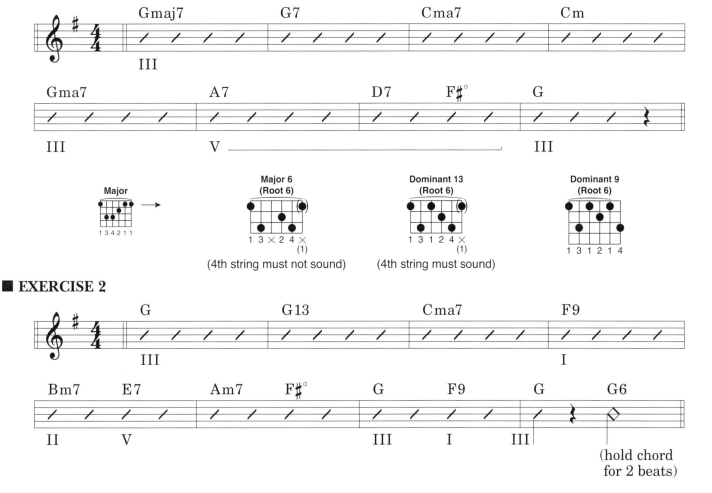

Major

Major 6 (Root 6)

Dominant 13 (Root 6)

Dominant 9 (Root 6)

(4th string must not sound)   (4th string must sound)

■ EXERCISE 2

G	G13	Cma7	F9

III   I

Bm7	E7	Am7	F♯°	G	F9	G	G6

II   V   III   I   III

(hold chord for 2 beats)

▌ You may substitute 6 and major 7 chords for major chords, and dominant 9 and 13 chords for dominant 7 chords.

Reading Studies

❚ Do not "practice" Reading Studies. Just read them.

G MAJOR 1 (FINGERING TYPE 2)

G MAJOR 2 (FINGERING TYPE 2)

❚ Continue on, without stopping, at the same tempo but in waltz time.

Speed not coming? Left-hand accuracy not consistent? Play any scale very slowly.
Watch your left hand. Force your fingers to remain poised over the fingerboard always in readiness.
Don't let them move too far away from the strings when not in use. Concentrate on this.

Blues in G (duet)

The 1st Guitar part of this duet is often played using the "muffled effect." This sound is produced by laying the right hand lightly along the top of the bridge. All strings being played must be kept covered. As this somewhat inhibits picking, the part should first be thoroughly practiced without the muffled effect (or "open").

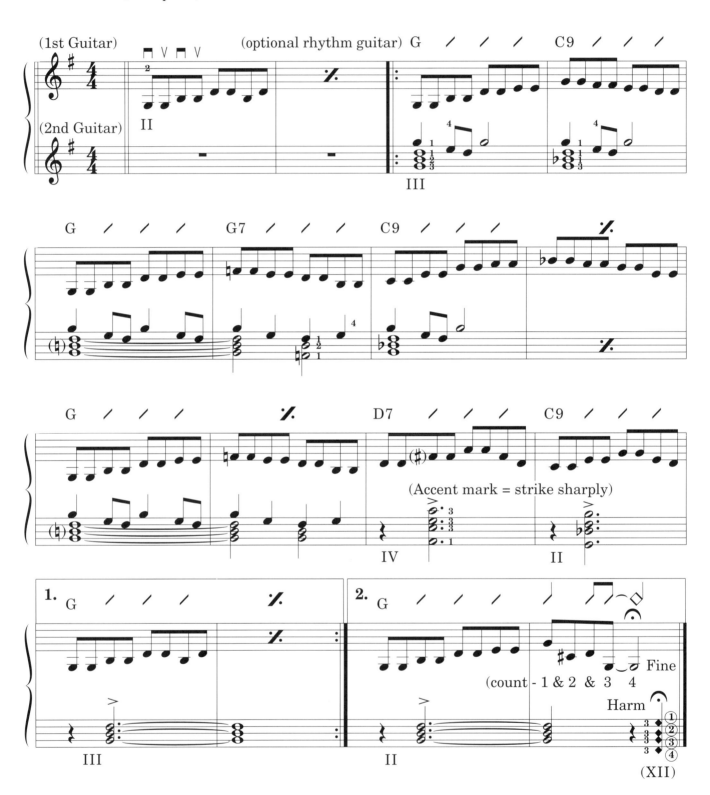

For a different rhythm feel, play all consecutive eighth notes as a ♩ ♪ rhythm.

Chord Etude No. 3

■ Observe position marks and fingerings, as they will make possible a smooth performance.

When moving from chord to chord, the best fingering is usually the one
that involves the least motion in the left hand.
Leaving one finger free for possible melodic additions is also an important factor.

Rhythm Accompaniment—Right-Hand Technique

Memorize these symbols.

- ⊓   Downstroke
- V   Upstroke
- (𝄾)   Release finger pressure (of left hand) immediately *after* chord sounds. Do not remove from strings.
- ╳   Strike deadened strings (fingers in formation on strings, but no pressure).
- >   Accent (strike sharply) with more force.

A basic Latin beat, which will work with the cha-cha, beguine, samba, and others.

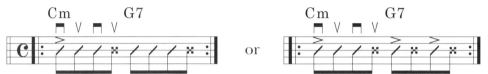

148   Track 53

Picking Etude No. 5

Hold down fourth finger throughout.

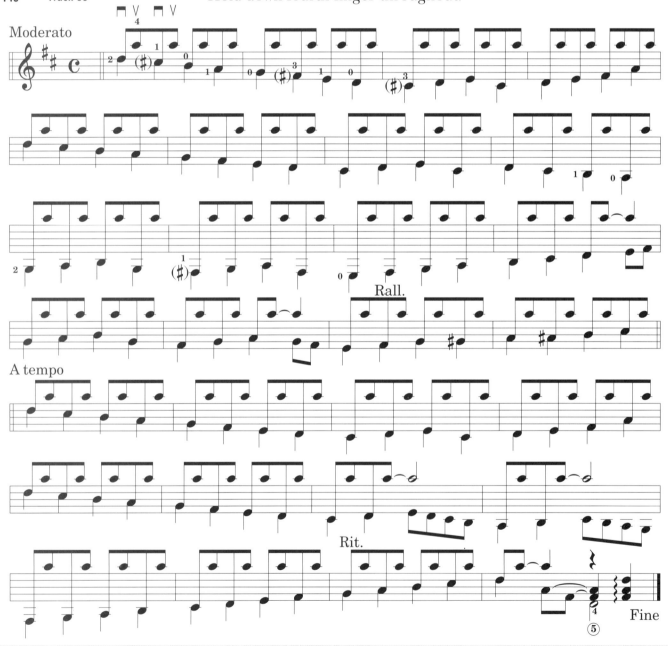

Review! Review!

Short and Sweet (duet)

149–151   Track 54

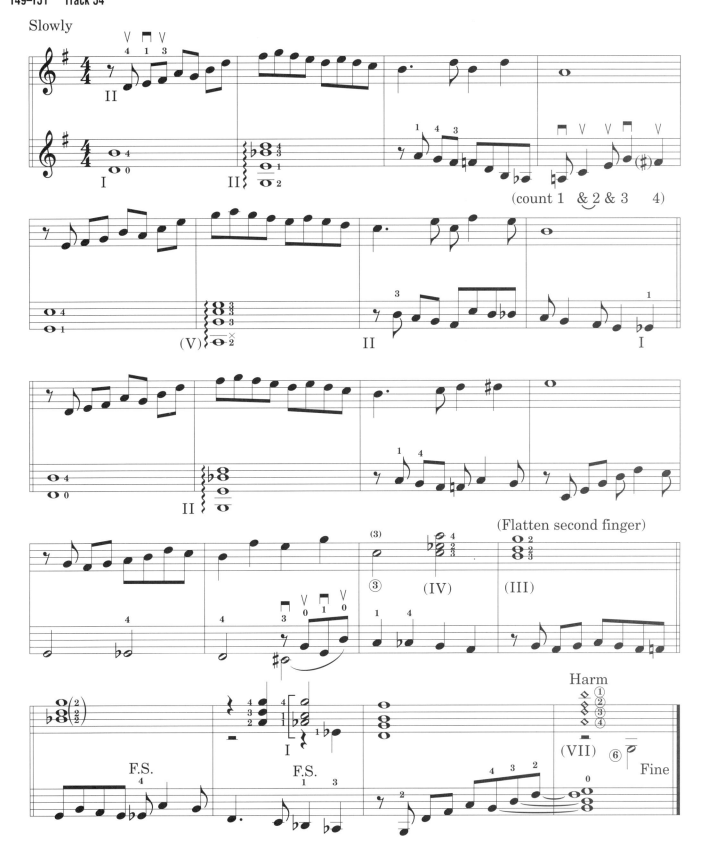

D Major Scale
(Fingering Type 3, Second Position)

EIGHTH-NOTE STUDY

ARPEGGIO STUDY

Also practice with alternate ⊓ V picking.

Chord Forms

154

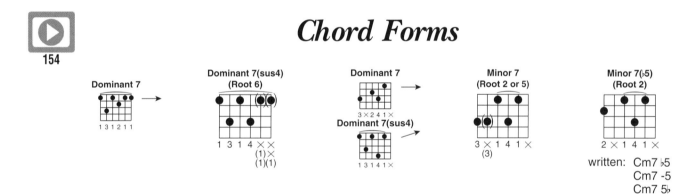

| Dominant 7 | Dominant 7(sus4) (Root 6) | Dominant 7 | Minor 7 (Root 2 or 5) | Minor 7(♭5) (Root 2) |

written: Cm7 ♭5
Cm7 -5
Cm7 5♭

◼ EXERCISE

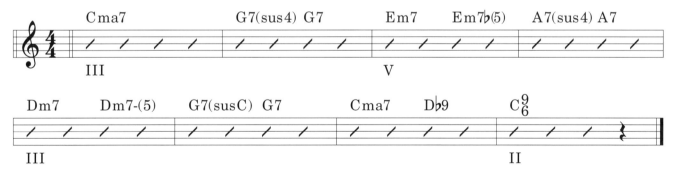

The sus4 refers to the 4th scale degree of the chord so named. The note name (for the 4th) is also used, e.g., G7susC. Sus4 may also be called (natural) 11. The root is on the same string as the sus4 form. For example, in the above exercise you may substitute symbols "G11" and "A11" for sus4.

Melodic Rhythm Study No. 1
Optional Duet With Rhythm Guitar

Be sure to count the rhythm until you can "feel" the phrase. Eventually you will be able to recognize (and feel) entire groups of syncopated notes. In the beginning you should pick *down* for notes falling on the beat, and *up* for those counted "and." This is a definite aid in learning to read these "off beat" rhythms. Later on, when syncopation is no longer a problem, you will vary your picking for the purpose of phrasing and accents.

✳ Rhythm Guitar: Use Latin beat.

✳ Rhythm Guitar [rhythm notation] or [rhythm notation]. Remember the substitutions possible on the dominant 7 and major chords.

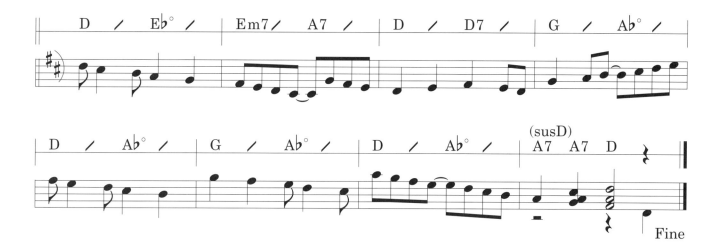

Chord Etude No. 4

Be sure to hold all notes for their full value.

Slowly, Freely

Staccato, Legato

157

A dot (.) above or below a note means "staccato" or short.

A line (−) above or below a note means "legato" or long.

Fine

Reading Studies

For reading only.

D MAJOR 1 (FINGERING TYPE 3)

D MAJOR 2 (FINGERING TYPE 3)

Fine

Reading music is a combination of instant note (and finger) recognition and playing the "sound" that you "see" in music (along with the relative time durations of the notes, of course). Try this: Play the tonic chord of these reading studies to get your ear in the proper key. Then try to sing the music to yourself as you play it. If your fingers have been over the fingering type enough times, they will automatically play whatever notes (sound patterns) you mentally "hear" on the page. This will take a great deal of time to master, but keep after it. It's worth it!

Dee-Oo-Ett (duet)

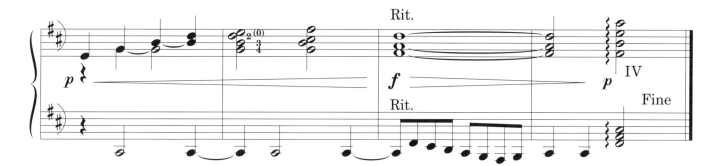

Chord Forms

Dominant 9

Dominant 9
(Root 5)

Diminished 7
(Root any string)

Major 6
(Root 6)

■ EXERCISE

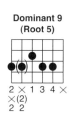

✿ The fingering will be given as shown here whenever two forms are possible in the same position (and also as an occasional reminder).

(Major 7)

Minor 6
(Root 2)

Dominant 9

Dominant 7(+5)
(Root 6)

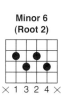

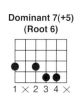

■ EXERCISE

▌ Latin beat—Be sure to release pressure where indicated ( ).

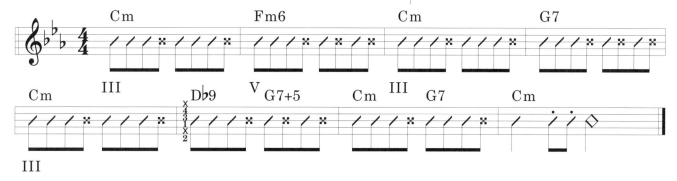

▌ The minor 6 form shown above may also be called a minor 7(♭5) (root 5th string).

Speed Study—Fingering Type 2

Maintain an *even tempo.* Play no faster than perfect coordination in both hands will allow. An increase in speed will come gradually.

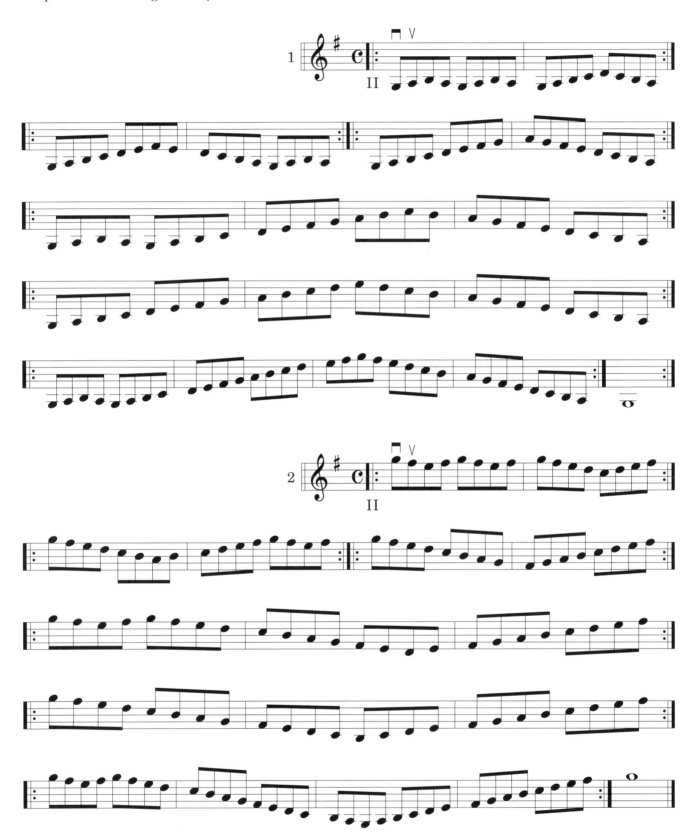

Speed Study—Fingering Type 3

Practice all speed studies as written and with ♪♩ rhythms. Also play them with and without repeats.

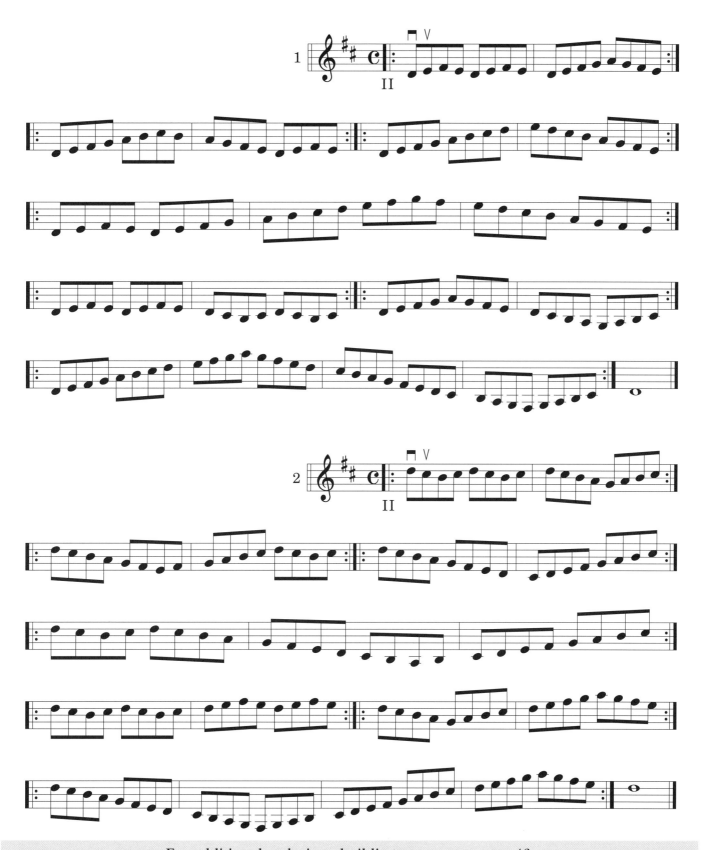

For additional technique-building patterns, see pg. 46.

A Major Scale
(Fingering Type 4, Second Position)

EIGHTH-NOTE STUDY

Double-sharp raises the note one tone (two frets)

Cancellation reminder (back to F♯, as in signature)

ARPEGGIO STUDY

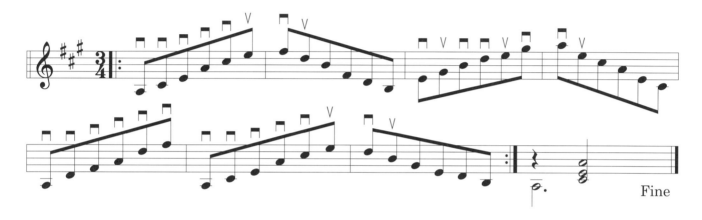

Also practice arpeggios with alternate ∏ ∨ picking.

Chord Etude No. 5

Fine

101

Reading Studies

❚ For reading only.

A MAJOR 1 (FINGERING TYPE 4)

A MAJOR 2 (FINGERING TYPE 4)

A MAJOR 3 (FINGERING TYPE 4)

Tres Sharp (duet)

172

Sixteenth Note Study

Count carefully. See pg. 31.

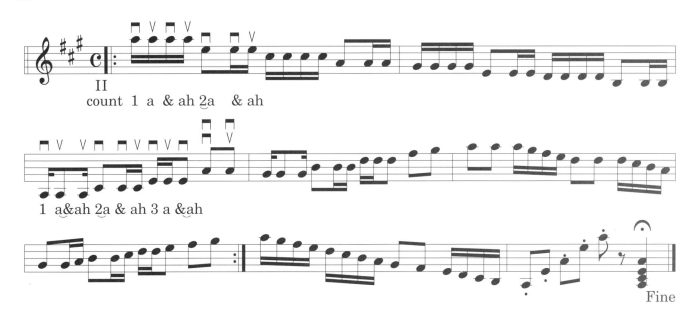

count 1 a & ah 2a & ah

1 a&ah 2a & ah 3 a &ah

Fine

Chord Forms

173

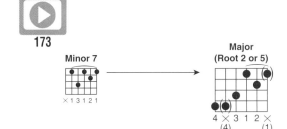

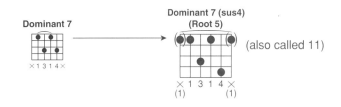

■ **EXERCISE**

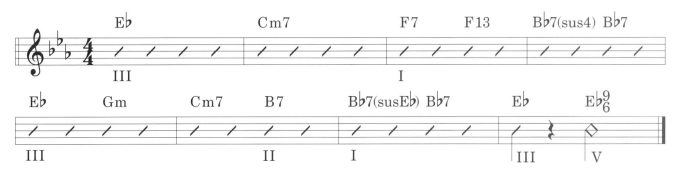

Speed Study—Fingering Type 4, Second Position

▌ As before, keep an even tempo. Play as written and with a ♪♪ rhythm, with and without repeats.

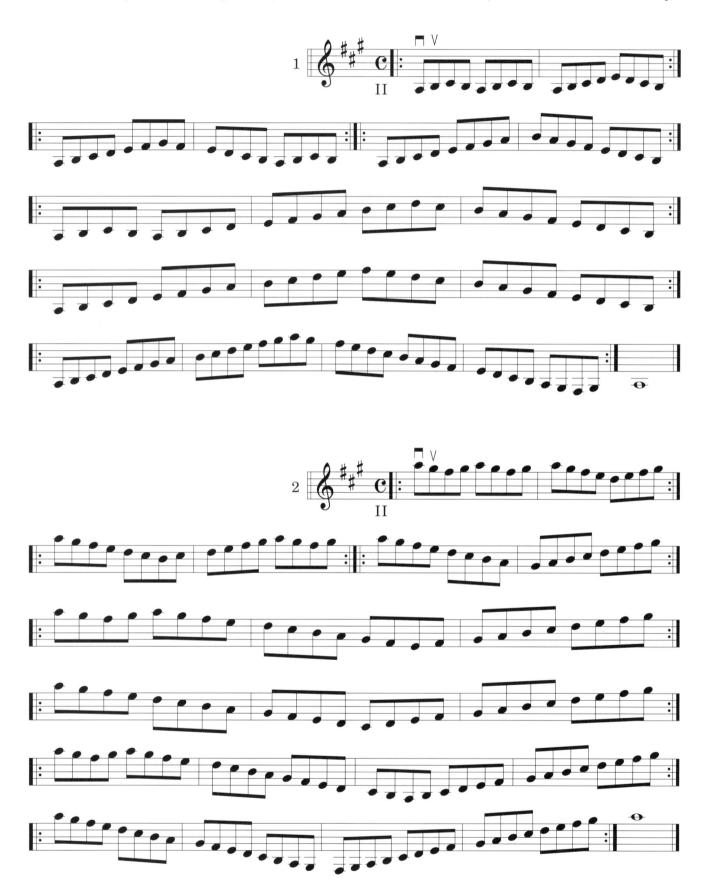

For additional technique-building patterns, see pg. 46.

Chord Forms

175

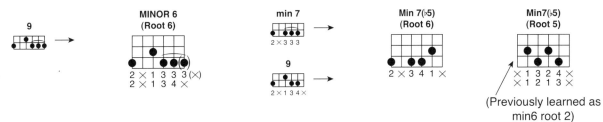

EXERCISE 1

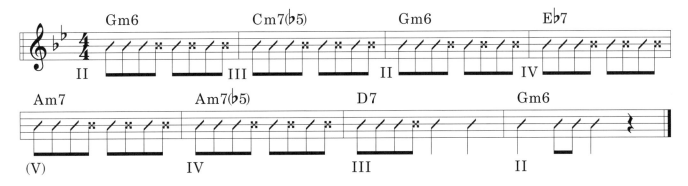

As the minor 6 and minor 7(♭5) forms tend to get confusing, study the following exercises, paying careful attention to the position marks. Play rhythm straight 4 (as written) and also practice using Latin beat. Experiment with various "pressure release" points to vary the accents.

EXERCISE 2

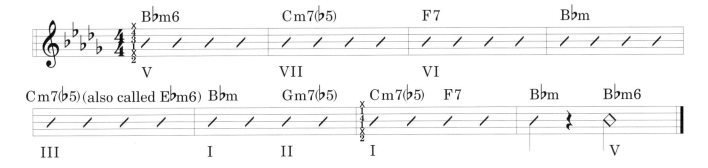

EXERCISE 3

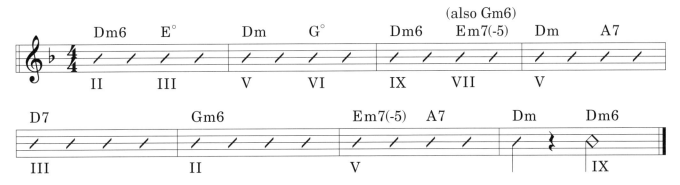

Transpose, write out, and practice all rhythm exercises one or more keys higher.

Second Position Review

Employing the five preceding major scales in position II.

176   Track 60

When played as a duet:
- Melody guitar play as written; rhythm guitar play Latin beat.
- Melody guitar play consecutive eighth notes as ; rhythm guitar play straight 4.

FINGERING TYPE 1

Chord Forms

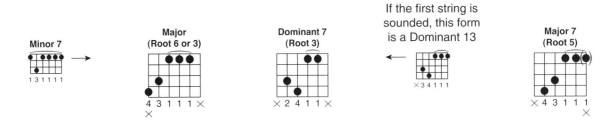

■ EXERCISE 1

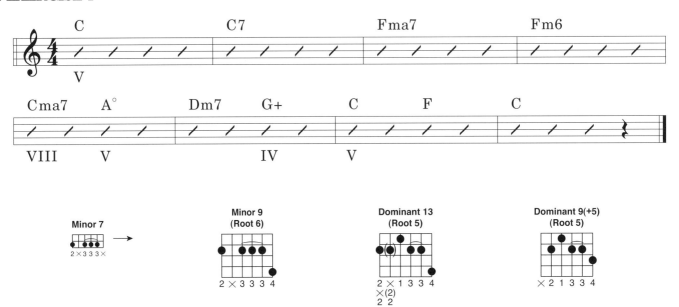

■ EXERCISE 2

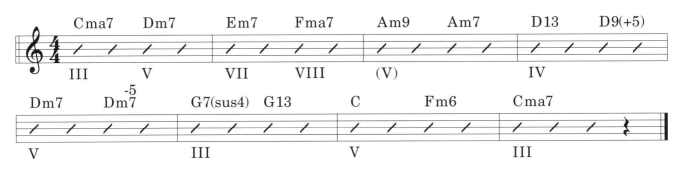

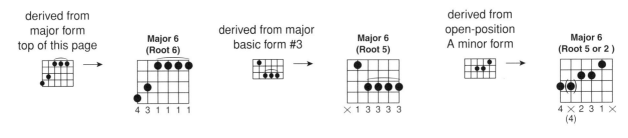

The third major 6 form shown here is, by far, the most valuable, as it does not use the first string, and therefore has a better rhythm sound.

Quarter-Note Triplets

Quarter-note triplets are very difficult to count. The most practical approach is to learn to "feel" them. This can be accomplished (as shown below) by playing two sets of eighth-note triplets using alternate picking and then two more sets of the same—but miss the string with the upstrokes of the pick.

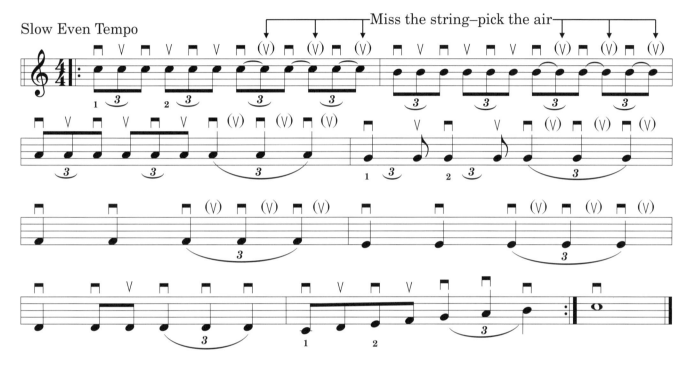

Tap your foot while playing this exercise. Keep at it until you can "feel" the  rhythm.

You are now able to read and play in five major keys in the second position. Actually, you can now play in five (major) keys in any position by using these same fingerings (Types 1, 1A, 2, 3, 4) on the higher frets.

Example: Position II major keys C, F, G, D, A

Position III C♯/D♭, F♯/G♭, A♭, E♭, B♭

Of course, you may not yet be able to read in these higher positions, as you have not seen the notes that correspond to these fingering patterns in any area of the fingerboard except the second position.
The following pages show the most used keys in the third position, first position (closed fingering, no open strings), and fourth position. You will be able to concentrate more on the notes, as by now, your fingers should know the patterns.

Major Scales in Third Position
(Most Used)

B-FLAT MAJOR (FINGERING TYPE 4)

E-FLAT MAJOR (FINGERING TYPE 3)

Fine

A-FLAT MAJOR (FINGERING TYPE 2)

Fine

D-FLAT MAJOR (FINGERING TYPE 1)

Double-flat lowers
note one tone

Cancellation
reminder–back to
B♭ as in signature

Fine

Third Position Review
Optional Duet With Rhythm Guitar
Employing the four preceding major scales in position III.

■ When played as a duet:
  • Melody guitar as written; rhythm guitar with optional Latin beat.
  • Melody guitar play consecutive eighth notes as a ♩ ♪ rhythm; rhythm guitar play straight 4.

114

TYPE 2

TYPE 1

Fine

115

Chord Forms

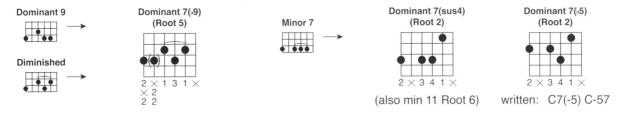

■ EXERCISE 1

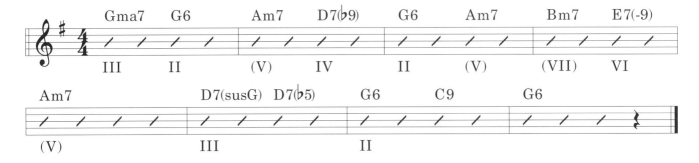

(The dominant 7(♭5) form shown above may also be named from the 6th string.)

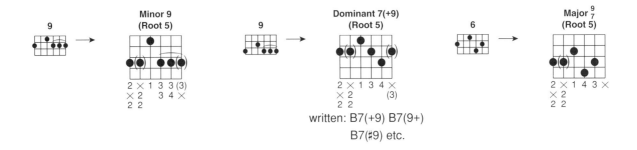

■ EXERCISE 2

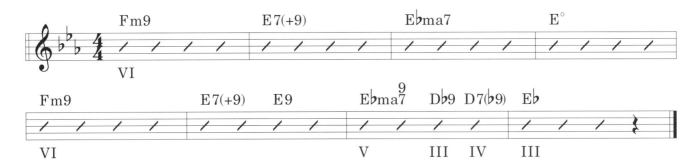

The E7(+9) chord used above would be called: E7(♯9), E7 raise 9, or E7 augmented 9. This explicit reference to the altered degree is important.

Major Scales in First Position
(Most Used)
No open strings.

A-FLAT MAJOR (FINGERING TYPE 4)

D-FLAT MAJOR (FINGERING TYPE 3)

First Position Review
Optional Duet With Rhythm Guitar
Employing the two preceding major scales in position I.

Melody guitar plays consecutive eighth notes as written and as ♩♪ rhythms. Rhythm guitar plays a waltz beat ♩ ♪ 𝄾 ♪ 𝄾 for both types of eighth-note rhythms.

Major Scales in Fourth Position
(Most Used)

G MAJOR (FINGERING TYPE 1A)

D MAJOR (FINGERING TYPE 1)

A MAJOR (FINGERING TYPE 2)

Fine

E MAJOR (FINGERING TYPE 3)

Fine

Chord Forms

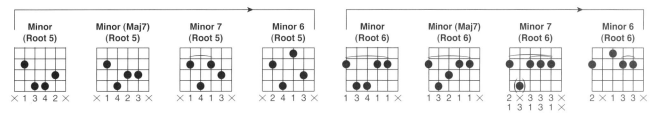

■ **EXERCISE 1**

These same minor chord sequences are often found written like this:

■ **EXERCISE 2**

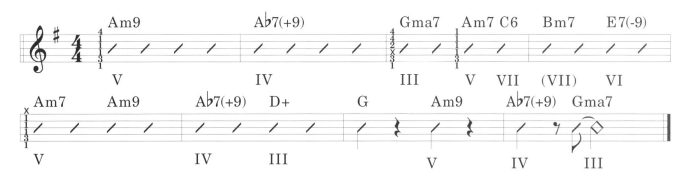

Substitution Tip: ♭5 and ♯5 forms are almost always interchangeable (also +9 and ♭9).

Fourth Position Review
Optional Duet With Rhythm Guitar
Employing the two preceding major scales in position IV.

Melody guitar plays consecutive eighth notes as written and as ♩♪ (3) rhythm. Rhythm guitar plays a waltz beat for both types of eighth-note rhythms.

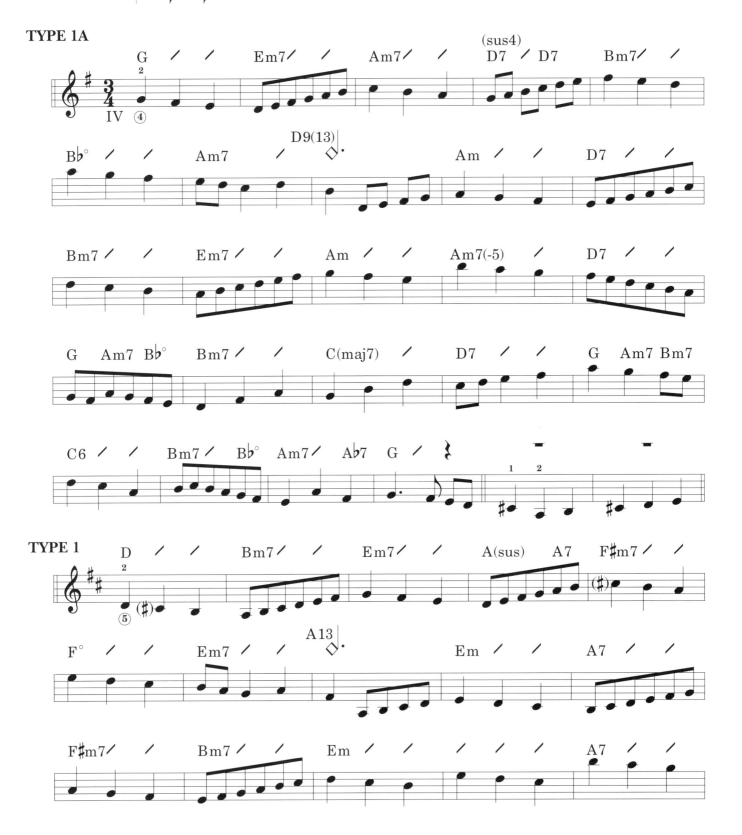

TYPE 2

TYPE 3

Fine

Find additional reading material. *Be sure it is easy to execute.* Then read five or more pages every day. Play each page *not more* than twice through. Do not practice, do not memorize, and do not use the same pages on consecutive days. Vary the material, and READ, READ, READ, READ.

Chord Forms

The root of this form is one fret below any fingered note. It has four possible names, like the diminished 7 chord.

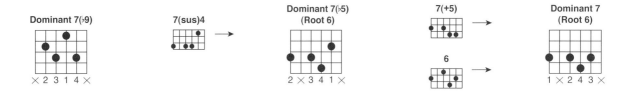

■ EXERCISE

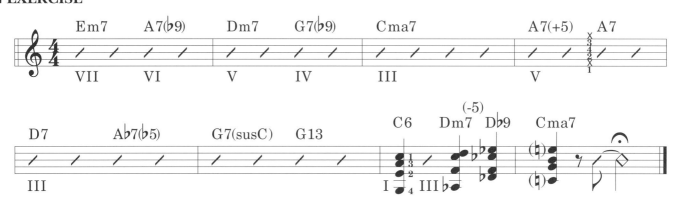

Author's Notes

All forms presented in this book that employ the 6th string (and therefore sound in part in the real bass register) have the root (first) or fifth chordal degrees sounding on the bottom. These are the "strongest" chord tones and *always sound right.*

You have probably seen some of these same forms elsewhere with different chord names indicated. Theoretically, these other names are also correct. However, the bass notes are "weak" chordal degrees and require special handling. This will be discussed thoroughly in a later section. Until then be careful of any forms that use the 6th string and do not have the root or fifth in the bass as they do not always sound right.

In an orchestral rhythm part, the chord symbols used generally indicate the total or complete harmonic structures, and it is not expected (nor is it possible) that you play all degrees at all times. Of course, you should try to play as close as possible to the written sequences. Actually, simplification by omitting some of the chordal degrees is the "norm." (It is best, for now, to omit the higher degrees.)

Examples: For C7+5(♭9) you may play: C7(+5)(omit the ♭9) or C+
              For G7 (♭9,13) you may play: G7(♭9)(omit the 13) or G7
              For F9(sus4) you may play: F7(sus4) (omit the 9)

Be very careful of substitutions, as they must be completely compatible with the chord(s) indicated. (More about this in later volumes.)

Now, in addition to the five major keys in the second position, you should be somewhat familiar with the most used major scales in positions I, III, and IV. You will have to do a great deal of reading in these areas, however, to really know them.

I cannot overemphasize the importance of learning the four major scale fingering types well, as they are the foundation for other kinds of scales. We will gradually add more (major) fingering patterns until, ultimately, we have twelve—one for each key in each position. At the same time, we will learn how to *convert previously practiced* major forms onto jazz minor, harmonic minor, etc.

Our next project (*Modern Method for Guitar, Volume II*) will be to learn the notes on the entire fingerboard by using all fingering types *in the same key.* This will require moving from position to position as we go through the patterns. The sequence of patterns will vary, depending upon the key signature. You will have a definite advantage in learning the fingerboard in this manner, as your fingers "know" the patterns and you can concentrate on the notes.

Remember, learning to play the guitar is an accumulative process. Regular, complete review is absolutely necessary for the gradual improvement and perfection of the techniques.

Index

SCALES: OPEN (FIRST) POSITION

SCALES: MOVABLE FINGERINGS (POSITION PLAYING)

SOLOS

SPEED STUDIES

A MODERN
METHOD
FOR GUITAR

william leavitt

volume

Introduction

This book is a continuation of *Modern Method for Guitar, Volume I.* Most of the terms and techniques are directly evolved from material presented there. For example, the entire fingerboard is covered at once in the five-position C major scale study. This is accomplished by connecting the four basic fingering patterns (Types 1, 2, 3, 4) and one derivative (Type 1A) that hopefully were mastered from the first book. (The sequence of fingering types will vary from position to position up the neck, depending upon the key.)

Study all the material in sequence, as I have tried to relate all new techniques and theoretical concepts to something already learned.

As in the previous volume, all music is original and has been created especially for the presentation and perfection of the lesson material.

Please be advised that the pages devoted to theory are not intended to replace the serious study of this subject with a competent teacher, but rather to intrigue the more inquisitive student, and maybe shed some light on the mysterious workings of music for guitar players in general.

Good luck and have fun.

Wm. G. Leavitt

It is important to learn the following material in consecutive order. The index on pg. 117 is for reference only and will prove valuable for review or concentration on specific techniques.

Contents
Section One

Section Two

SECTION ONE

Four Basic Major-Scale Fingering Patterns

  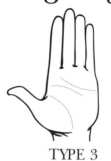 

TYPE 1   TYPE 2   TYPE 3   TYPE 4

■ *(s)*: Finger Stretch

Remember: Do not move entire hand.

TYPE 1   All out-of-position scale tones played with first-finger stretches (See *Vol. I,* pg. 60.)

C Major

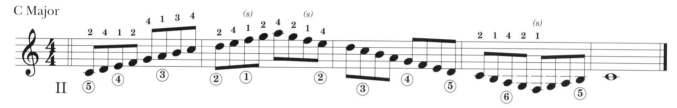

TYPE 2   No finger stretches necessary for scale tones

G Major

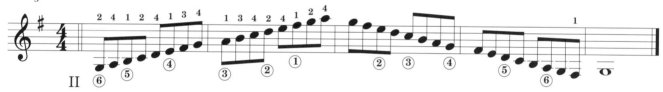

TYPE 3   No stretches

D Major

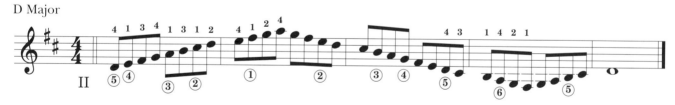

TYPE 4   All out-of-position scale tones played with fourth-finger stretches

A Major

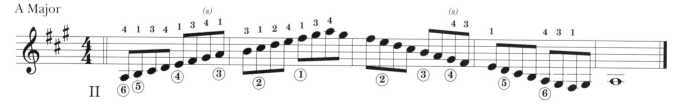

All scales (major and minor, etc.) will be derived from these four basic major-scale patterns. Ultimately, five major keys will be possible in each position with Type 1 and its four derivative fingering patterns: 1A, 1B, 1C, and 1D. This also applies to Type 4 and its derivatives: 4A, 4B, 4C, and 4D. Fingering Types 2 and 3 have no derivative major fingering patterns.

C Major—Ascending (Five Positions)

FINGERING TYPE 1

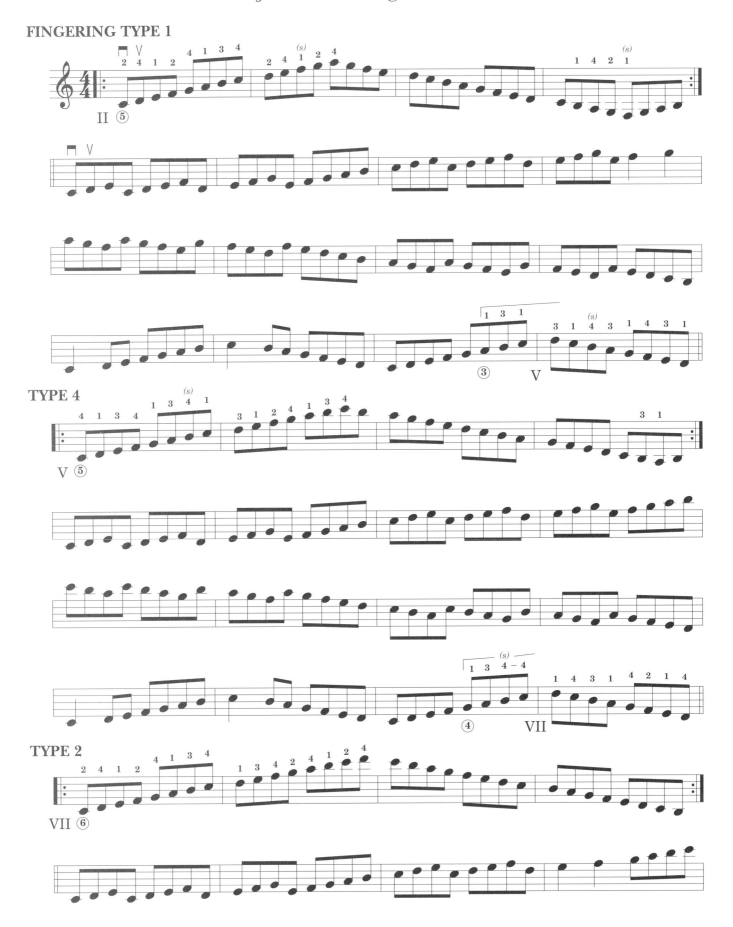

TYPE 4

TYPE 2

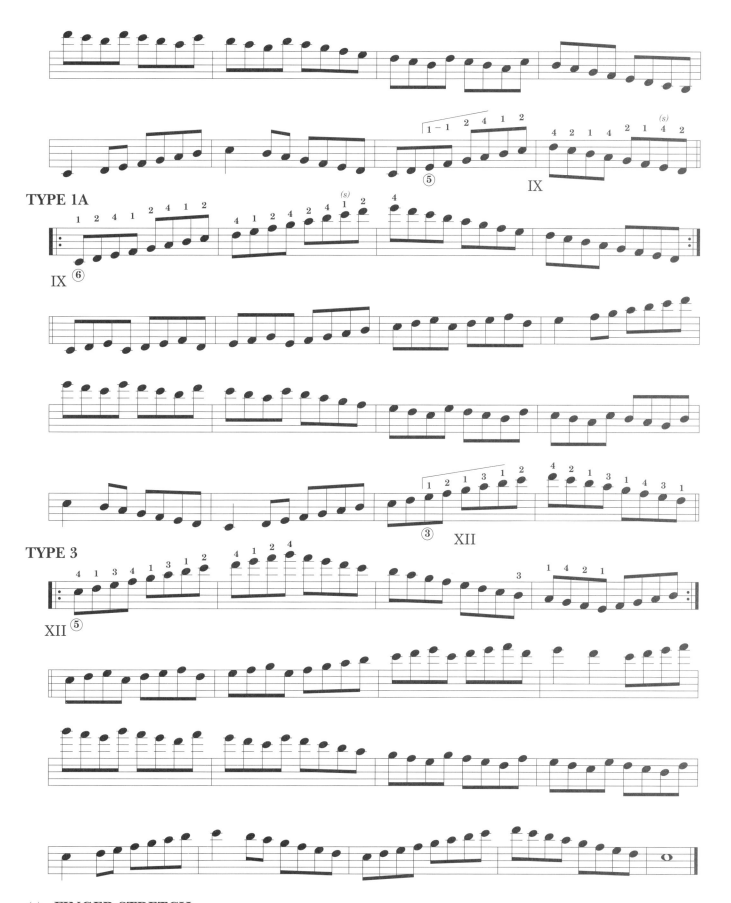

TYPE 1A

TYPE 3

(s): **FINGER STRETCH**

C Major—Descending (Five Positions)

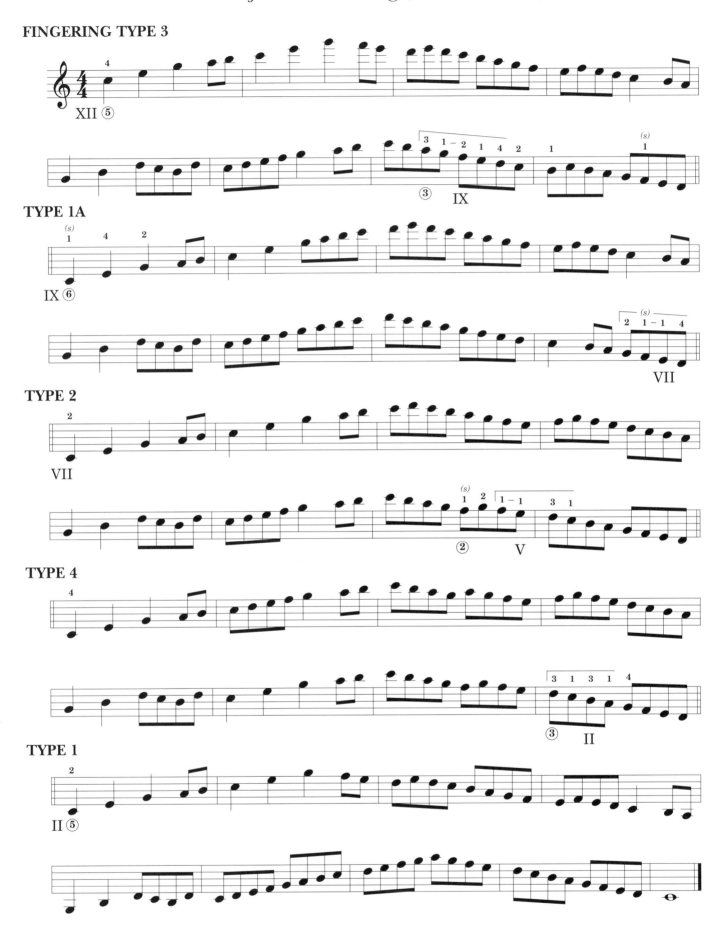

Getting Up There (duet)

Chord Etude No. 6

Mod. Slow

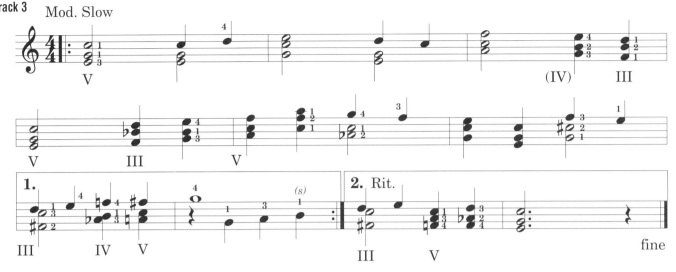

Observe fingering carefully.

Melodic Rhythm Study No. 2

This is a notation comparison, not a duet.

¢ is referred to as "Alla Breve," "Cut Time," or "In Two."

¢ or 2/2: Half note (♩) gets one beat

2/4: Quarter (♩) note gets one beat

Triads (Three-Note Chords)

CONSTRUCTION FROM MAJOR SCALES

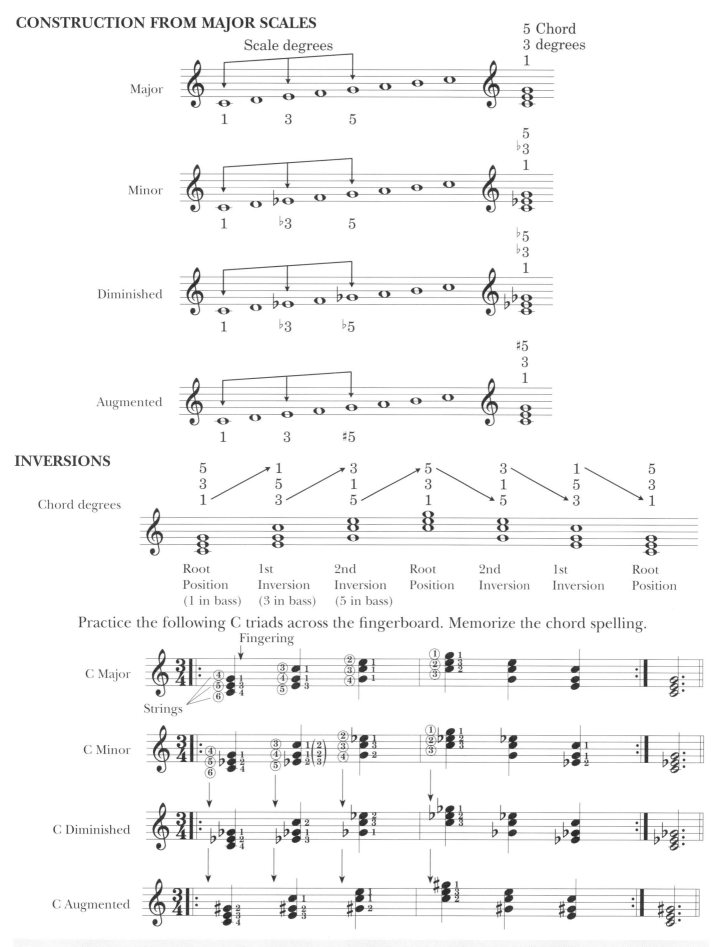

INVERSIONS

Practice the following C triads across the fingerboard. Memorize the chord spelling.

Note common finger and string relationships between most forms.

F Major—Ascending (Five Positions)

FINGERING TYPE 1A

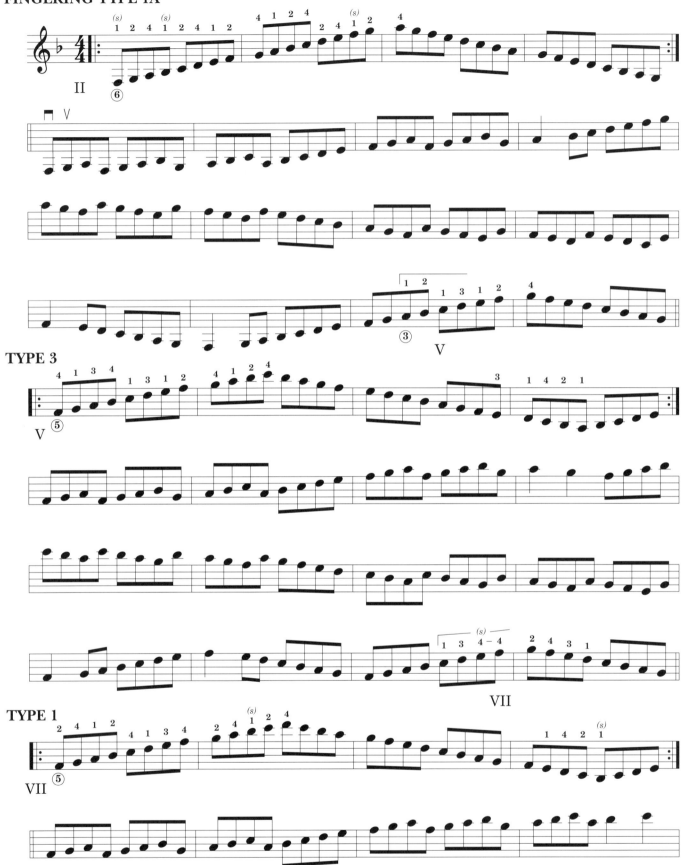

TYPE 3

TYPE 1

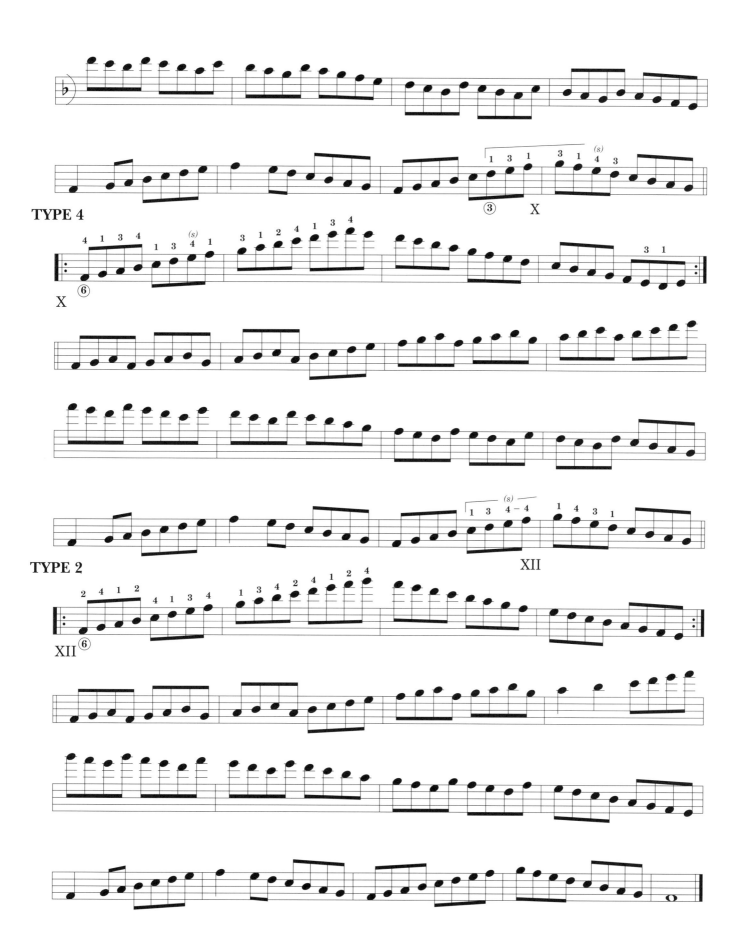

F Major—Descending (Five Positions)

FINGERING TYPE 2

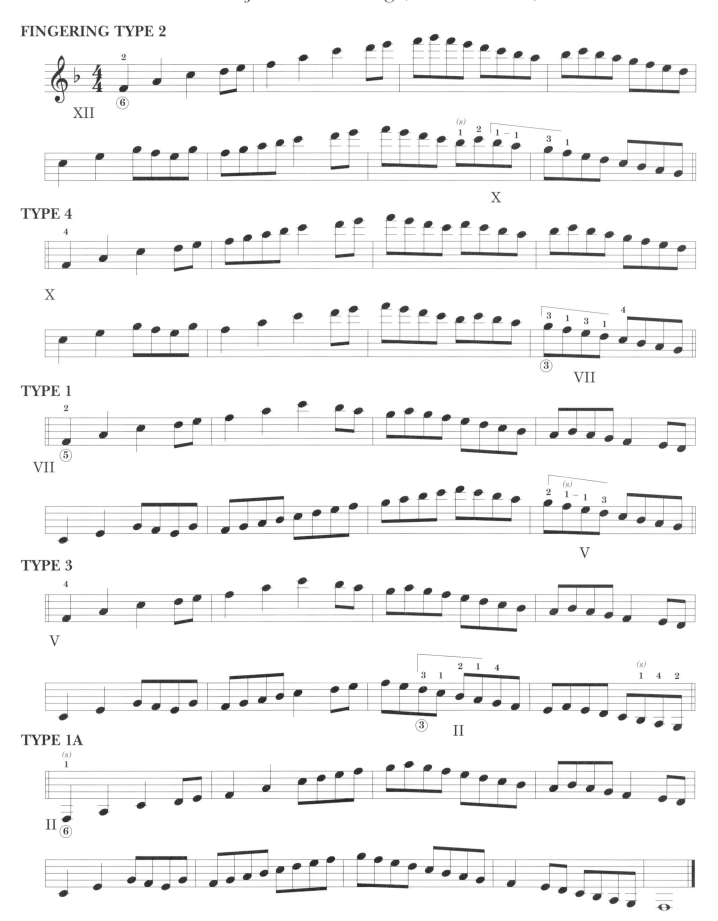

TYPE 4

TYPE 1

TYPE 3

TYPE 1A

Another Waltz for Two (duet)

Track 4

Chord Forms

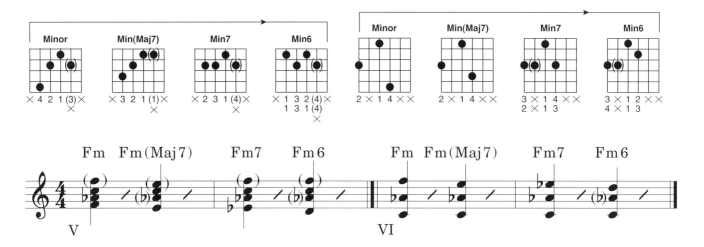

*Also see *Vol. I,* pg. 121.

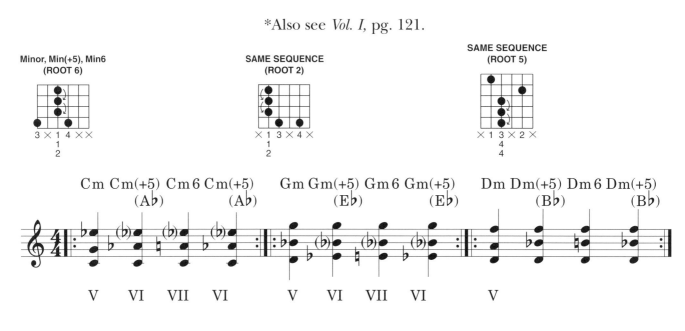

Speed Study

Keep tempo constant throughout.

To practice other fingering patterns, play "Speed Study" as written, but change the key signature to A, D, G, and C.

Triads

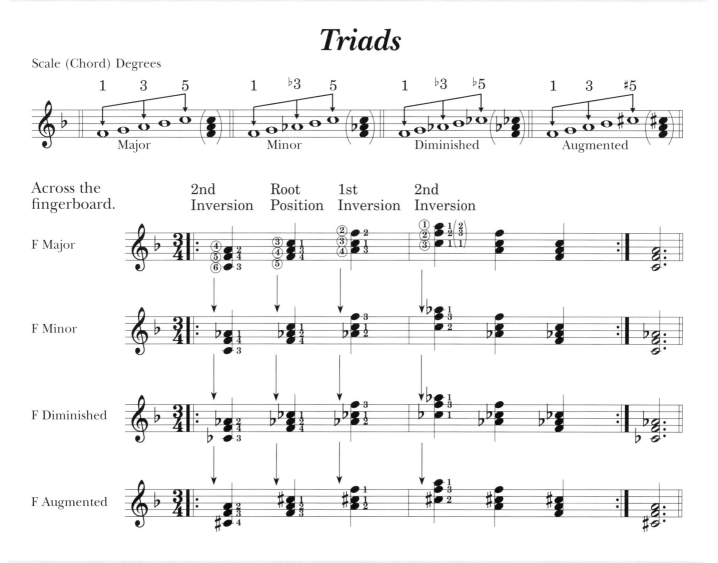

Observe the fingering: Note common finger(s) between most forms.

Rhythm Guitar—The Right Hand ($\frac{4}{4}$ and 2 Beat)

For a good rhythm section blend, all notes of a chord must seem to explode into sound at the same instant. This can be accomplished by a combination of downward, rotary forearm and loose wrist motion, as if flecking something from the back of your hand. The pick must travel very quickly across the strings to match the sound of the production of a pizzicato note on the bass violin.

NOTATION: ⊓ Downstroke

V Upstroke

× Strike muffled strings; fingers in formation

, Release pressure immediately after chord sounds

All strokes labeled "Basic" are usually best when used with a guitar alone or with an incomplete rhythm section.

Basic Stroke:
Four, Four, and Two Beat

Orchestral:
Four, Four

Chord duration must
match notes of bass violin.

The "Chop"
(often slightly amplified)

For use with organ groups
and similar small combos.

■ **EXERCISE**

Practice in all three styles, with emphasis on the orchestral stroke.

The principal difficulty in the above orchestral stroke is in producing the sharp, explosive attack while keeping the chord duration long.

Orchestral
"Two Beat"

❋ It is sometimes advisable in practice (and in use) to lightly hit the (muffled) top strings on the returning upstroke where rests are indicated.

■ **EXERCISE**

Be sure to practice at slow, medium, and fast tempos. When learning this style of rhythm playing, it is necessary to tap the foot. First tap on beats 1 and 3, and later tap on 1, 2, 3, and 4.

Orchestral Fast to Very Fast "Four"

Tap the foot "in two" (i.e. on beats 1 and 3)

Make the upstroke sound as much like the downstroke as possible by favoring the lower strings with the returning upstroke of the pick. There will be a slight natural accent on beats 2 and 4, because the downstroke hits the heavy string first. This is good, as it is comparable to the drummer's use of the hi-hat cymbal on these beats.

■ **EXERCISE**

This right-hand technique is difficult to master but is extremely valuable. It allows you to maintain very bright tempos (steady as a rock) with very little tightening up.

Chord Etude No. 7

$\frac{3}{8}$: Eighth note (♪) gets one beat

All notes connected by a curved line must be kept ringing.

Moderately Fast Waltz

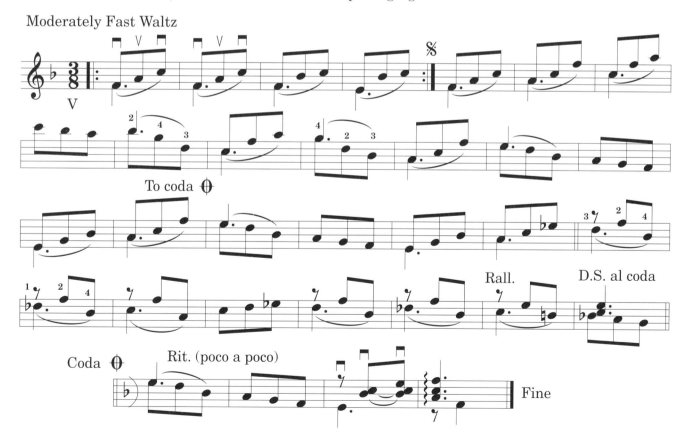

17

G Major—Ascending (Five Positions)

FINGERING TYPE 2

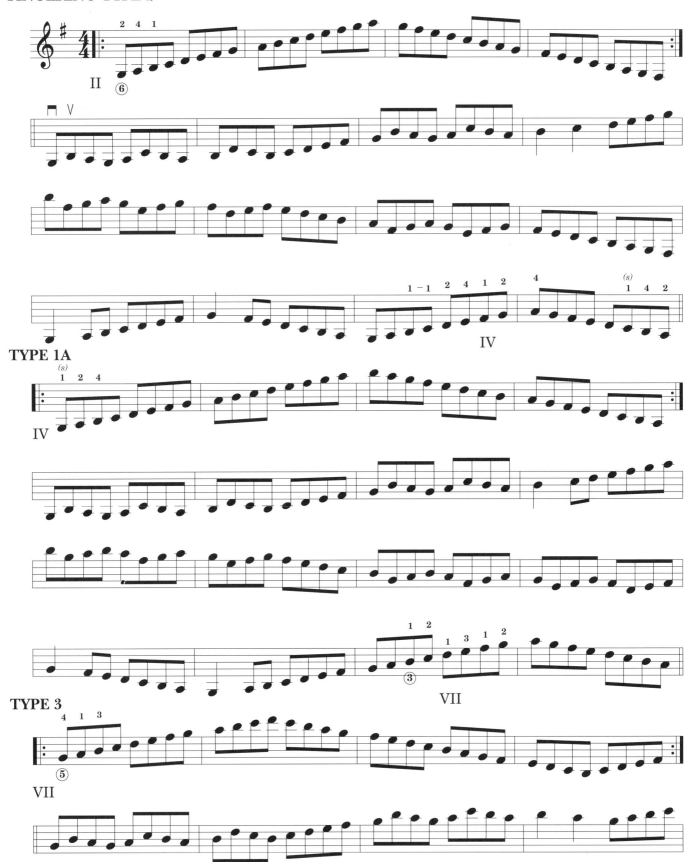

TYPE 1A

TYPE 3

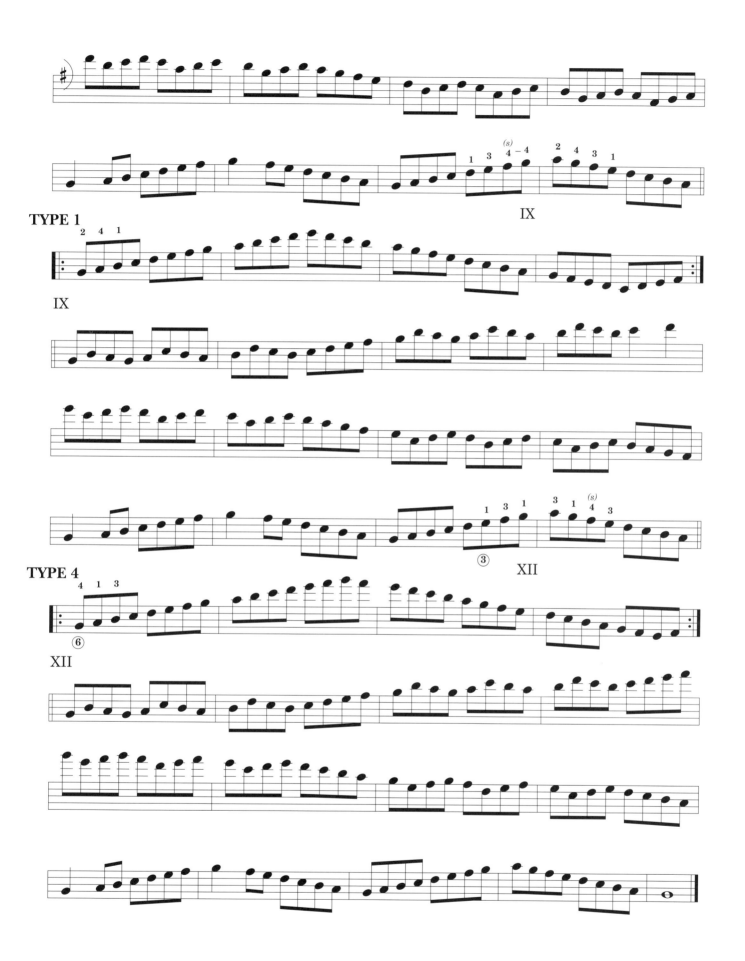

TYPE 1

IX

TYPE 4

XII

G Major—Descending (Five Positions)

FINGERING TYPE 4

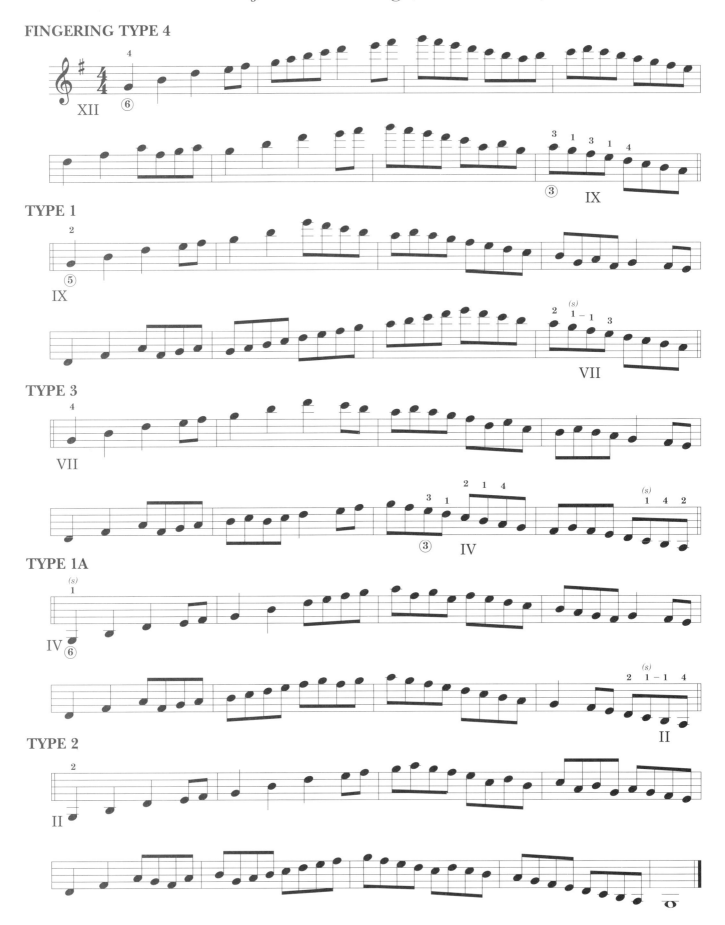

TYPE 1

TYPE 3

TYPE 1A

TYPE 2

Sea-See-Si (duet)

Note durations are relative to tempo. Sixteenth notes will not sound fast if the tempo is slow.

Chord Forms

A.R. = Assumed Root

Most of the chord form pages from here on are highly concentrated. I recommend that you practice one line at a time while going on with the note studies on the following pages. Keep coming back periodically until all forms and sequences are mastered.

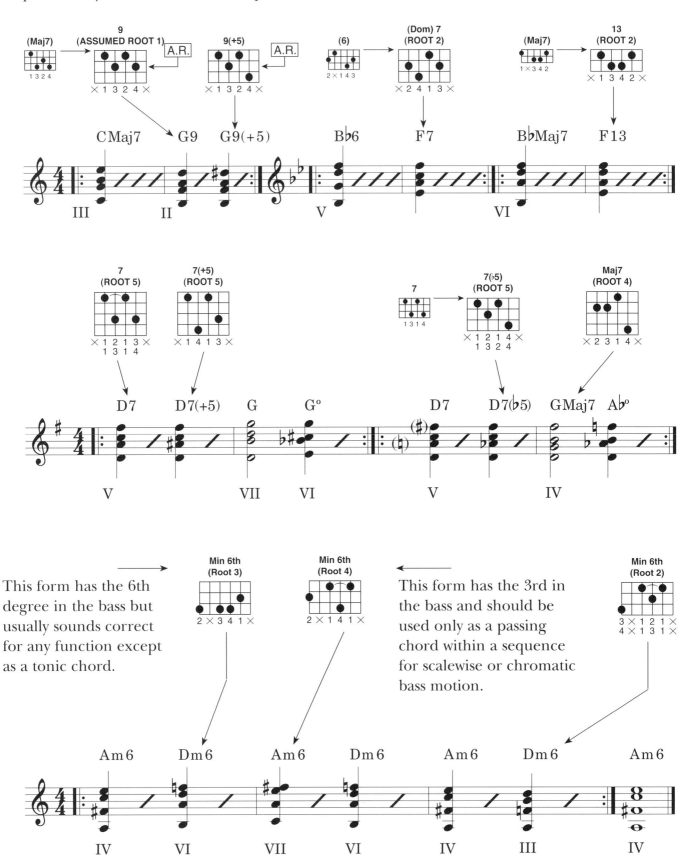

This form has the 6th degree in the bass but usually sounds correct for any function except as a tonic chord.

This form has the 3rd in the bass and should be used only as a passing chord within a sequence for scalewise or chromatic bass motion.

22

Triads

Scale (Chord) Degrees

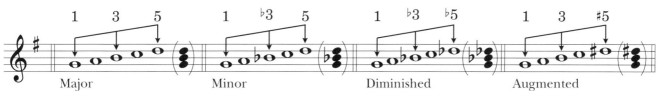

Across the fingerboard.

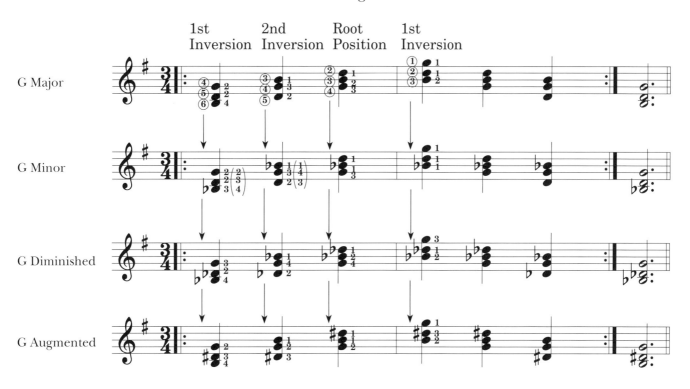

Finger Stretching Exercises

D Major—Ascending (Five Positions)

FINGERING TYPE 3

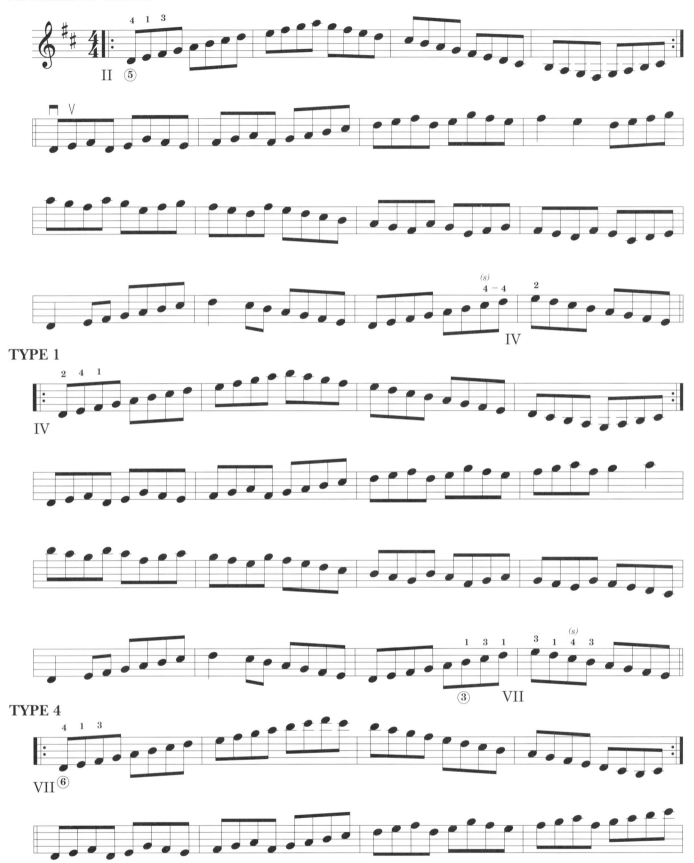

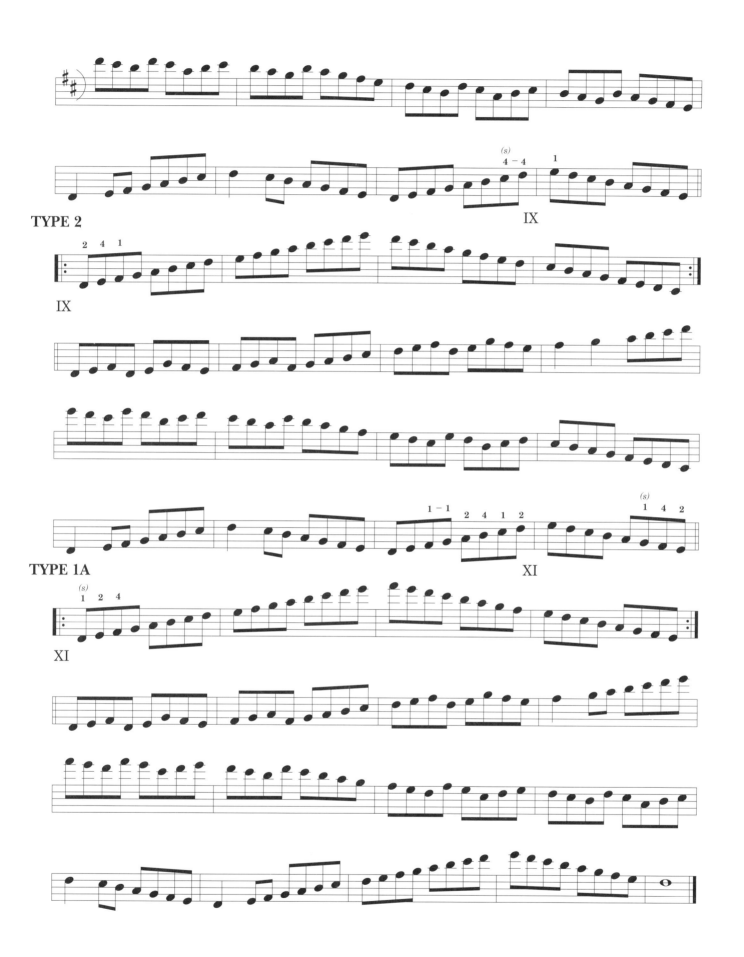

TYPE 2   IX

IX

TYPE 1A   XI

XI

D Major—Descending (Five Positions)

FINGERING TYPE 1A

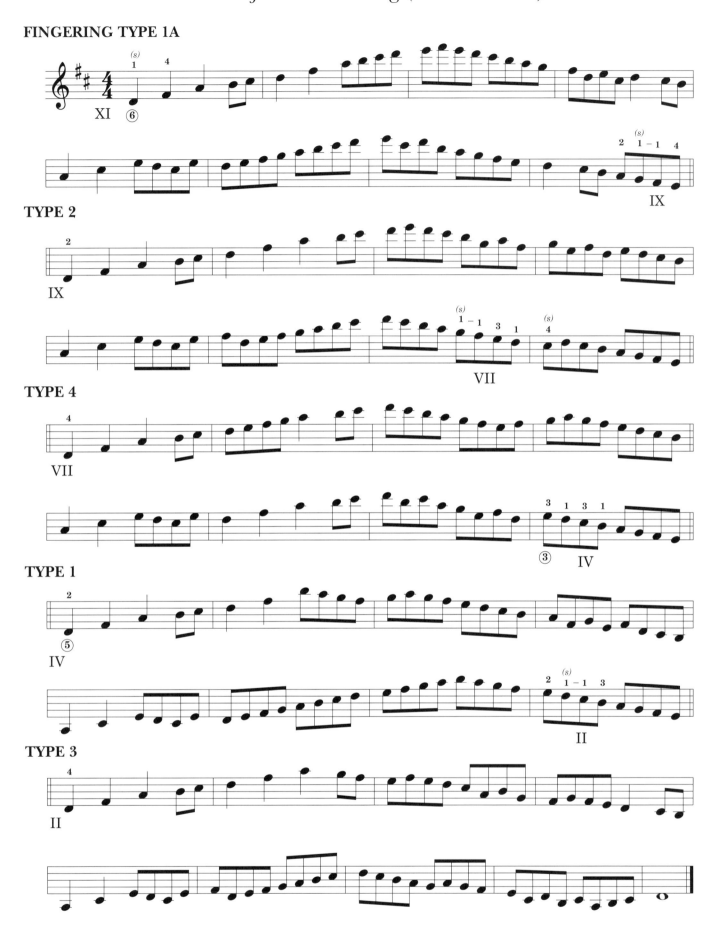

TYPE 2

TYPE 4

TYPE 1

TYPE 3

Melodic Rhythm Study No. 3 (duet)

Intervals

Interval: The number of whole and half steps between two notes.

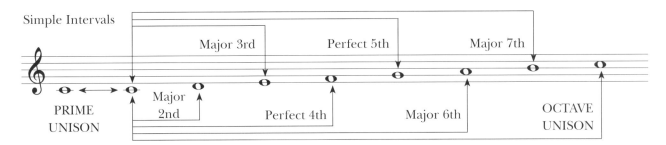

The above numbers represent the scale and chord degrees, as well as the interval from the tonic.

- If the top note is a member of the major scale of the bottom note, the interval is called: major 2nd, major 3rd, major 6th, major 7th, or perfect 4th, perfect 5th, perfect octave.

- Intervals one half step smaller than major are called *minor.* Intervals one half step smaller than *perfect* or a whole step smaller than major are called *diminished.* Any major or perfect interval expanded by one half step is called *augmented.*

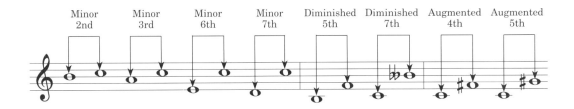

When only the numerical term (3rd, 4th, etc.) is used, major and perfect intervals are intended. Minor, diminished, and augmented intervals must be specifically named.

Compound intervals (larger than one octave) are described by the same terms as simple intervals (one octave or less) from which they are derived. (Example: Major and minor 2nd plus an octave = major and minor 9th.)

Compound Intervals

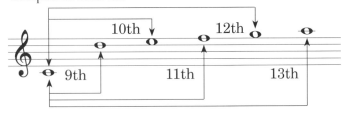

Triads

Scale (Chord) Degrees

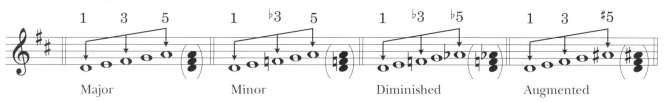

As you move across and up the fingerboard, carefully observe fingerings and strings.

D Major

Root 1st 2nd Root
Pos. Inv. Inv. Pos.

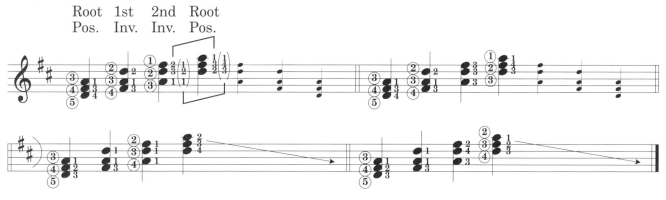

D Minor

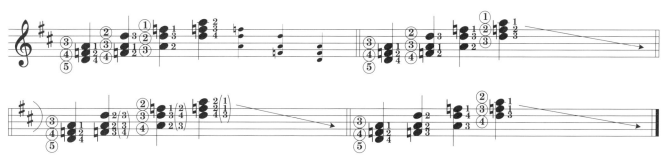

D Diminished

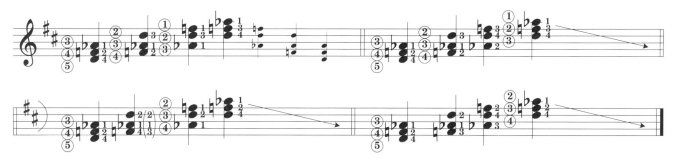

D Augmented

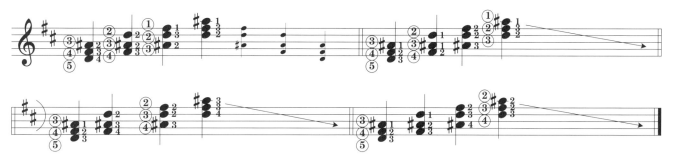

A Major—Ascending (Five Positions)

FINGERING TYPE 4

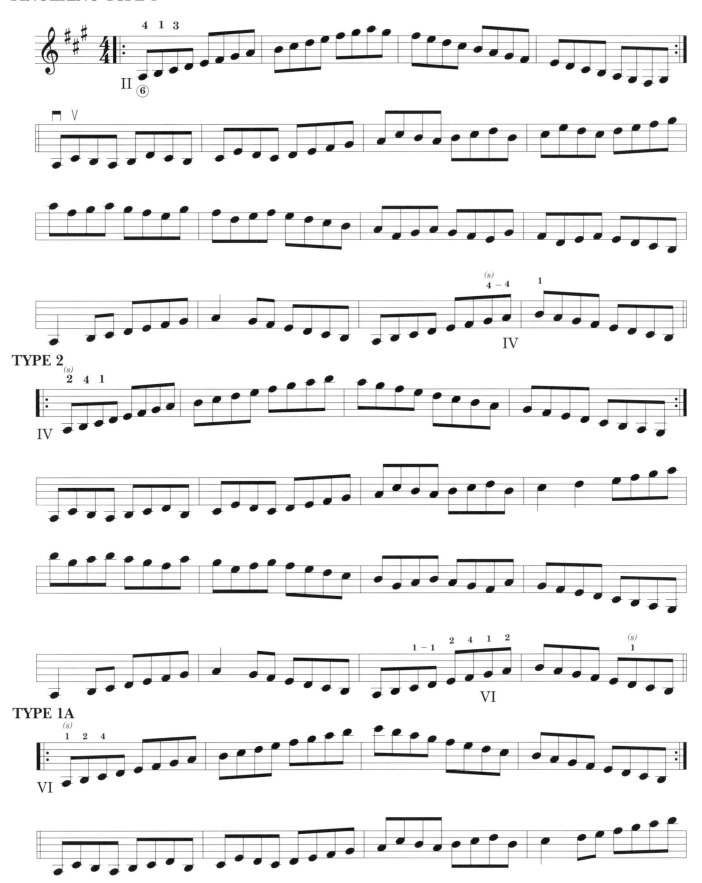

TYPE 2

TYPE 1A

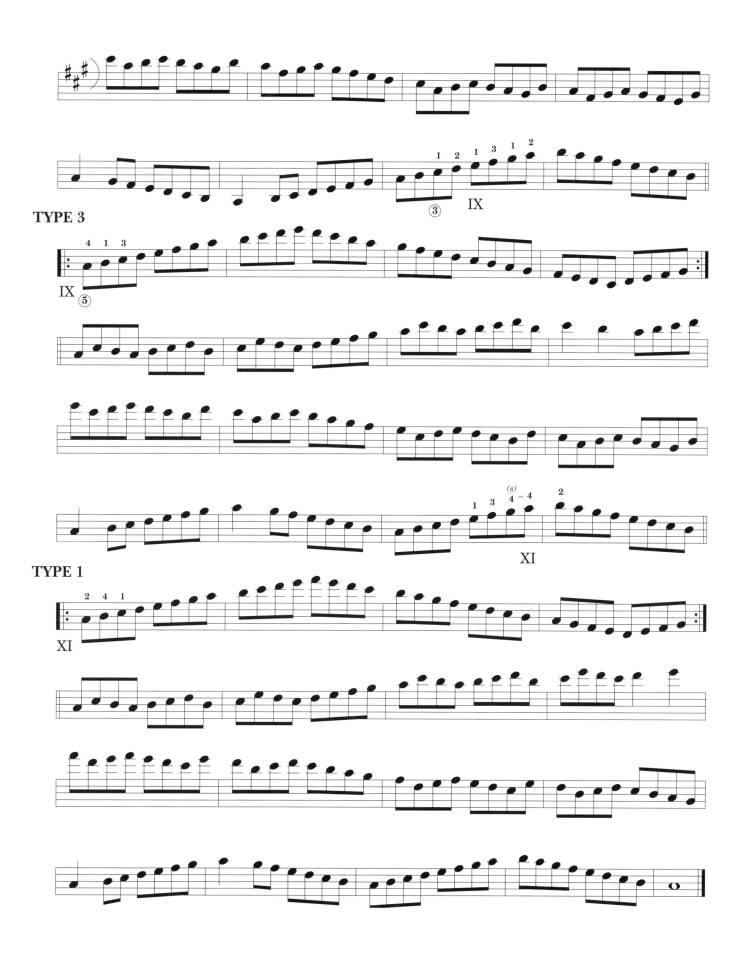

TYPE 3

TYPE 1

A Major—Descending (Five Positions)

FINGERING TYPE 1

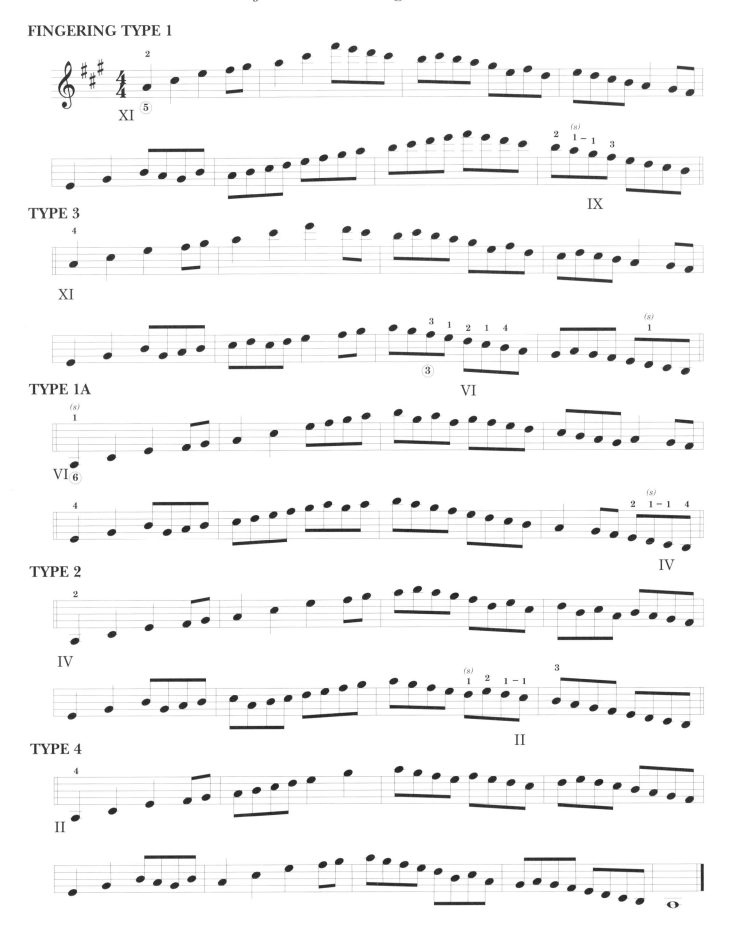

TYPE 3

TYPE 1A

TYPE 2

TYPE 4

Track 7

Chord Etude No. 8

Rubato

II   (V)   (VII)   III ——— II

1.

2.

II

Fine

Rhythm Guitar—Right Hand (Rock-Style Ballad)

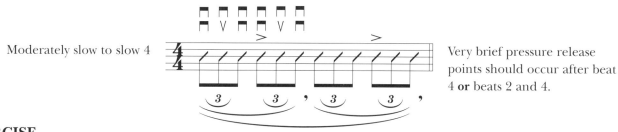

Moderately slow to slow 4

Very brief pressure release points should occur after beat 4 **or** beats 2 and 4.

■ **EXERCISE**

Observe notation.

G6   Ab°   D7sus4   D7(b5)   G6

simile (continue in similar manner)

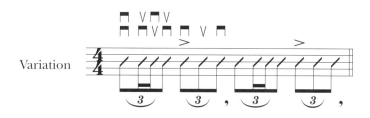

Variation

■ **EXERCISE**

Observe notation.

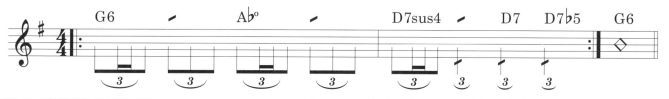

G6   Ab°   D7sus4   D7   D7b5   G6

These strokes are used with regular acoustic and amplified (high-register) rhythm playing. Observe notation.

Chord Forms

A.R.: Assumed Root

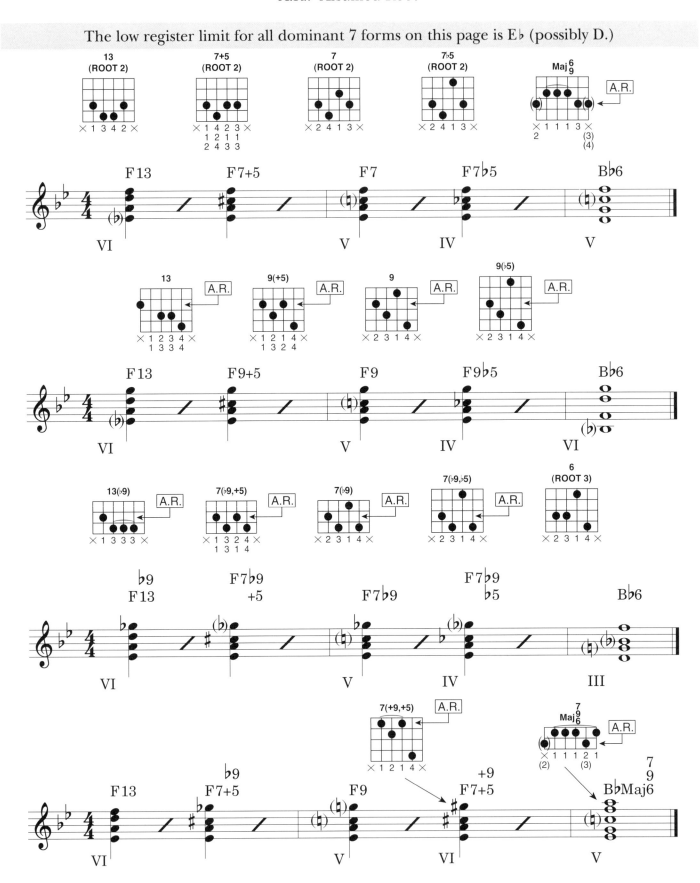

Do not be concerned with the theoretical explanation of the more complex chords. They will be covered in a later section. Most important for now is the physical ability to perform them and eventually memorize all forms, chord types, and root locations.

These are the same forms as those shown on the opposite page. The roots are different and the sequence is reversed. Considerable time will be required to really learn them.

The low register limit for all dominant 7 forms on this page is A♭ (possibly G). Also, all ♭5s on this and the preceding page may be considered Augmented 11 (+11).

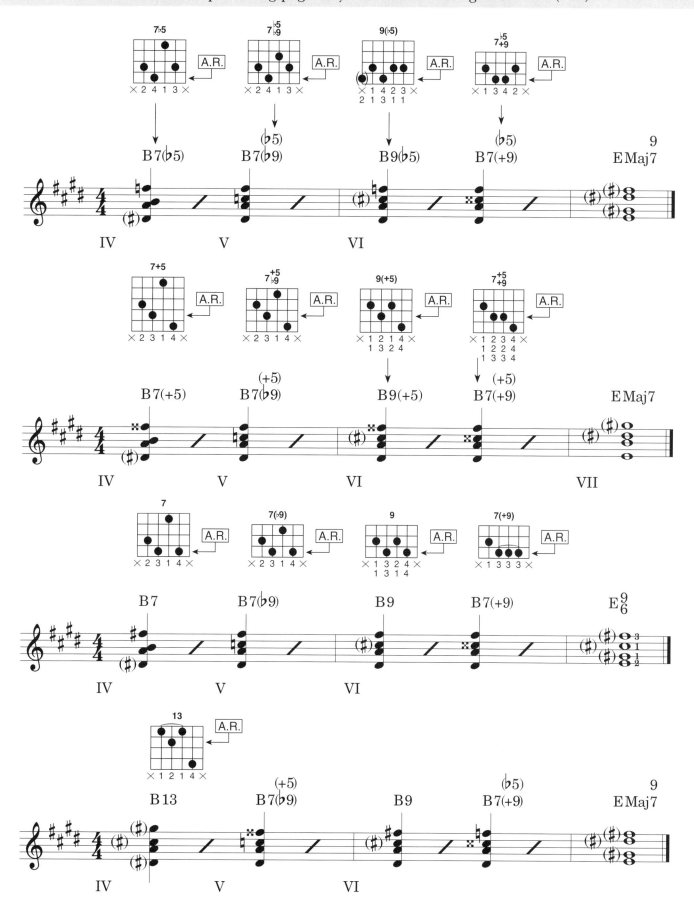

35

Tranquility (duet)

Sustain all notes full value.

Triads

Scale (Chord) Degrees

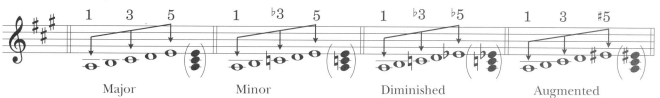

As you move across and up the fingerboard, carefully observe fingerings and strings.

A Major

A Minor

A Diminished

A Augmented

Bb Major—Ascending (Five Positions)

FINGERING TYPE 4

TYPE 2

TYPE 1A

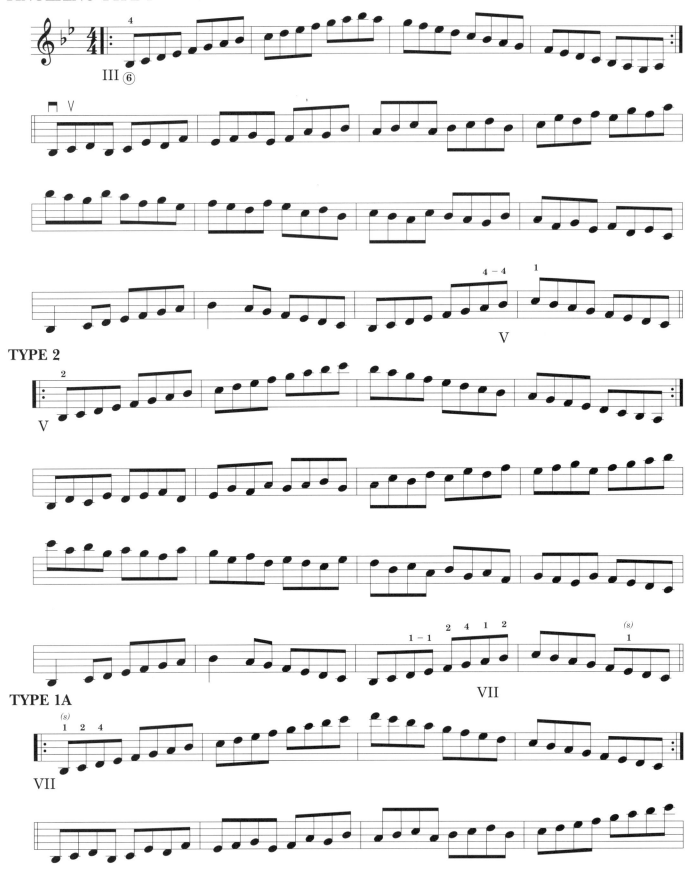

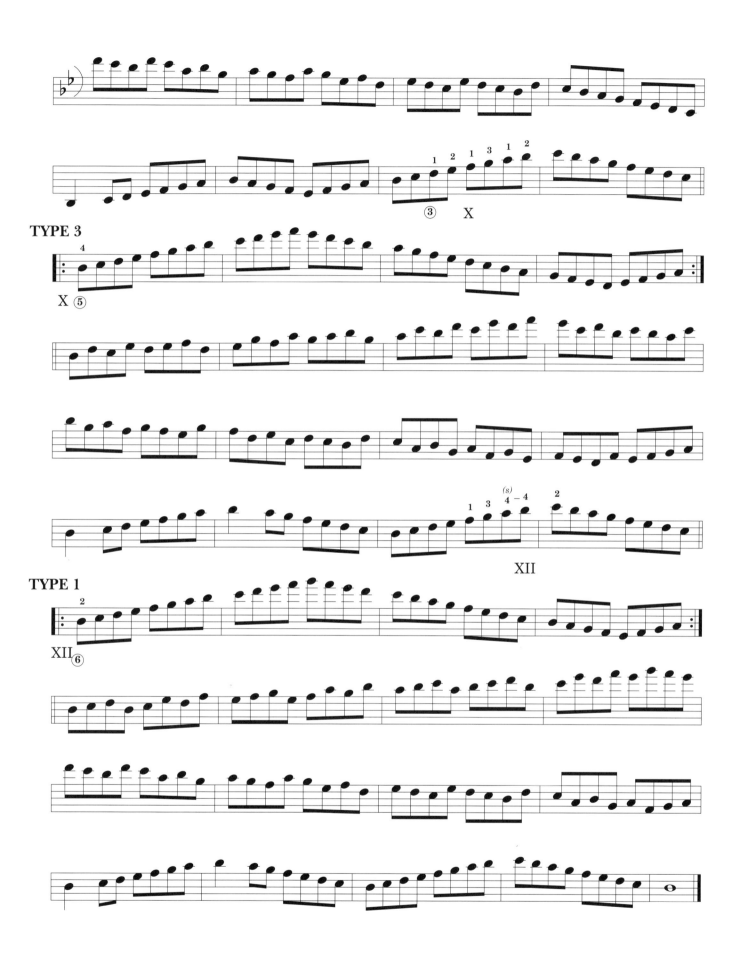

B♭ Major—Descending (Five Positions)

FINGERING TYPE 1

TYPE 3

TYPE 1A

TYPE 2

TYPE 4

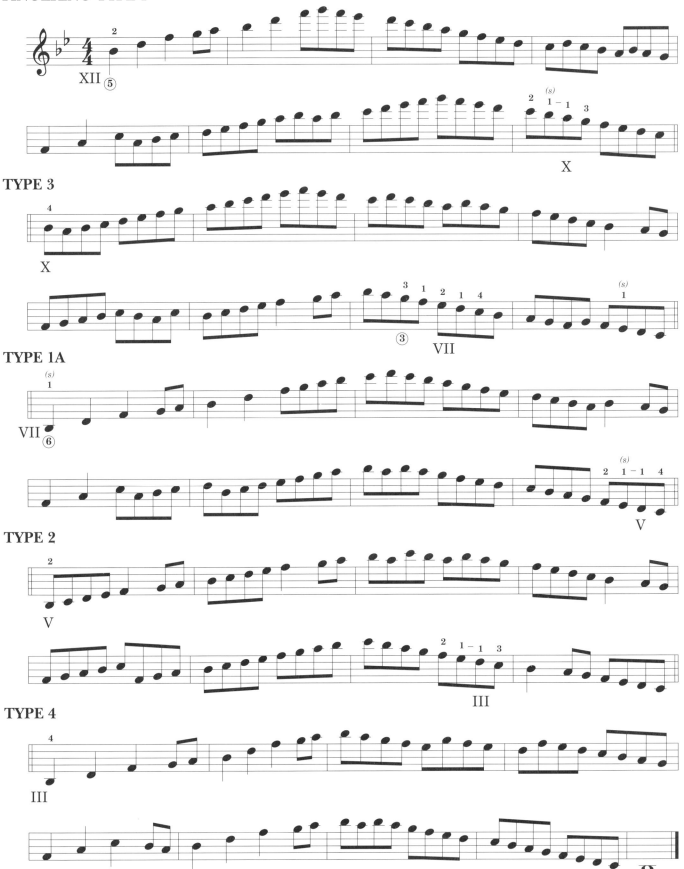

Waltz in B♭ (duet)

Melodic Rhythm Study No. 4

This is a notation comparison, not a duet.

A fast waltz is often best counted "in 1." Beats 2 and 3 are merely felt. 6/8 is usually counted "in 2," each measure being divided in half (like two fast waltz measures). However, a slower 6/8 is counted 1-2-3-4-5-6. Each eighth note gets one full beat.

Note durations are relative to tempo and time signatures.

Finger Stretching Exercises

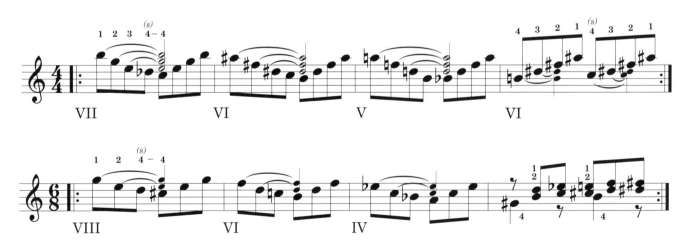

Triads

Scale (Chord) Degrees

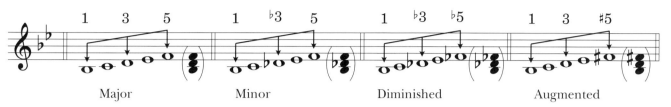

As you move across and up the fingerboard, carefully observe fingerings and strings.

Pentatonic (Five-Note) Scales

A good preparation for arpeggio studies.

MAJOR (1, 2, 3, 5, 6 OF MAJOR SCALE)

Tremolo Study

Tremolo: Quick repetition of the same note.

At first, practice very slowly and evenly. Later, gradually increase the tempo, but keep it steady throughout. Practice all "Loco" (in the same octave as written) and also 8va (one octave higher than written).

Observe picking.

■ **EXERCISE 1**

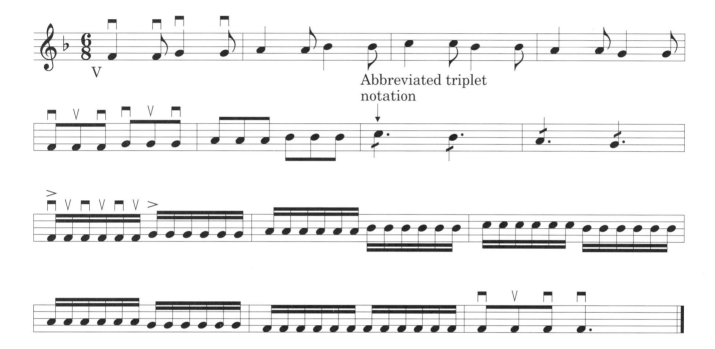

Abbreviated triplet notation

■ **EXERCISE 2**

Abbreviated eighth note notation

Abbreviated 16th note notation

Abbreviated 32nd note notation

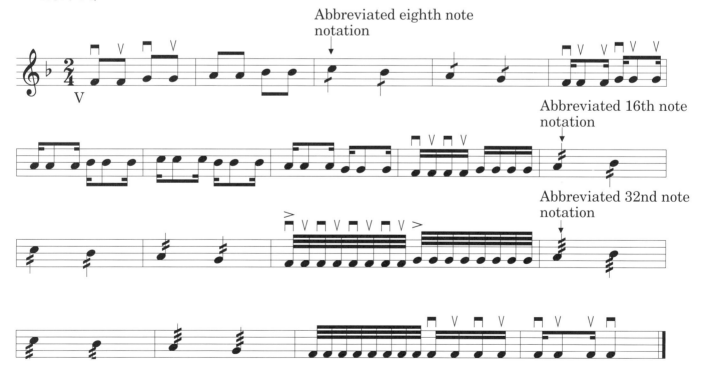

45

E♭ Major—Ascending (Five Positions)

FINGERING TYPE 3

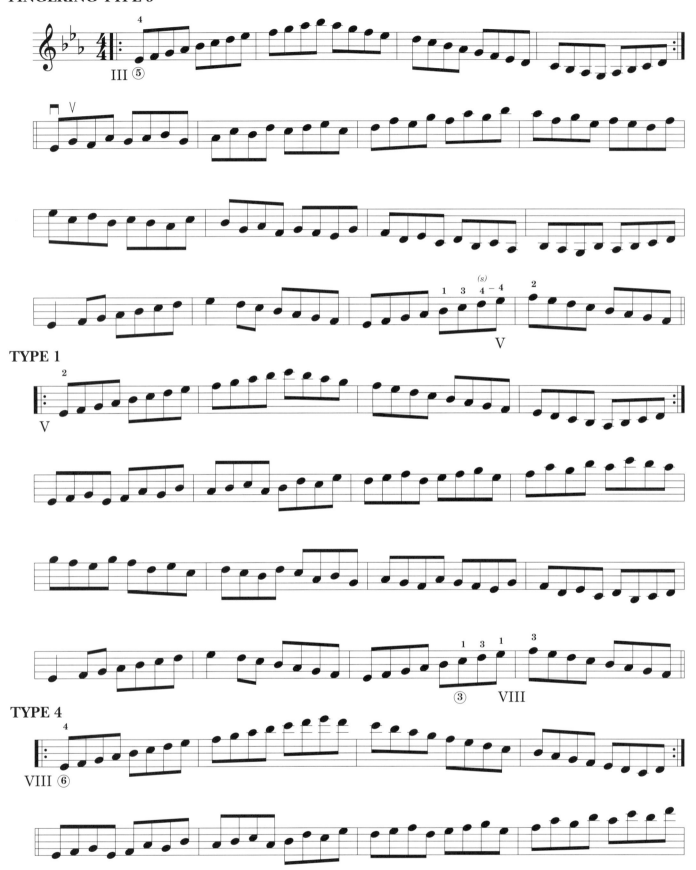

TYPE 1

TYPE 4

46

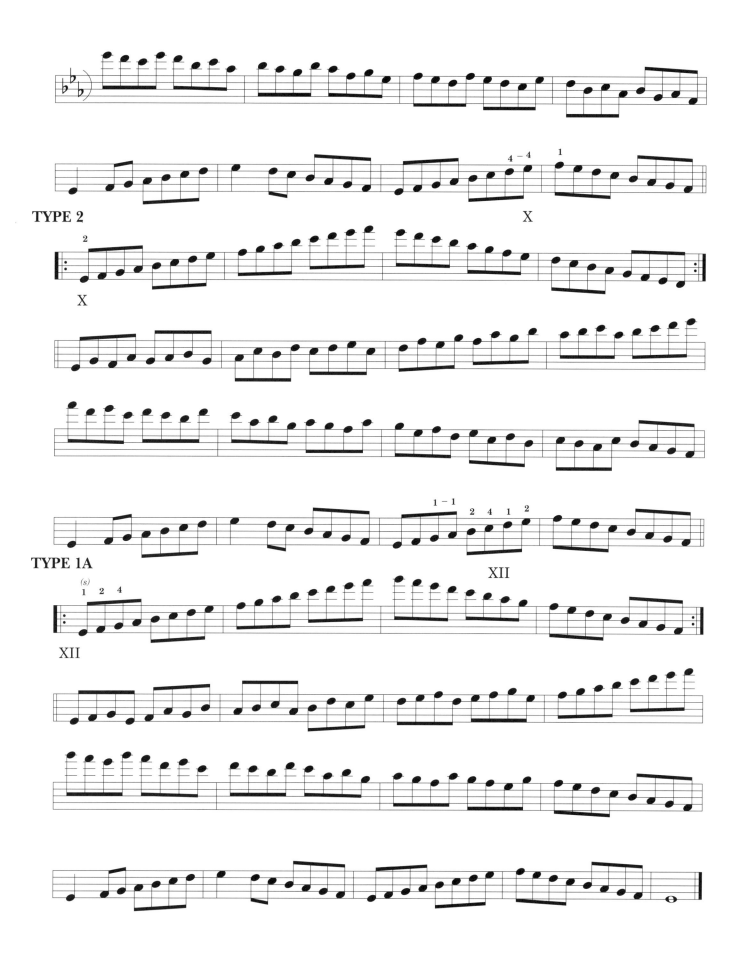

TYPE 2

X

X

TYPE 1A

XII

XII

47

E♭ Major—Descending (Five Positions)

FINGERING TYPE 1A

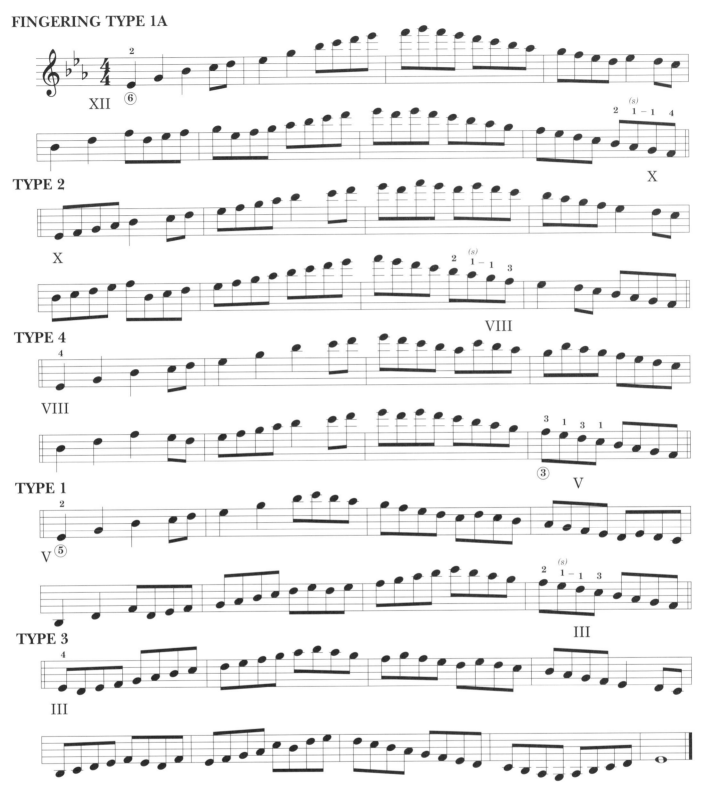

By transposing the preceding five-position major scale studies up or down one half step (one fret or one position), all major scales are now possible.

EXAMPLES: D major position II to D♭ major position I; E♭ major position III to E major position IV.

These same seven (five-position) studies can be used for practice if you merely change the key signatures and position marks. As before, additional reading material must be used to learn these new keys.

Chord Forms

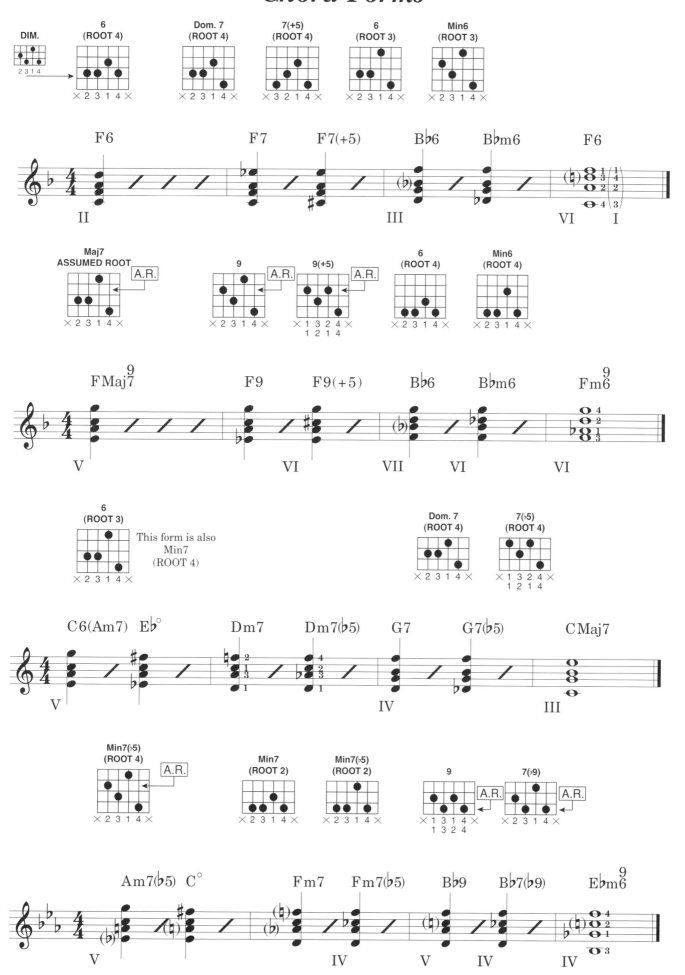

Major Scale Review—Positions II, III, V

The construction of a major scale (upwards) from any note is accomplished
by using the following series of whole and half step intervals.
(1 = half step, 2 = whole step):

```
2 2 1 2 2 2 1          2 2 1 2 2 2 1          2 2 1 2 2 2 1
C D E F G A B C        F G A B♭ C D E F       G A B C D E F♯ G
```

Observe the half steps between the 3rd and 4th, 7th and 1st scale degrees in
all major scales. These interval relationships account for the presence
of flats or sharps in the various keys.

Triads

Scale (Chord) Degrees

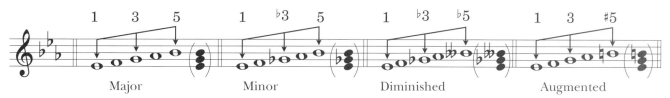

Major   Minor   Diminished   Augmented

As you move up and across the fingerboard, carefully observe fingerings and strings.

Eb Major

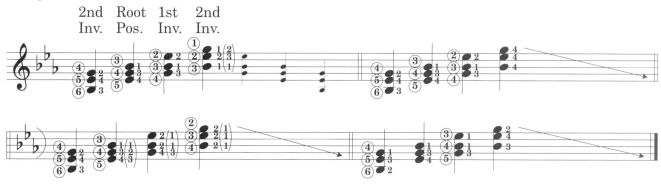

Eb Minor

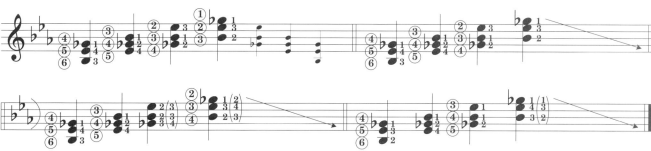

Eb Diminished

Eb Augmented

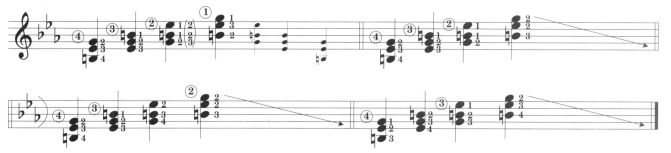

Theory: Diatonic Triads (Major Keys)

Diatonic: All notes belong to the key signature.

1.) There are seven notes in every major scale and seven chords common to each key. These diatonic chords are constructed upwards in thirds from each scale tone. The structures (major, minor, diminished, resulting from the scale) will be as follows in all major keys:

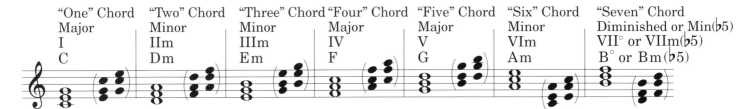

"One" Chord	"Two" Chord	"Three" Chord	"Four" Chord	"Five" Chord	"Six" Chord	"Seven" Chord
Major	Minor	Minor	Major	Major	Minor	Diminished or Min(♭5)
I	IIm	IIIm	IV	V	VIm	VII° or VIIm(♭5)
C	Dm	Em	F	G	Am	B° or Bm(♭5)

Roman numerals are used to represent these chord structures. (Be careful not to confuse them with position marks.) You must memorize the names and structures in all major keys.

2.) The principal chords and cadences (chord sequences) in major keys are:
- I-V-I, called **Authentic Cadence**, or C-G-C in the key of C.
- I-IV-I, called **Plagal Cadence**, or C-F-C in the key of C.
- Combined I-IV-V-I, **Authentic Cadence**, or C-F-G-C in the key of C.

❂ The II minor chord sometimes replaces IV in the preceding combined authentic cadence: I-IIm-V-I, or C-Dm-G-C in the key of C.

3.) There are three basic chordal sounds in every major key that are represented by these diatonic chord structures, and the following specific terms are used to name them:
- **Tonic:** I chord
- **Subdominant:** IV chord
- **Dominant:** V chord

There are also names for the chords built on all other scale degrees, but we will not discuss them here as they have no direct bearing on the three basic sounds, and they are usually referred to by number, i.e., the "two" (II) chord, the "three" (III) chord, the "six" (VI) chord, etc.

4.) The seven chords in a major key are related to each other with regard to the three basic chordal sounds. The I, IIIm, and VIm all produce a tonic sound. The IIm and IV chords produce a subdominant sound, and the V and VIIm(♭5) produce a dominant sound. These facts will be very important later on for chord substitutions and scale relationships in improvisation.

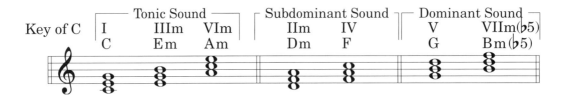

	Tonic Sound			Subdominant Sound		Dominant Sound	
Key of C	I	IIIm	VIm	IIm	IV	V	VIIm(♭5)
	C	Em	Am	Dm	F	G	Bm(♭5)

Memorize chord names and diatonic structures in all major keys.

Diatonic Triads
Key of G Major
Arpeggios and Scales

FINGERING TYPE 2

▌ (Also play in position IV, FINGERING TYPE 1A.)

Key of F Major

FINGERING TYPE 3

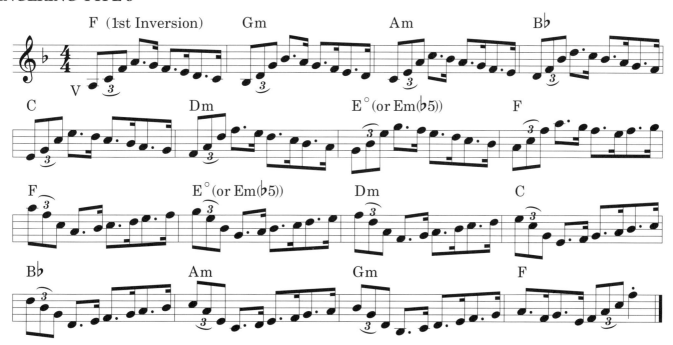

When two consecutive notes are played by the same finger on adjacent strings, "roll" the fingertip from one string to the next. Do not lift the finger from the string.

Key of B♭ Major

FINGERING TYPE 4

Key of E♭ Major

FINGERING TYPE 1

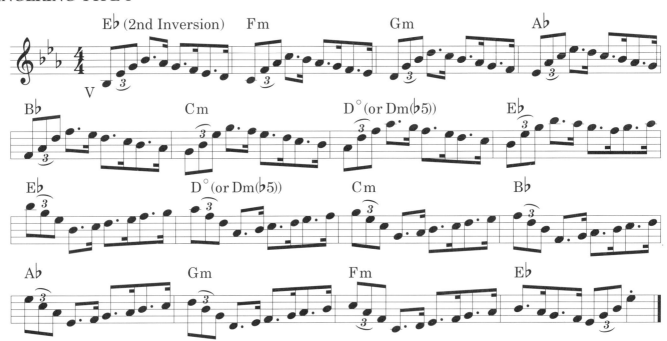

5th Position Study (duet)

(Play as)

■ EXERCISE (MAJOR TRIADS)

This exercise moves up and down the fingerboard, through all inversions on the same three strings (including all four sets of three adjacent strings).

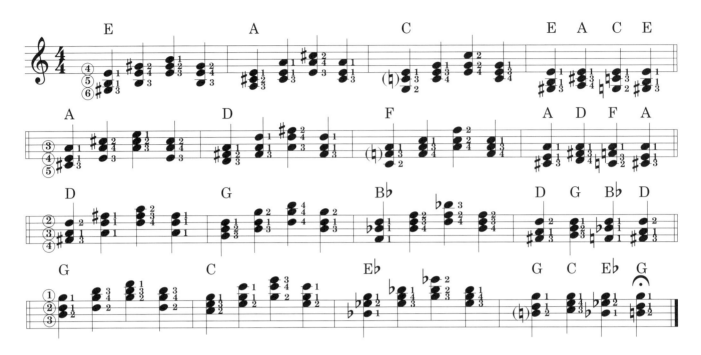

■ EXERCISE (MINOR TRIADS)

This exercise moves up and down the fingerboard, through all inversions on the same three strings (including all four sets of three adjacent strings).

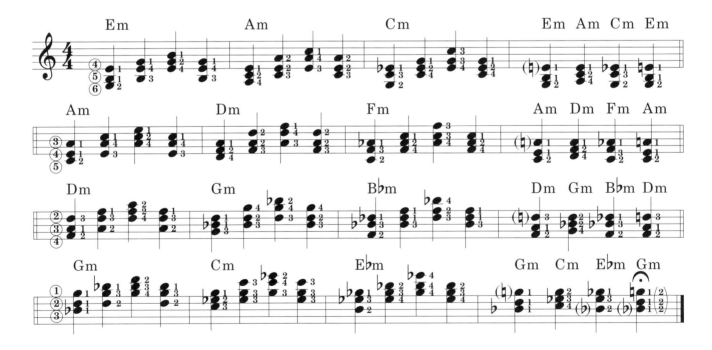

SECTION TWO

One-Octave Arpeggios—Triads
Fingering derived from scales—Across the fingerboard.

Transpose on the guitar by moving up the fingerboard (do not write out), and practice the preceding arpeggios in the following keys: A, B♭, C, D, and E♭. Thoroughly memorize all chord spellings.

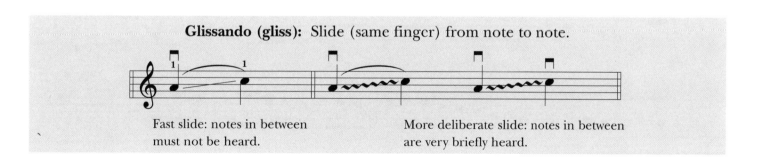

Glissando (gliss): Slide (same finger) from note to note.

Fast slide: notes in between must not be heard.

More deliberate slide: notes in between are very briefly heard.

59

Real Melodic (or Jazz) Minor Scale

The real melodic minor scale is derived from the preceding major scale forms by merely lowering the 3rd degree (note) one half step (one fret). This is a tonic major-to-minor relationship. All notes in this melodic minor scale remain the same—ascending and descending.

In the real melodic (or jazz) minor studies on the following pages, tonic major key signatures are used to simplify the conversion from major to minor. All playing positions are exactly the same.

You must practice these minor scales carefully, as at first they are difficult to "hear." They are worth putting considerable effort into, as they play a very large part in improvisation. (Application will be discussed later.)

C Real Melodic Minor (Five Positions)

FINGERING DERIVED FROM TYPE 1

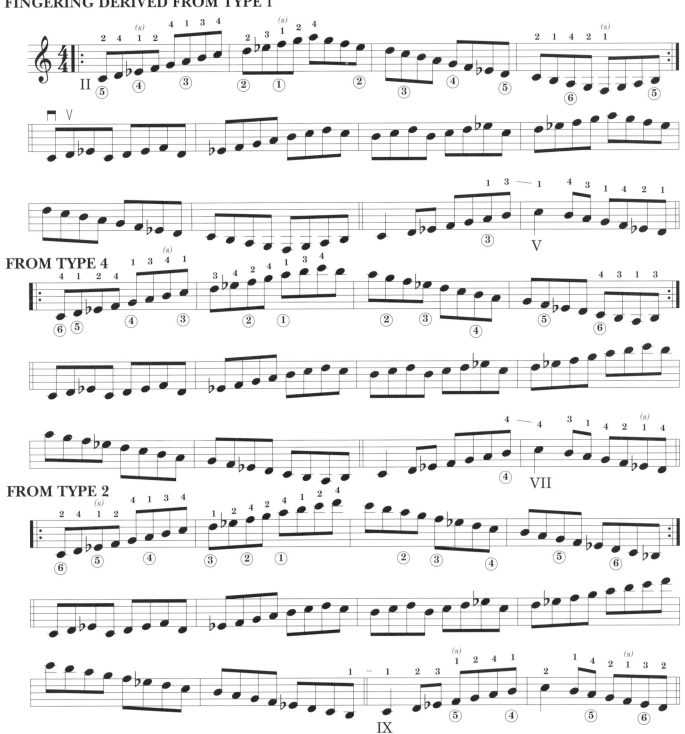

FROM TYPE 4

FROM TYPE 2

FROM TYPE 1A

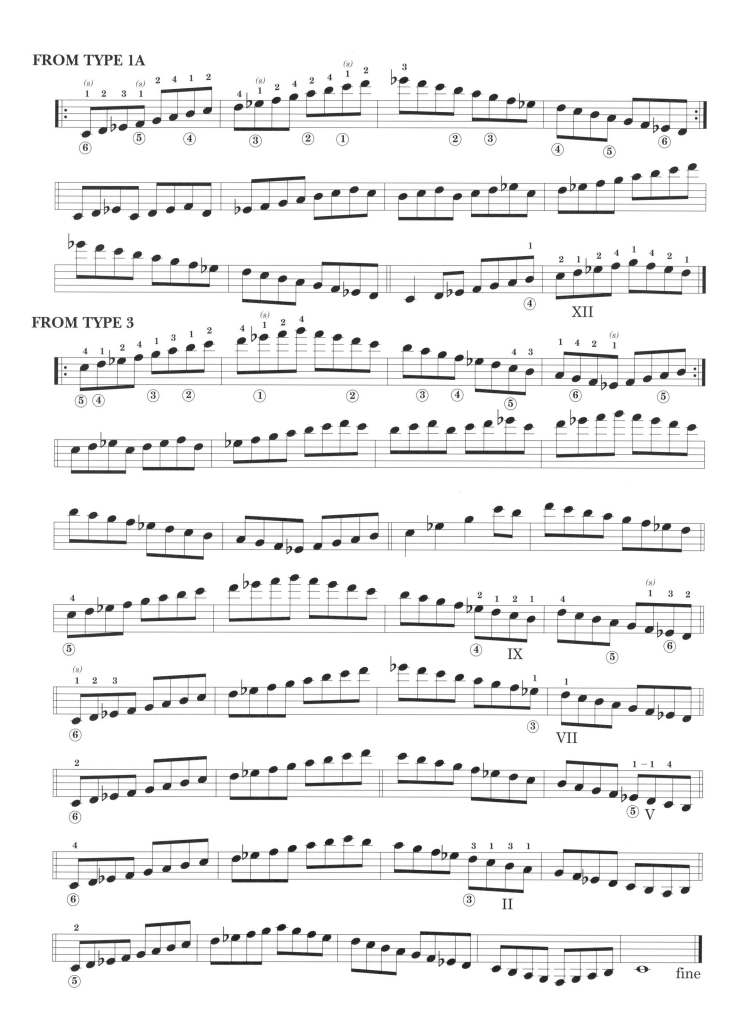

FROM TYPE 3

61

Rhythm Guitar—The Right Hand (Shuffle)

Basic Stroke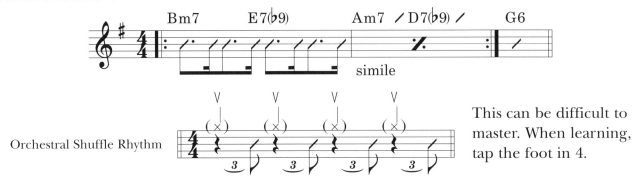

A very stable beat, but most practical with an incomplete rhythm section, as all accents fall "on the beat."

■ **EXERCISE**
▌ Observe notation.

▌ This stroke accents the off-beats and therefore adds a great deal more to a rhythm section.

Orchestral Shuffle Rhythm

This can be difficult to master. When learning, tap the foot in 4.

■ **EXERCISE**
▌ Observe notation.

▌ The preceding shuffle rhythm strokes also apply to rhythm parts in 6/8.

Observe notation.

Speed Study

Tempo must be constant throughout.

For practice with other fingerings, change the signature to C, F, D, and A.

Chord Forms

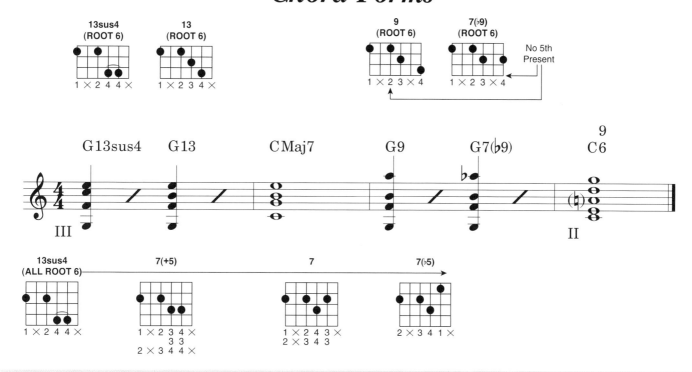

When the ♭5 of any dominant 7 form falls on the 1st, 2nd, or 3rd strings, you may consider it an augmented 11.

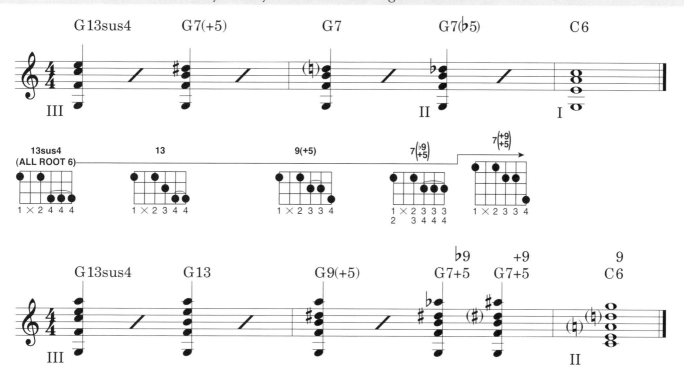

■ EXERCISE

Play through this exercise using some of the above forms. Carefully observe the fingerings (and their relationships to each other).

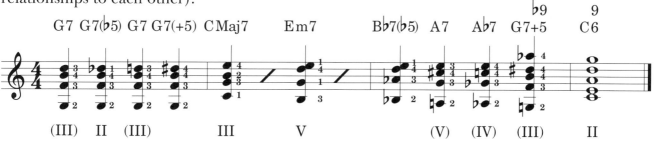

Melodic Rhythm Study No. 5 (duet)

One-Octave Arpeggios—Triads

Fingering derived from scales—Across the fingerboard.

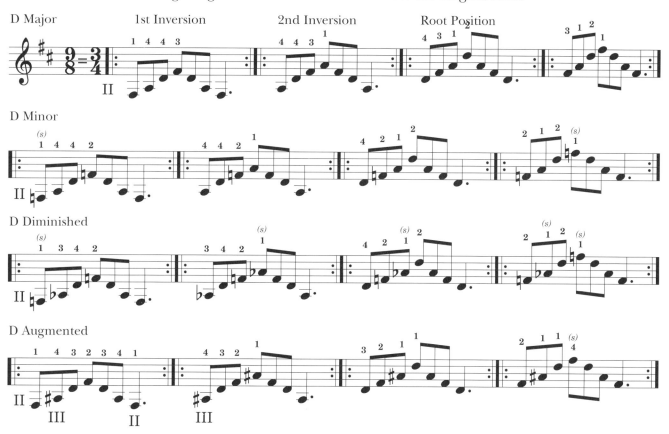

■ Transpose and play in the keys of E♭, F, G, A, and B♭.

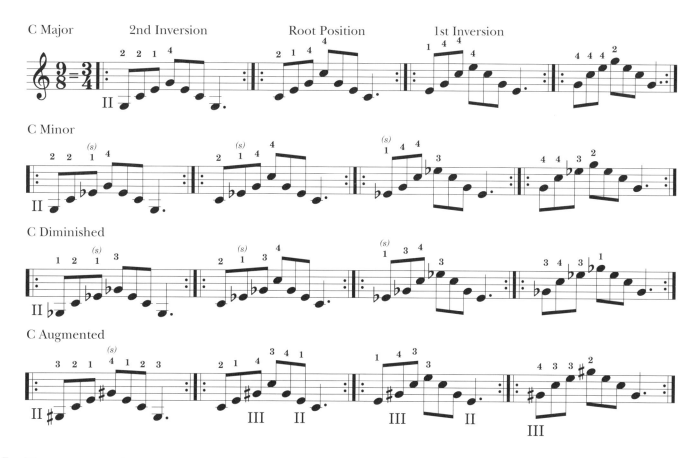

■ Transpose and play in keys of D, E♭, F, G, and A.

F Real Melodic Minor (Five Positions)

FINGERING DERIVED FROM TYPE 1A

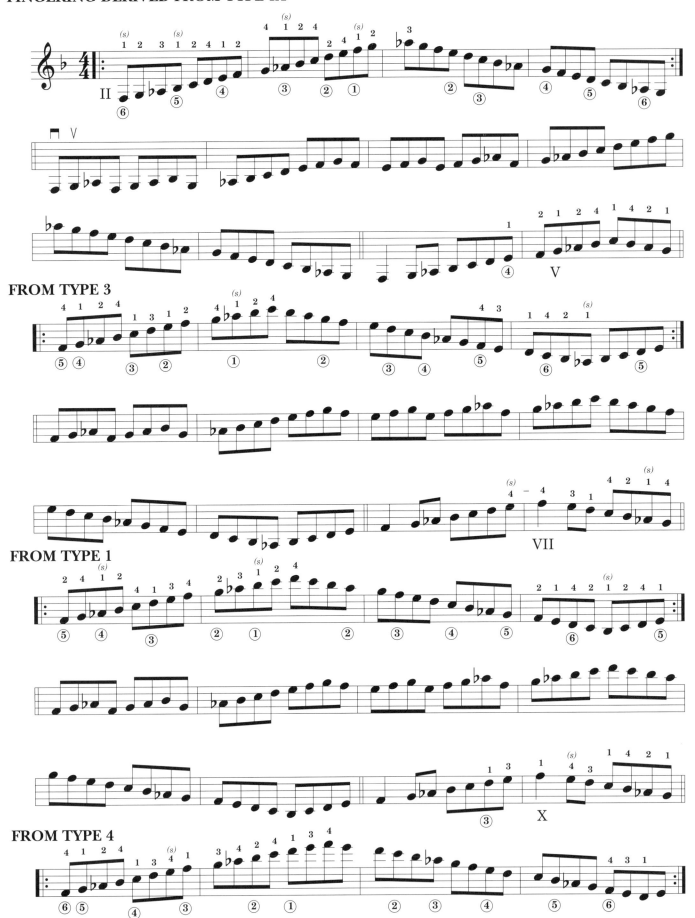

FROM TYPE 3

FROM TYPE 1

FROM TYPE 4

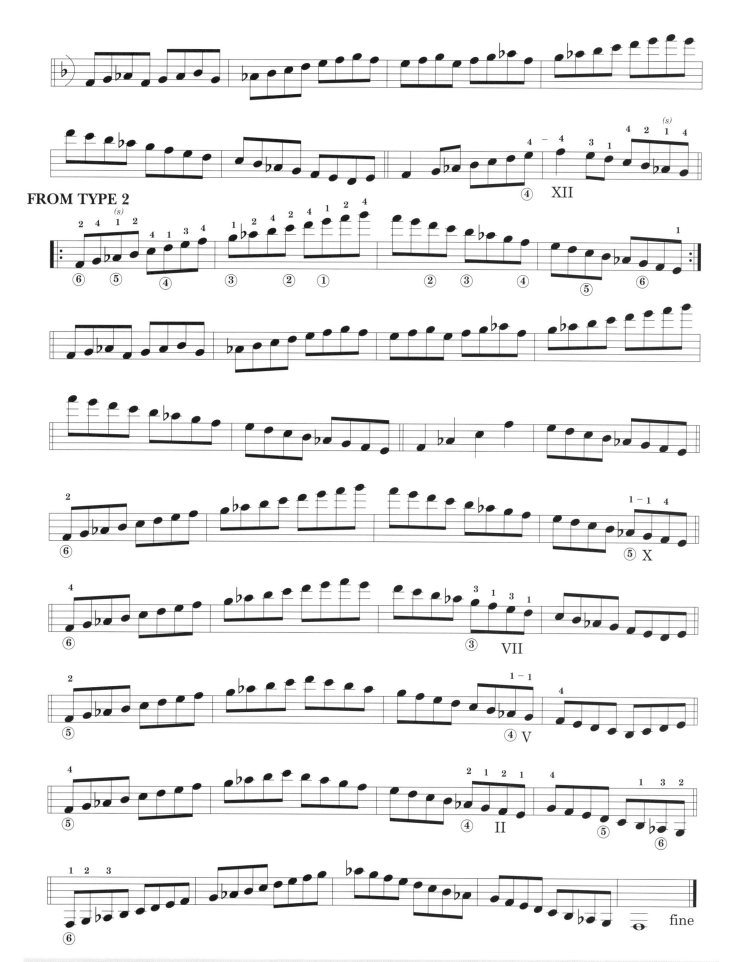

FROM TYPE 2

For additional practice on real melodic minor scales, refer to *Volume I*. Play reading and speed studies with lowered 3rd scale degree.

5th Position Study No. 2 (duet)

Track 12

One-Octave Arpeggios—Triads

Fingerings derived from scales—Across the fingerboard.

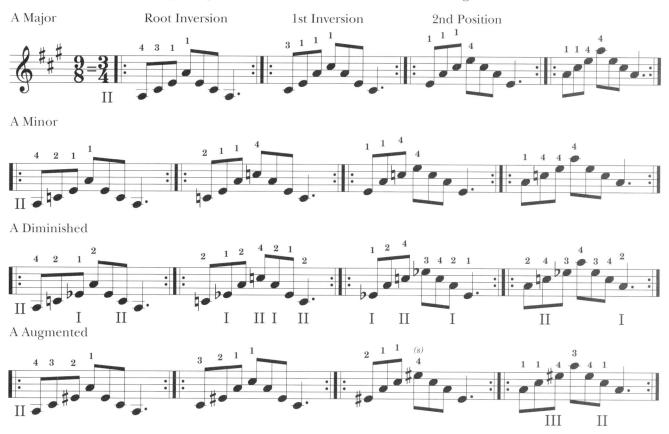

- Transpose and play in the keys of B♭, C, D, E♭, and F.

Fingering derived only partly from scales—Across and up the fingerboard.

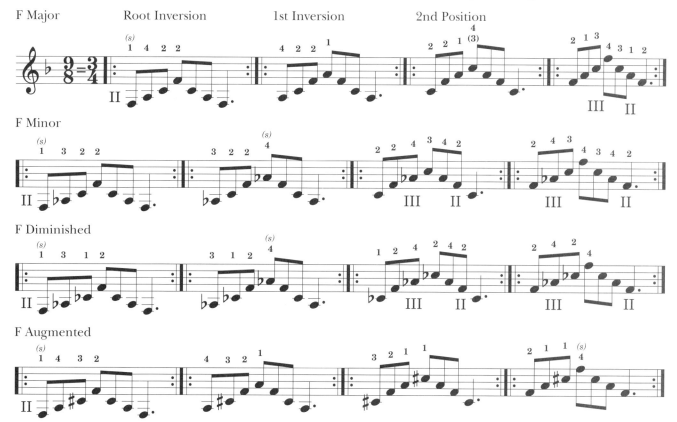

- Transpose and play in the keys of G, A, B♭, C, and D.

Chord Forms

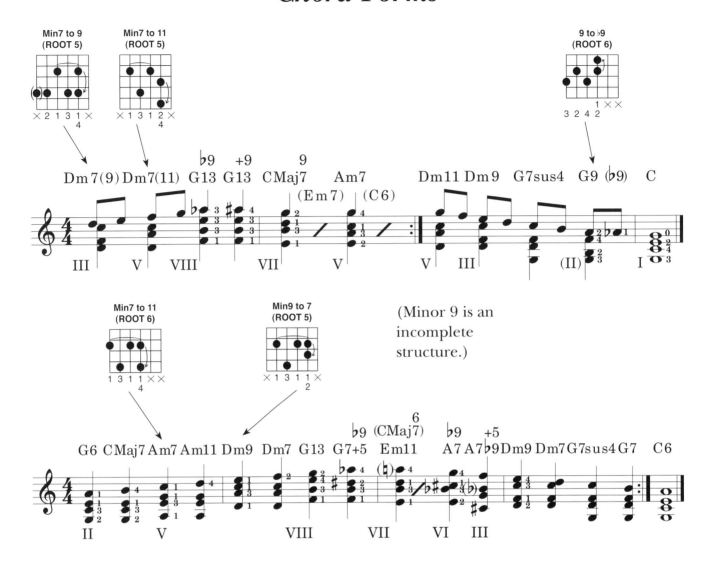

(Minor 9 is an incomplete structure.)

Slur

Ascending: Indicated by a curved line over two or more notes. Pick only the first note and drop the finger(s) of the left hand sharply on the string to produce the remaining note(s).

Descending: Prepare the entire group of notes with the fingers of the left hand in place. Pick only the first note with the right hand. Remove the left hand fingers from the remaining notes of the slur, drawing them toward the palm so as to actually pick the string again.

When blending electric guitar with horns, it is usually best to gliss from note to note when a slur is indicated. This produces no attack whatsoever on the second note and therefore is more "horn-like." (Be careful not to mistake a phrasing mark for a slur. A phrasing mark generally encompasses a large group of notes and indicates a legato or smooth performance of them.) You can also expect the horn player to break the phrase or breathe at the end of a phrasing mark. For a perfect blend you must perform accordingly. Commas are also used to indicate where to break a phrase or "breathe."

Trill

A trill is the effect created by rapidly alternating a note with the next diatonic note above it. Pick only the principal note, drop the finger for the next note sharply on the same string. Then, draw it off toward the palm, actually picking with the left-hand finger, to keep the string vibrating.

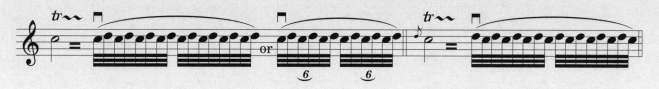

Theory: Diatonic 7th Chords (Major Keys)

❚ All diatonic chords within a key are built upwards in thirds.

1.) By adding another note a third above the diatonic triads, we construct all four-part chords common to a major key. (See diatonic triads, pg. 54.)

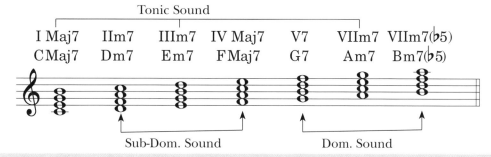

The VIIm7(♭5) is sometimes called "half diminished" (∅). Observe the chord relationships producing the tonic, subdominant, and dominant sounds.

Also: The IIIm7 is often found as an intermediate chord in a subdominant sequence.

EXAMPLES

IV	IIIm7	IIm7	(V7 I) ...	IIm7	IIIm7	IV	(V7 I)
FMaj7	Em7	Dm7	(G7CMaj7)..	Dm7	Em7	FMaj7	(G7 CMaj7)

2.) Because of a conflict with the root in the melody, the four-part structures used on the I and IV are often 6th chords, built from major scale degrees 1, 3, 5, and 6. You might say this is a result of the substitution of VIm7 over the root of the I chord and IIm7 over the root of the IV chord: Am7 = C6; Dm7 = F6.

3.) Substitution of IIIm7 or VIm7 for I, IIm7 for I, IIm7 for IV, and VIIm7(♭5) for V7 are especially valuable when creating moving bass lines with strong chordal degrees (I and V) supporting the harmonic structures.

EXAMPLE:

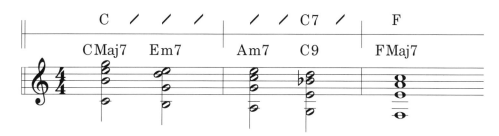

All diatonic chords (names and structures) must be memorized, in all keys.

Arpeggios—Diatonic Sevenths

All four-part chords, all inversions—Key of G major.

FINGERING TYPE 1A

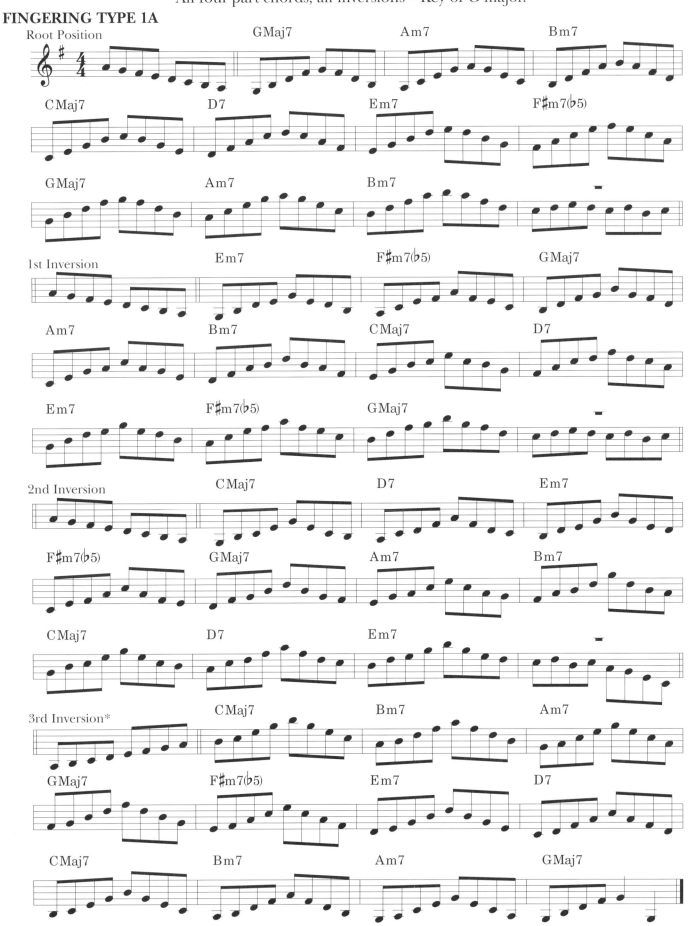

✱ 3rd Inversion: 7th in the bass

Arpeggios—Diatonic Sevenths

All four-part chords, all inversions—Key of C major.

FINGERING TYPE 4

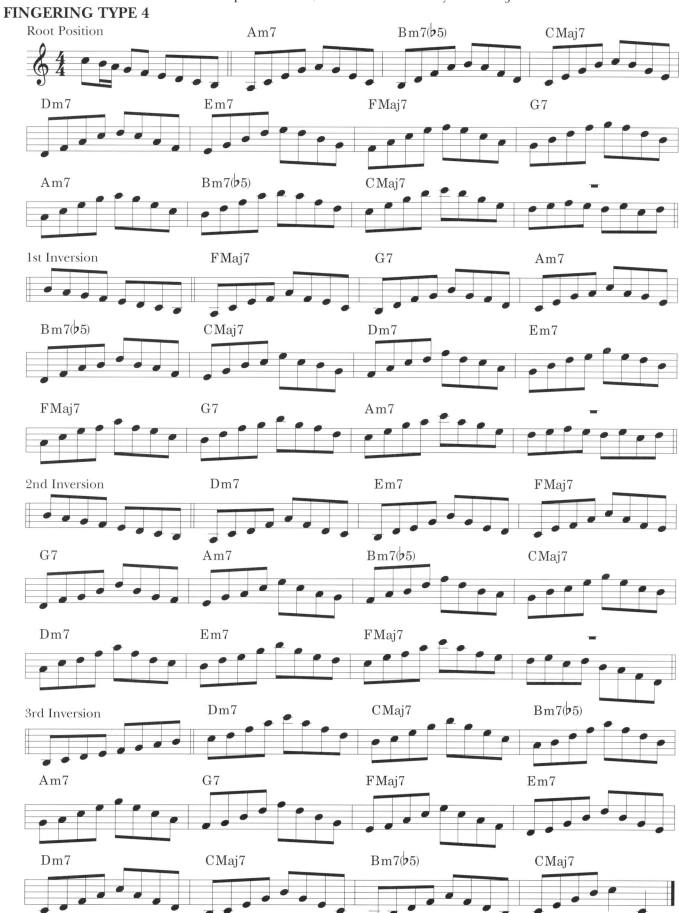

▍ (See bottom of pg. 55.)

G Real Melodic Minor (Five Positions)

FINGERING DERIVED FROM TYPE 2

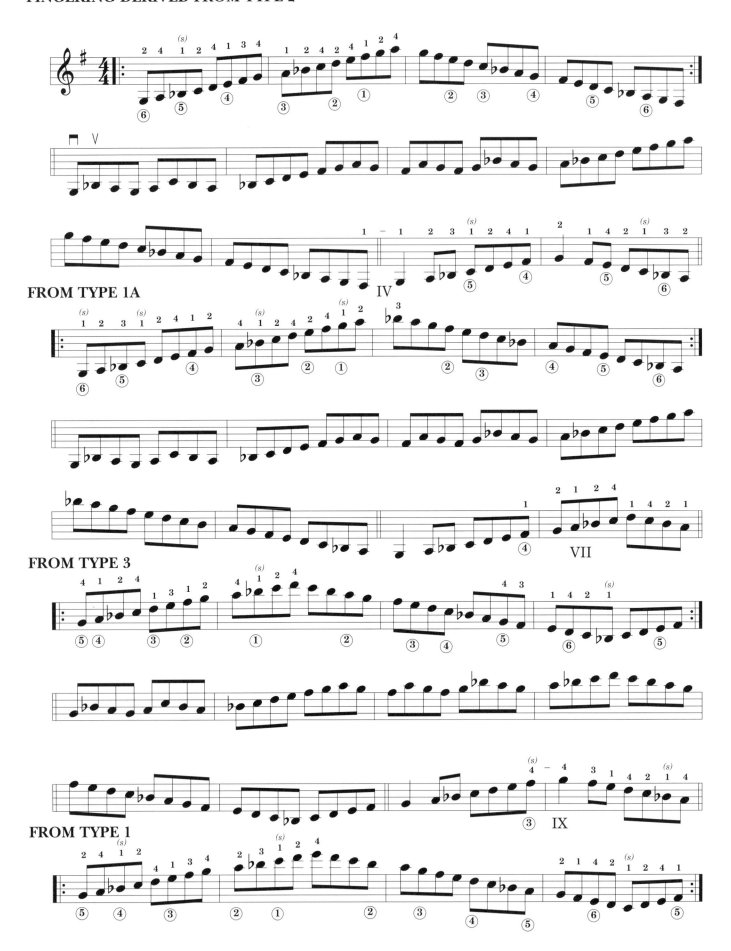

FROM TYPE 1A

FROM TYPE 3

FROM TYPE 1

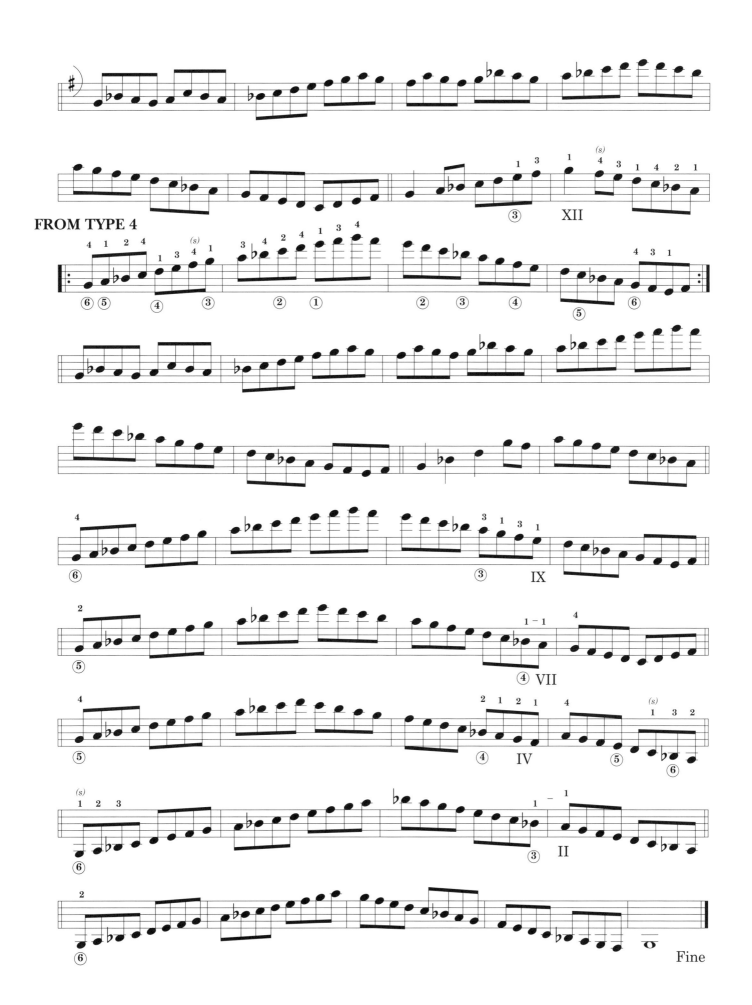

FROM TYPE 4

Chord Forms

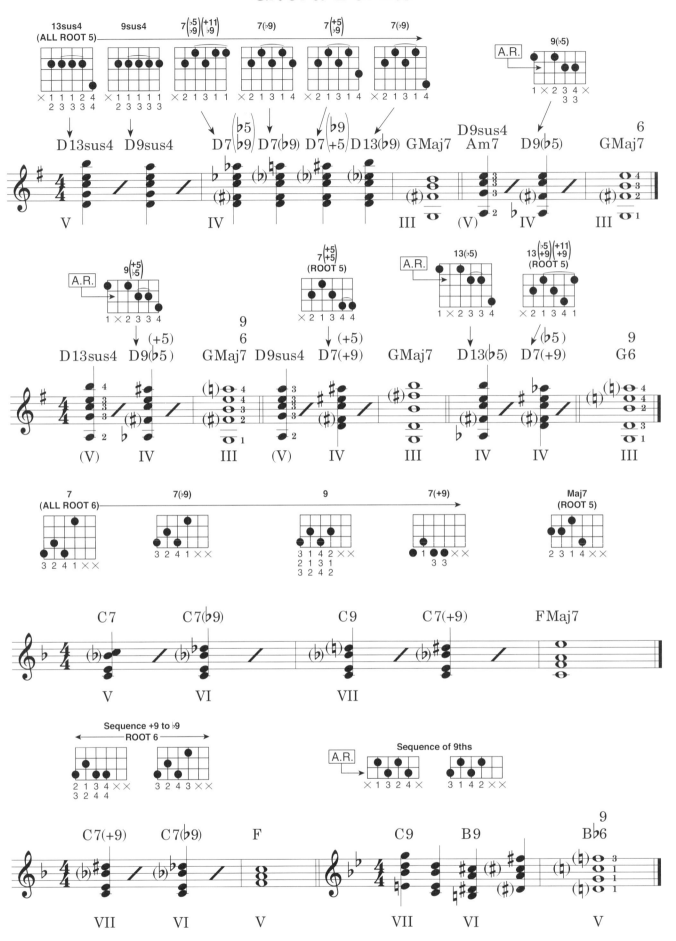

Two-Octave Arpeggios
C Major Triad from the Root
Fingering derived from scales and chords—Across and up the fingerboard.

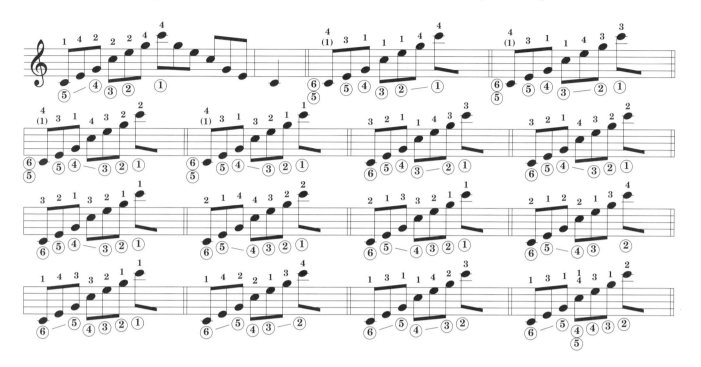

Practice all forms in all possible keys.

Chord Etude No. 9

77

The Wanderer (duet)

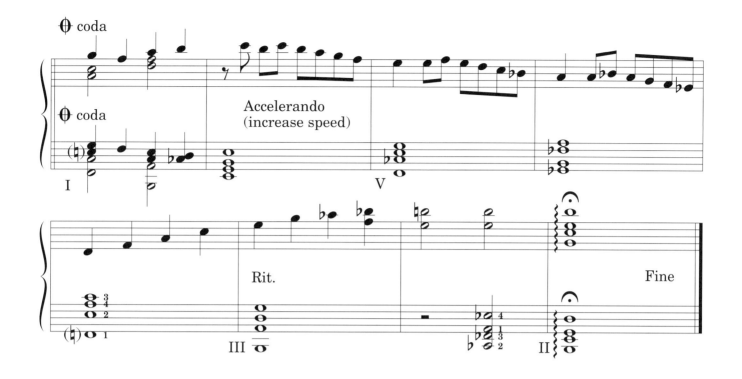

Rhythm Guitar—The Right Hand (Waltz)

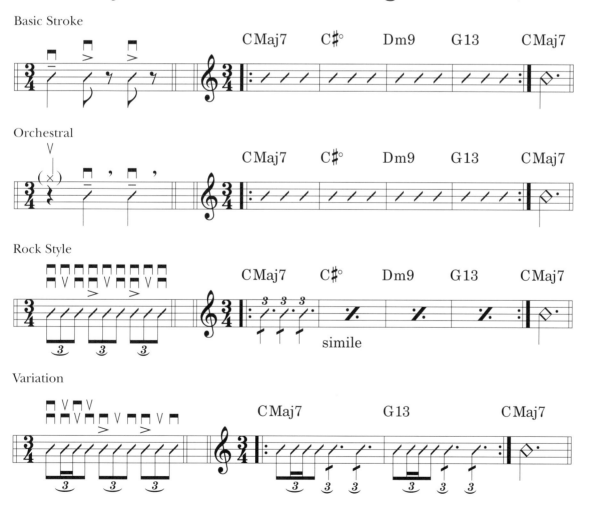

Arpeggios—Diatonic Sevenths

All four-part chords, all inversions—Key of F major.

FINGERING TYPE 3

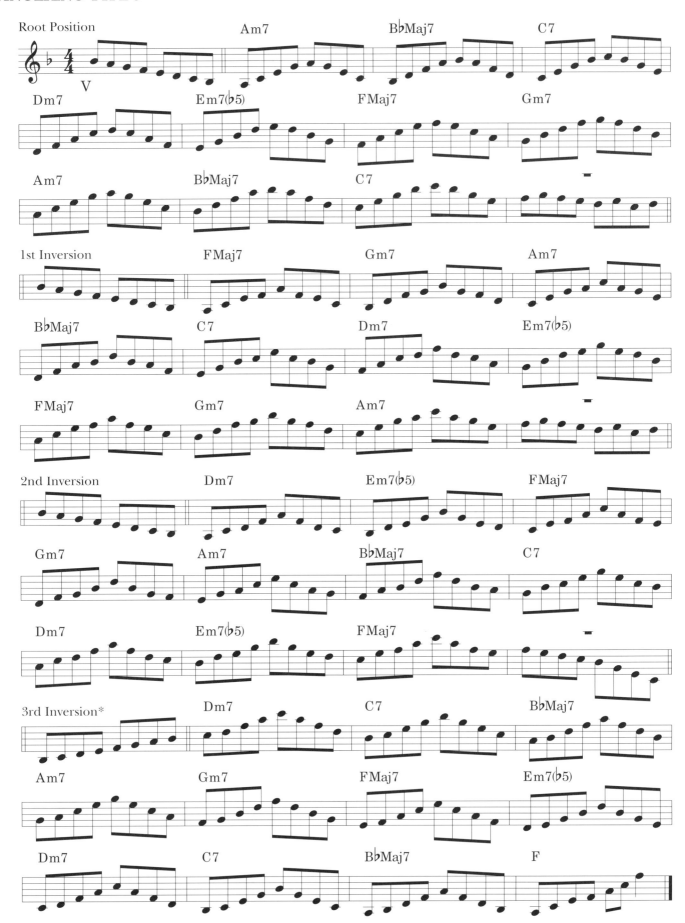

Theory: Chord-Scale Relationships

For improvisation.

WITH DIATONIC CHORD STRUCTURES

All the notes of a major scale may be used melodically over the seven chord structures contained in that key. However, any scale tone one half step above a chord tone (1, 3, 5, 7 in diatonic harmony) must be of short duration and used only in passing to a chord tone next to it.

EXAMPLE:

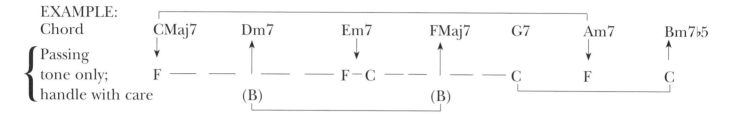

Melodic ideas may be created from scale tones in any order, providing you do not start with, or "lean on," the passing tones discussed above.

Improvisation: The spontaneous creation of music while playing, usually within the confines of the harmonic content of a song. (All available notes are drawn from chord tones and related scales.)

Before all-out (no holds barred) improvisation is attempted on the chords to a song, it is best if you stay close to the melody and fill in only during notes of long duration.

EXAMPLE:
Straight Melody

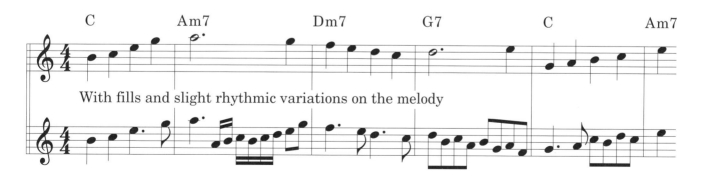

With fills and slight rhythmic variations on the melody

D Real Melodic Minor (Five Positions)

FINGERING DERIVED FROM TYPE 3

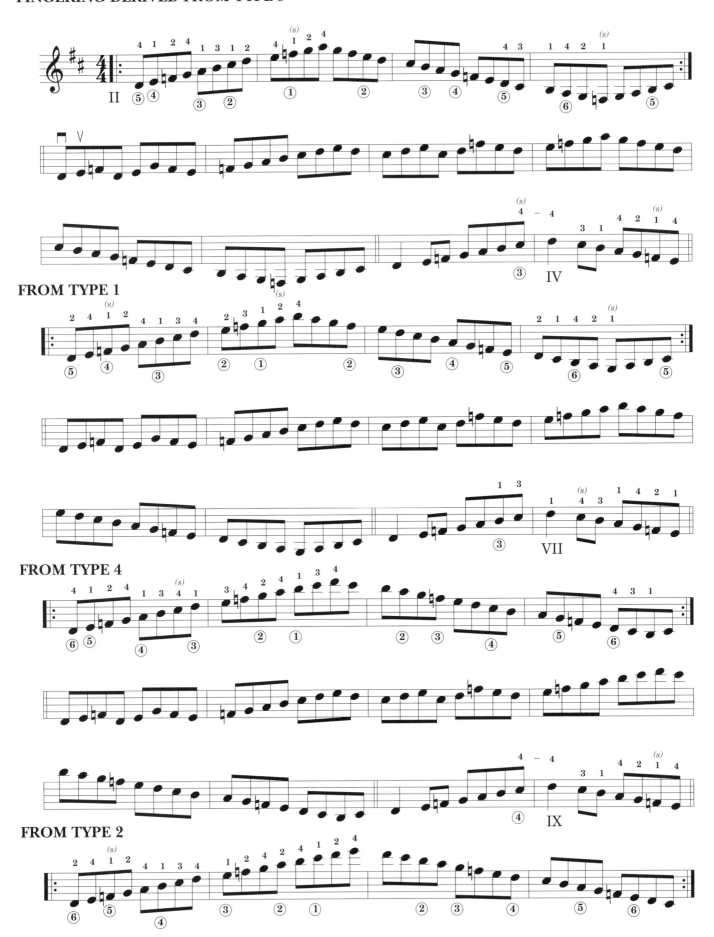

FROM TYPE 1

FROM TYPE 4

FROM TYPE 2

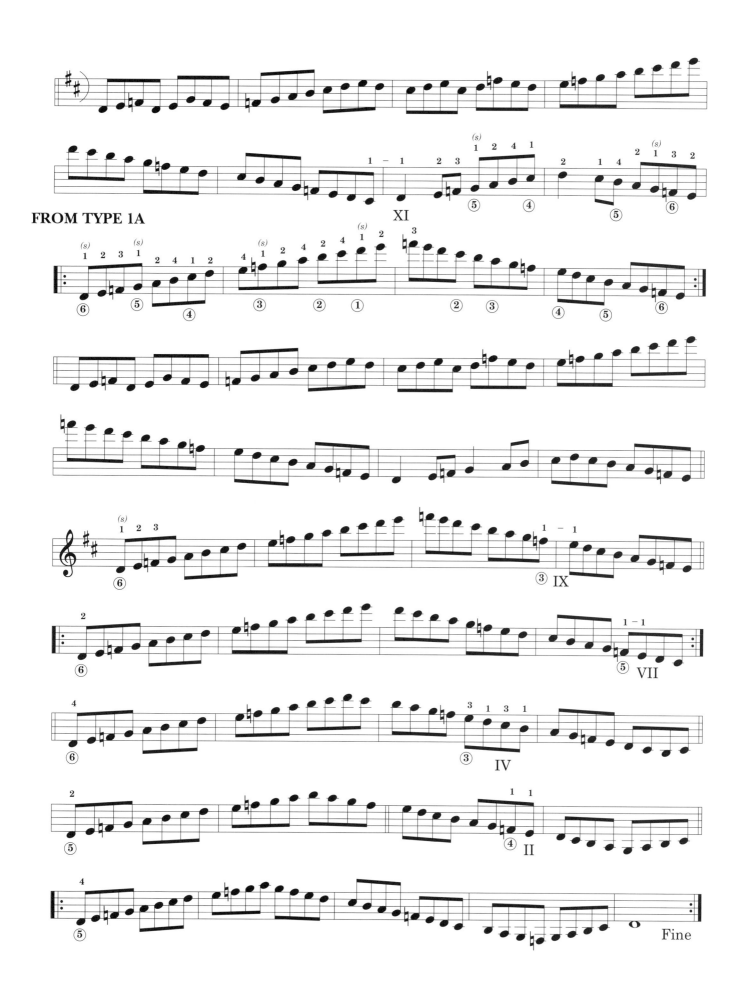

FROM TYPE 1A

83

Chord Forms—3rd in the Bass

I define the real bass (sounding) range as any note lower in pitch from C, 5th string (3rd fret) or C, 6th string (8th fret).

Any chord voiced with the 3rd degree in the bass has a weak chordal sound, and should be used only when leaping to a new inversion of the same chord, or as a passing chord to produce scalewise or chromatic bass motion.

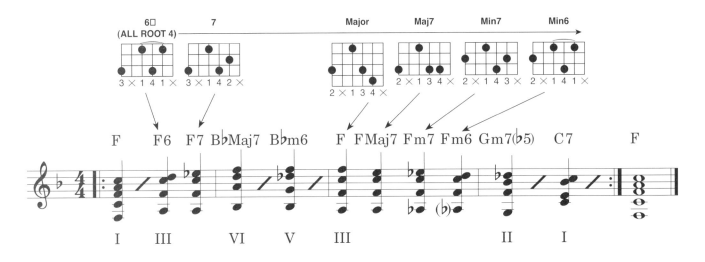

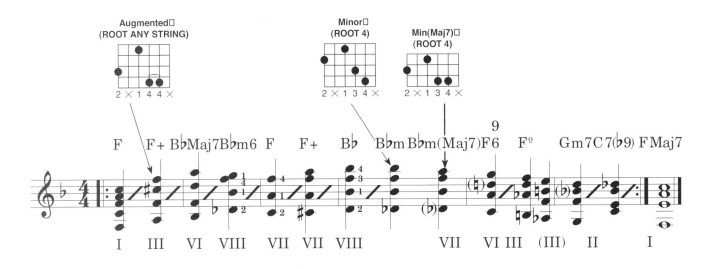

Chord Etude No. 10

Track 15

84

Two-Octave Arpeggios

G Major Triad from the 3rd

Fingering derived from scales and chords—Across and up the fingerboard.

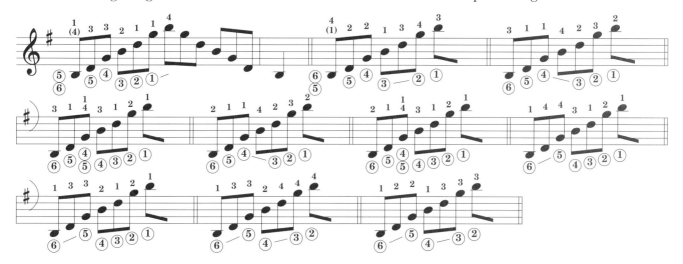

F Major Triad from the 5th

Across and up the fingerboard.

Practice all forms in all possible keys.

Rhythm Guitar—The Right Hand (Jazz Waltz)

Arpeggios—Diatonic Sevenths

All four-part chords, all inversions—Key of B♭ major.

FINGERING TYPE 2

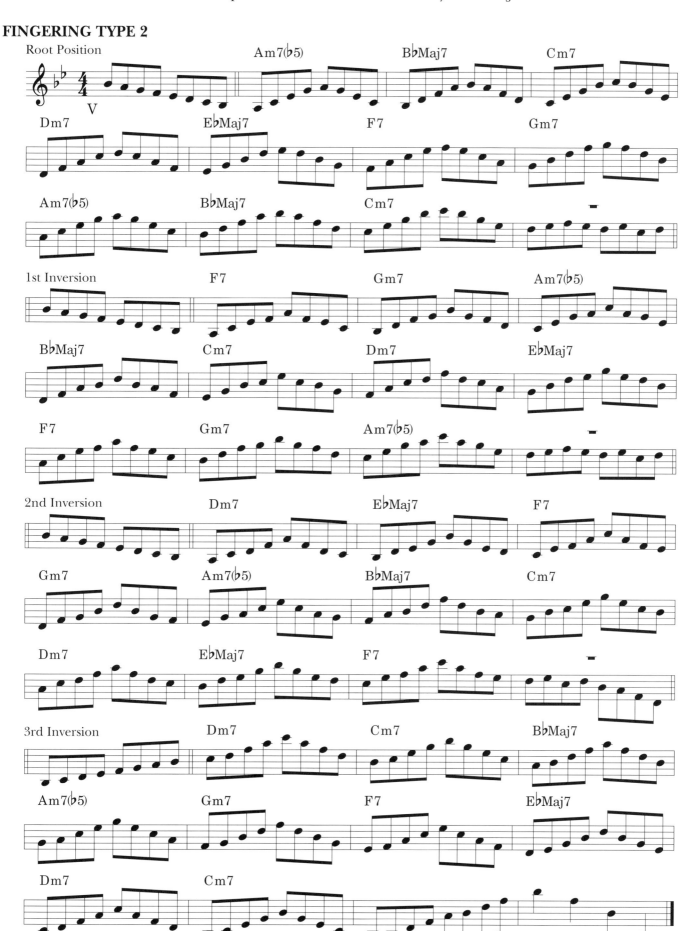

A Real Melodic Minor (Five Positions)

FINGERING DERIVED FROM TYPE 4

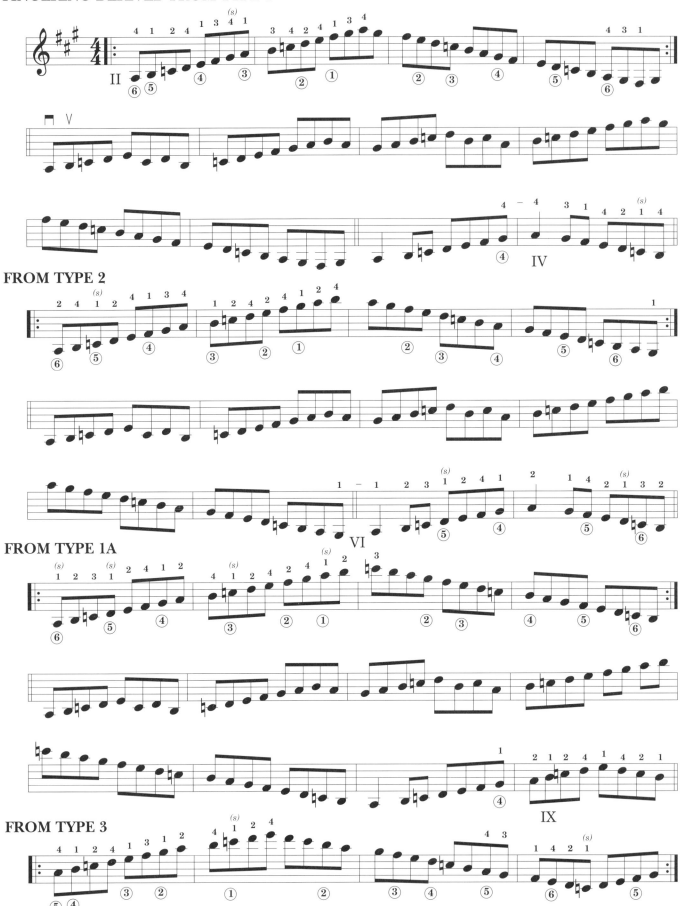

FROM TYPE 2

FROM TYPE 1A

FROM TYPE 3

88

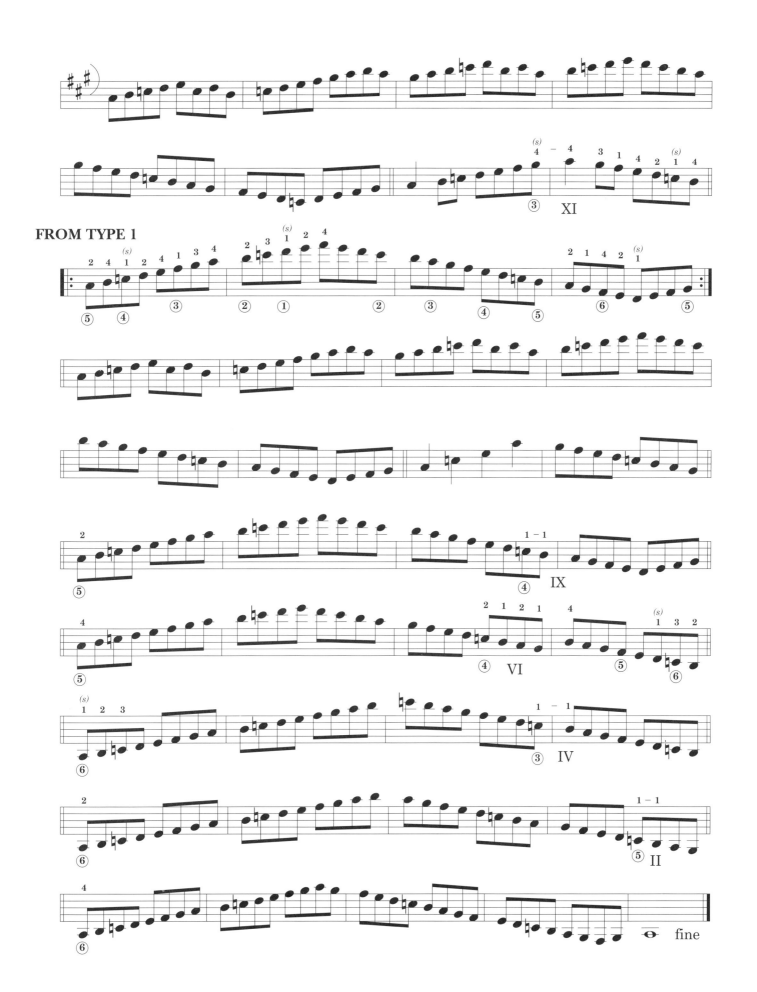

FROM TYPE 1

Chord Forms

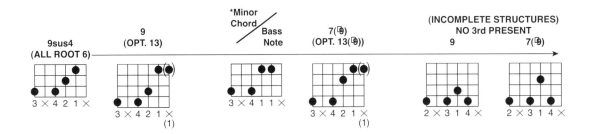

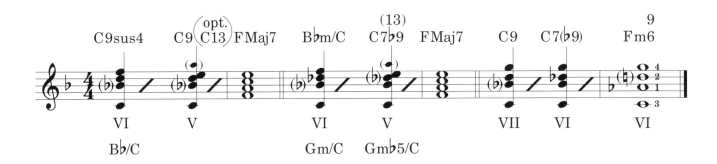

✺ This is a way to notate symbols for chord structures that might be difficult to name any other way. The basic chord sound is represented above the diagonal line; the bass note it is to be played over is indicated below it.

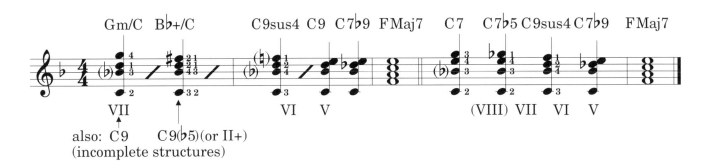

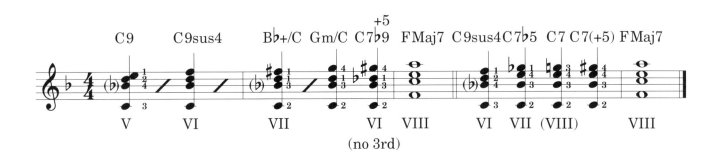

Two-Octave Arpeggios

C Minor Triad from the Root

Fingering derived from scales and chords—Across and up the fingerboard.

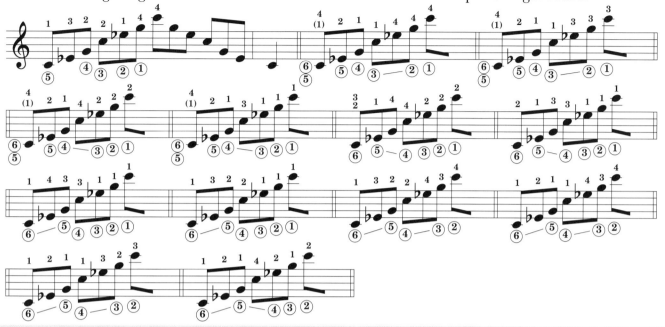

Practice all forms in all possible keys.

Appoggiatura (Grace Notes)

The unaccented appoggiatura takes its duration from the preceding beat.

(written)   (played)   (written)   (played)

The accented appoggiatura (usually shown with no slash through the hook) falls directly on the beat.

It is best written out in full.

(written)   (played)   (written)   (played)

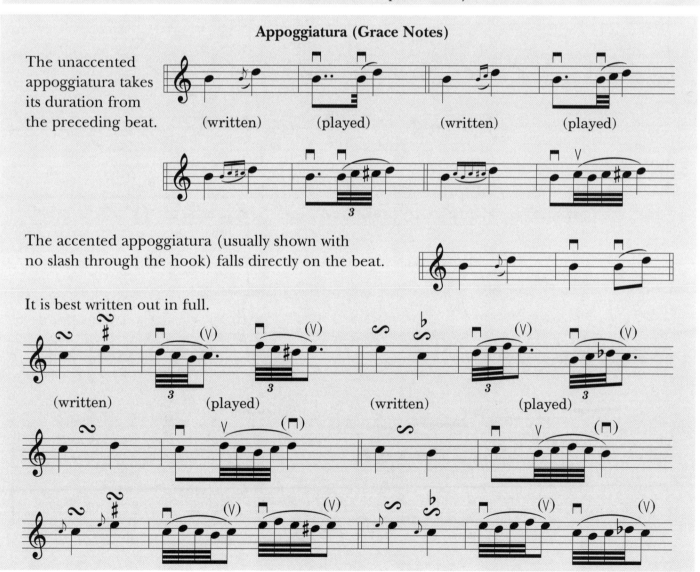

Melodic Rhythm Study No. 6 (duet)

Latin beat optional.

Rhythm Guitar—The Right Hand
(Cha-cha and Beguine)

Cha-cha: Basic and Orchestral

Orchestral

(Tap the foot in "2")

Variations
Basic and Orchestral

1.   2.   3.

Beguine: Basic Stroke

Variation
1.   2.   3.

Beguine: Orchestral

This stroke is difficult to master, but it is very important to right-hand development.
When learning, tap the foot on beats 1, 3, and 4, or 1, 2, 3, and 4.

■ **EXERCISE**

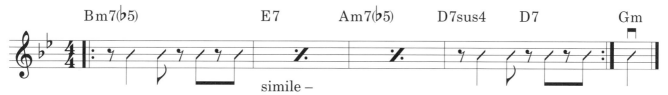

simile –

93

Arpeggios—Diatonic Sevenths

All four-part chords, all inversions—Key of E♭ major.

FINGERING TYPE 1

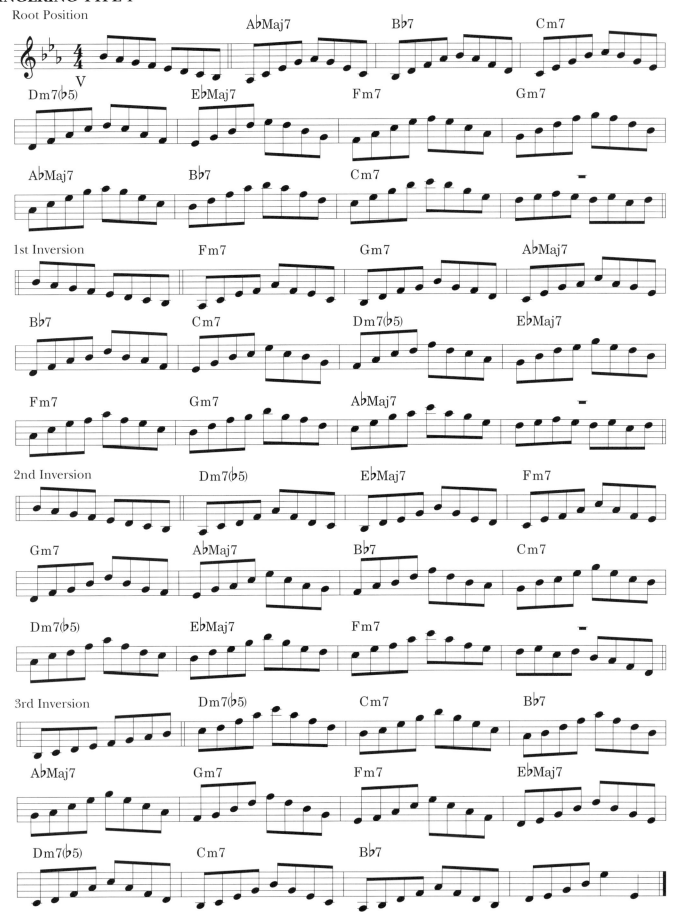

Theory: Chord-Scale Relationships

For improvisation.

- It is very rare when a song remains completely diatonic harmonically, from beginning to end.
- Any chord that does not conform to the diatonic structures actually is a modulation to another key (or scale) for its duration.
- Sometimes a series of nondiatonic chords completely changes the key for a period of time. (This is why there will be references to "the key of the moment" in some of the following discussions on chord-scale relationships.)
- Remember this: The ear has memory but no eyes. Therefore the sound of what has gone before has a definite influence on which scales belong to certain chords in particular situations (but what is yet to sound has no bearing whatsoever).

Modulation: The change of key within a composition or arrangement.

Nondiatonic Minor 7 and Major 7 Chords

1.) Any minor 7 chord not in the key of the moment usually tends to sound like a IIm7 of whatever key it is the 2nd diatonic structure of. (A nondiatonic minor 7 chord actually performs the function of modulation more thoroughly than dominant 7 chords.) Use the major scale from one whole step below the chord name for nondiatonic minor 7.

EXAMPLE:

Chord	C	Cm7	Dm7	G7	Ebm7	Ab7	Abm7	Db7	C
Scale	CMaj	BbMaj	CMaj	⟶	DbMaj	⟶	GbMaj	⟶	CMaj

2.) Any major chord that is not in the key (of the moment), not preceded by modulation, and with a nondiatonic root, tends to sound like a IV chord of whatever key it is the 4th diatonic structure of. Use the major scale from the 5th chordal degree of the major chord with a nondiatonic root.

EXAMPLE:

Chord	C	Eb(Maj7)	Dm7	G7	Ab(Maj7)	Db(Maj7)	C
Scale	CMaj	BbMaj	CMaj	⟶	EbMaj	AbMaj	Cmaj

3.) Any major chord not in the key (of the moment), not preceded by modulation, and with a scale tone root, tends to sound like a I (tonic) chord. Use the major scale from the chord name of the nondiatonic major chord with a scale-tone root.

EXAMPLE:

Chord	C	E(Maj7)	G9susC	G7	C
Scale	CMaj	EMaj	CMaj	⟶	⟶

The major scale constructed from the 5th chordal degree may be used with any major chord at any time, but the chord-scale relationship on those with diatonic roots will be less perfect and will sound farther "out."

Also: Minor 7 chords are occasionally tonic chords in disguise, so don't overlook the possibility of nondiatonic minor 7 chords actually being a IIIm7 or VIm7 for I. (See pg. 71.)

7th Position Study (duet)

Solo in G

B♭ *Real Melodic Minor (Five Positions)*

FINGERING DERIVED FROM TYPE 4

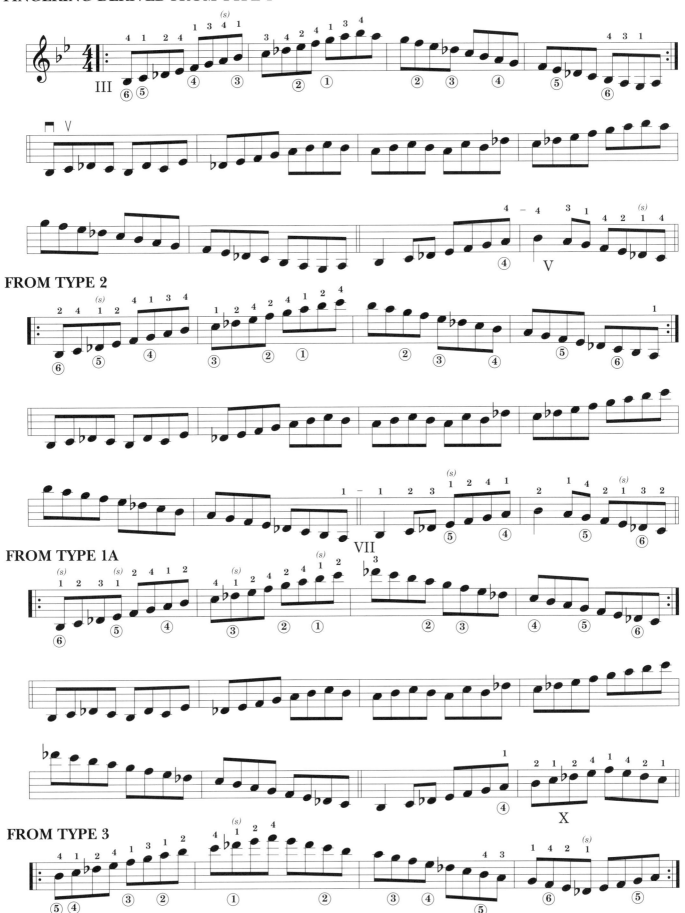

FROM TYPE 2

FROM TYPE 1A

FROM TYPE 3

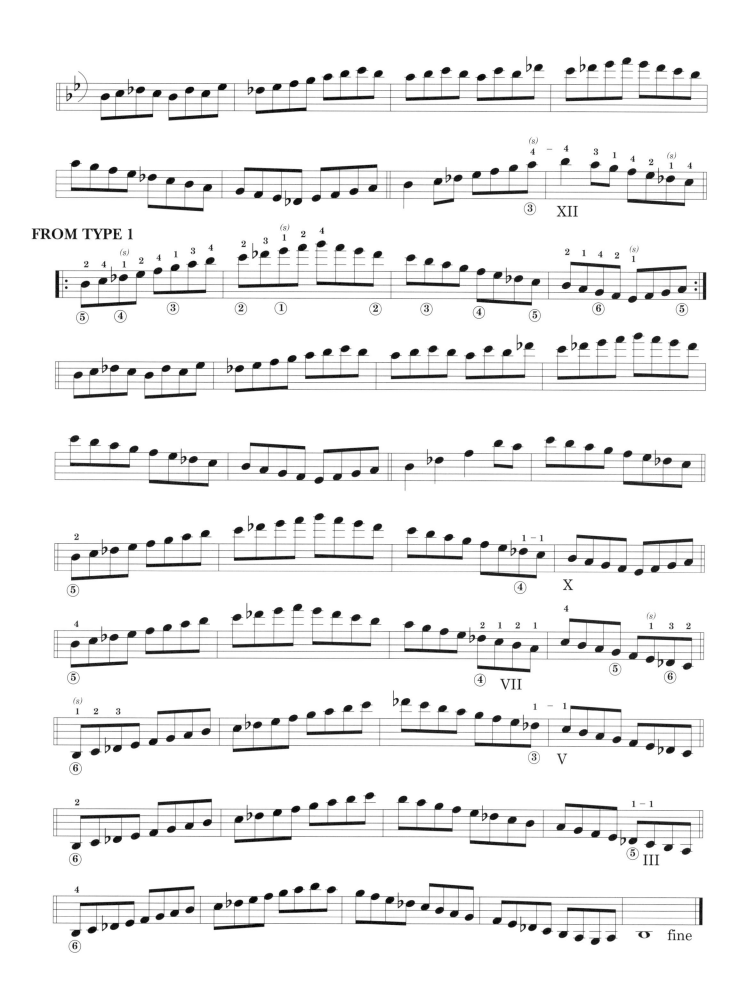

FROM TYPE 1

99

Chord Forms—7th in the Bass

Bass (sounding) range: From approximately C (5th or 6th strings) on down in pitch.

Chord voicings with the 7th degree in the bass have very weak chordal sounds. These forms (like those with the 3rd in the bass) may be used for inversion leaps or as passing chords, but their use must be well justified—such as in a strong descending bass line—or they will sound "wrong."

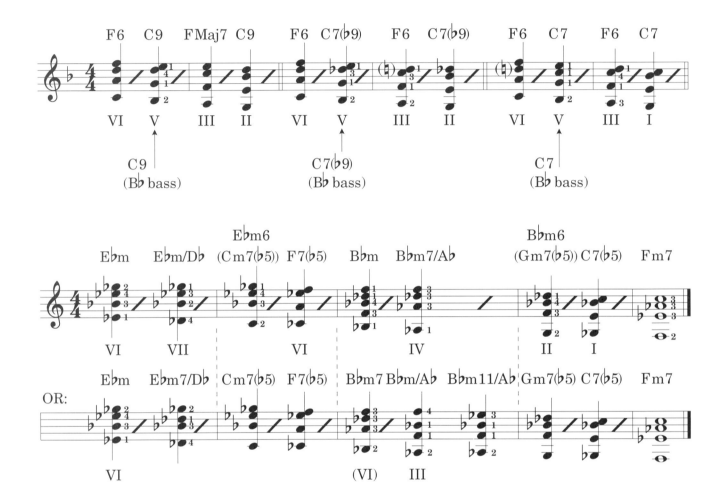

Chord Etude No. 11

Track 19

Two-Octave Arpeggios

G Minor Triad from the 3rd

Fingering derived from scales and chords—Across and up the fingerboard.

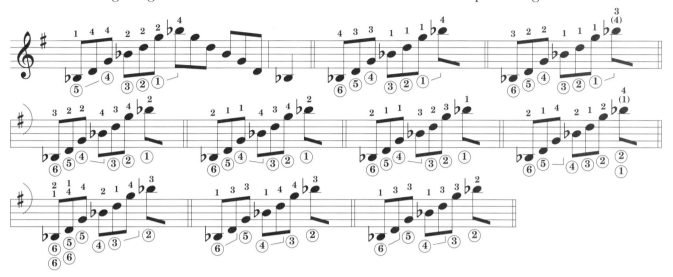

F Minor Triad from the 5th

Across and up the fingerboard.

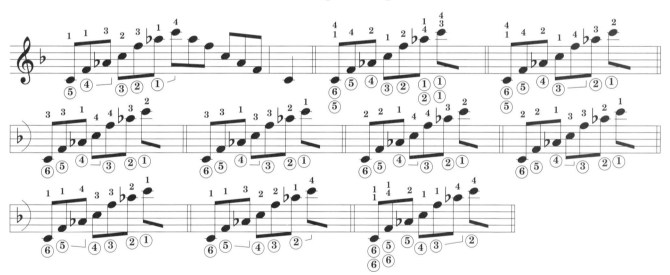

Practice all forms in all possible keys.

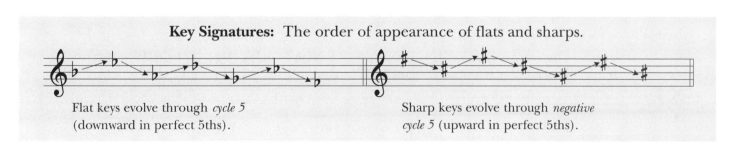

Key Signatures: The order of appearance of flats and sharps.

Flat keys evolve through *cycle 5* (downward in perfect 5ths).

Sharp keys evolve through *negative cycle 5* (upward in perfect 5ths).

Theory: Chord-to-Chord Motion
A Brief Discussion

DESCRIPTIONS AND TERMS

1.) Chord sequences (cadences) are represented by numerical terms or numbers that indicate the chords and their structures in the key of the moment. If a single number is used to represent a chord, the structure is assumed to be diatonic (in the indicated key).

EXAMPLE

II-V-I in C = Dm7-G7-C

II-V-I in F = Gm7-C7-F

2.) Nondiatonic structures are represented by two numbers and, if necessary, a descriptive term or symbol.

EXAMPLE

	"one"	"six-seven"	"two-seven"	"five-seven"	"one"
(Key of C)	I	VI7	II7	V7	I
	C	A7	D7	G7	C

	"one"	"one sharp diminished"	"two"	"flat two-seven"	"one"
(Key of C)	I	I#°	IIm7	♭II7	I
	C	C#°	Dm7	D♭7	C

3.) Chord sequences are also described in another way. The word "cycle" followed by a number indicates the interval (distance) from chord root to chord root. In the most common chord progressions (cycle 5, cycle 3, cycle 7), the interval is figured downward. Notice in the following examples that, in use, the direction of bass notes is optional, but the chords have been constructed from the notes a 5th, 3rd, or 7th below.

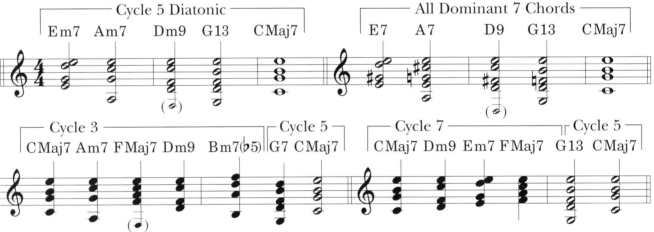

4.) When chord root motion goes up a 3rd, 5th, or 7th, it is called a negative cycle 3, negative cycle 5, or negative cycle 7. (One sequence of two chords is common; further extension of negative cycles is less common.)

Both of the above methods of indicating chord motion are extremely valuable, especially in memorizing and transposing the chords to songs.

EXAMPLE: (First 16 bars)

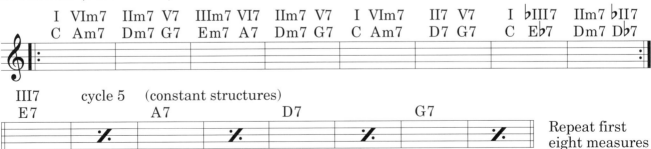

102

Chromatic Scale

The chromatic scale consists of twelve notes, one half step apart.

FINGERING PATTERN 1

Across fingerboard—no position change.

Examples of application shows use of chromatic scales over augmented and diminished (optional dominant 7(♭9)) chords. Observe the way that sixteenth notes and triplets are used to ensure that the first attack of each beat is a chord tone.

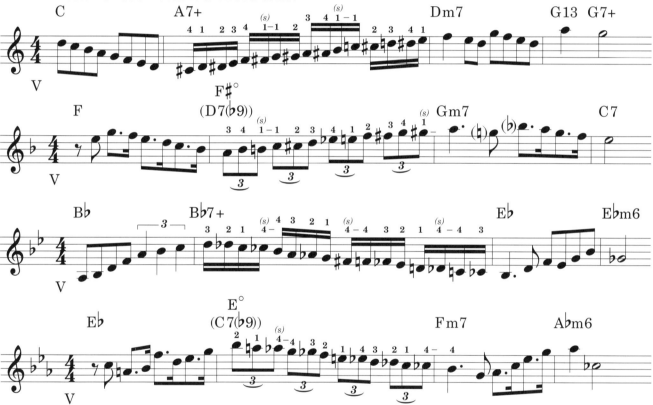

FINGERING PATTERN 2

Across fingerboard—with position changes.
This is less practical than the fingering shown above, as the use of this pattern must be pre-set in order to come out in the proper position.

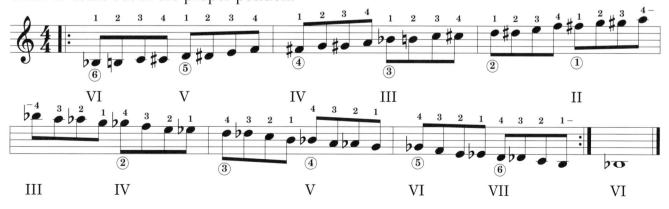

E♭ Real Melodic Minor (Five Positions)

FINGERING DERIVED FROM TYPE 3

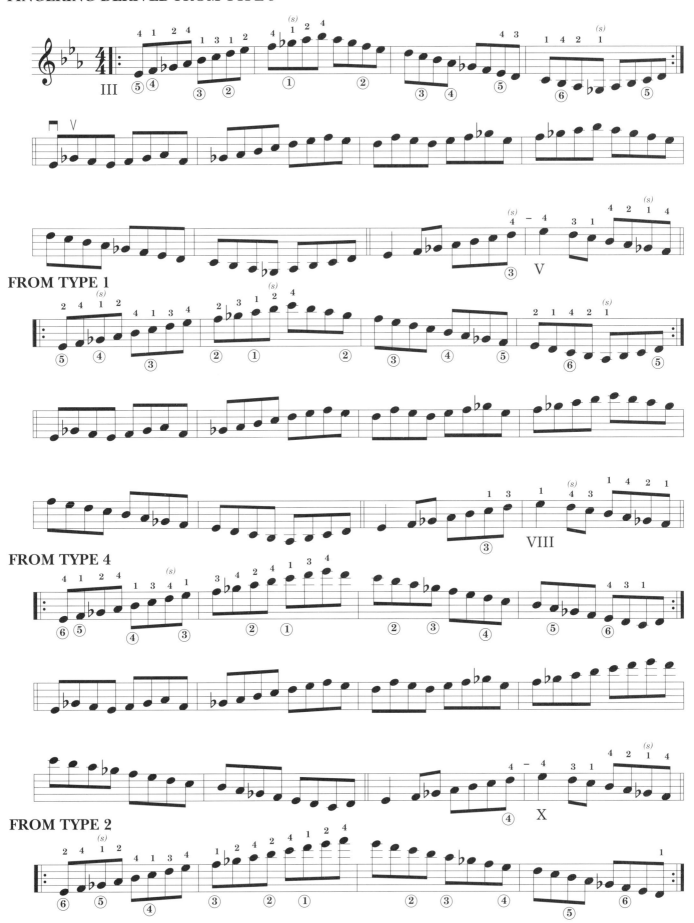

FROM TYPE 1

FROM TYPE 4

FROM TYPE 2

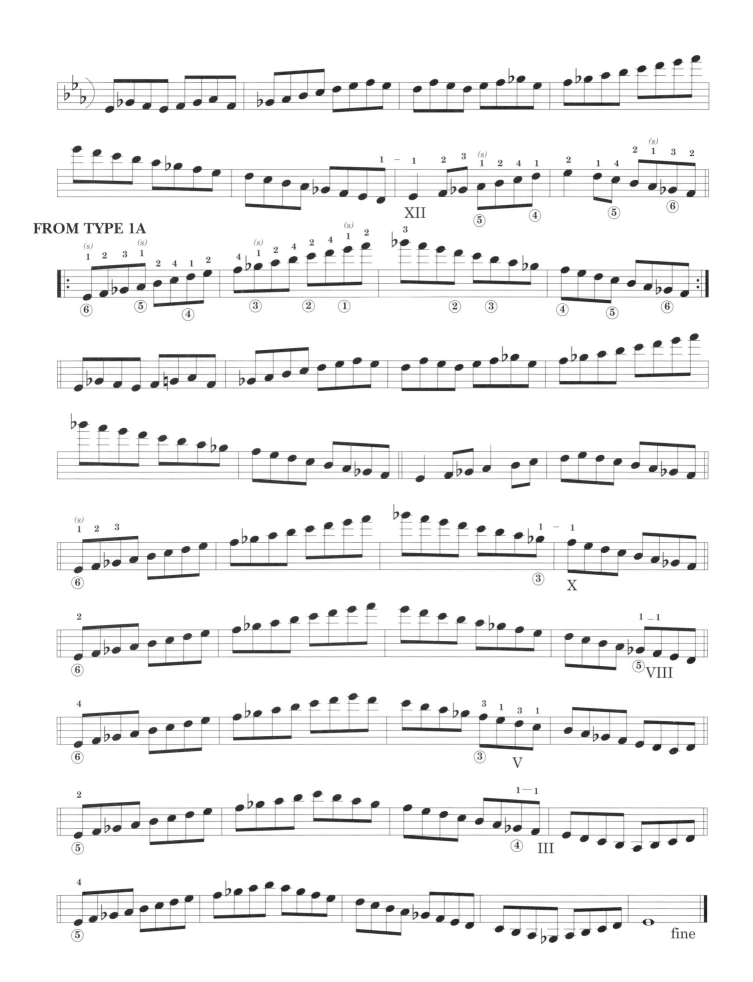

FROM TYPE 1A

Chord Forms

**Diminished 7
(with added high degrees)**

Diminished 7 chords may be named from any chord tone. High degrees (two frets above any diminished chord tone) give you the name of the four dominant 7(♭9) chords with the same sound.
(Gdim = A7(♭9) = B♭dim = C7(♭9) = D♭dim = E♭7(♭9) = Edim = F♯7(♭9))

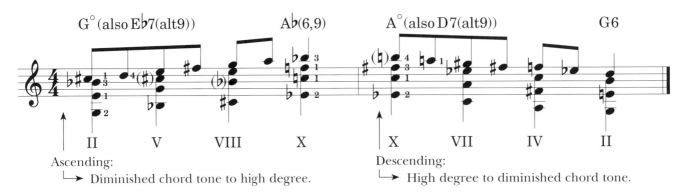

Ascending:
→ Diminished chord tone to high degree.

Descending:
→ High degree to diminished chord tone.

**Diminished 7
(with added high degrees)**

High degrees on diminished 7 chords may also be thought of as the note one fret below any diminished chord tone. (They will be the same four notes as those found two frets above.)

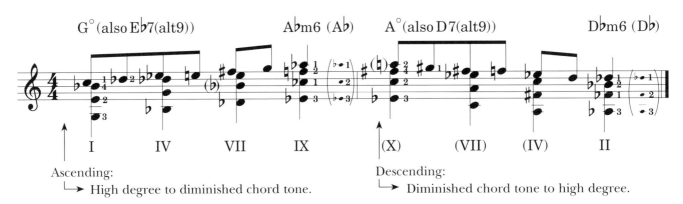

Ascending:
→ High degree to diminished chord tone.

Descending:
→ Diminished chord tone to high degree.

Chord Etude No. 12

Track 20

Speed Study

Tempo must be constant throughout.

For practice with other fingerings, change the key signature to C, F, D, and A. Also use speed studies for real melodic minor scales. Practice all suggested keys with ♭13.

Two-Octave Arpeggios

C Diminished Triad from the Root

▐ Across and up the fingerboard.

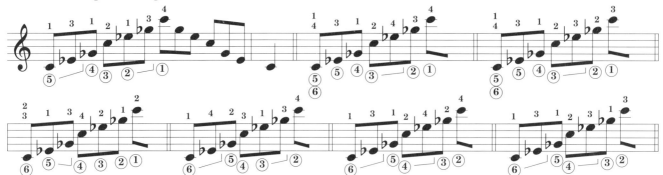

G Diminished Triad from the 3rd

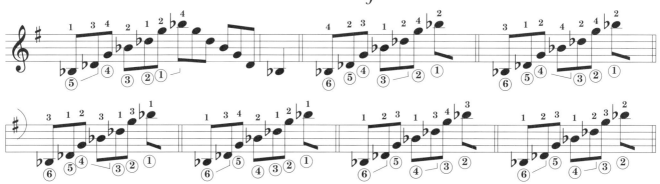

F Diminished Triad from the 5th

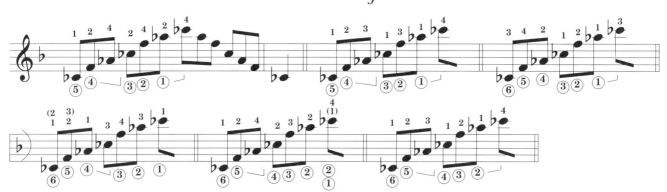

Practice all forms in all possible keys.

Melodic Rhythm No. 7 (duet)

Whole Tone Scales

The whole tone scale consists of six notes, a whole step apart. Each scale tone can be considered the tonic. Therefore only two whole tone scales exist.

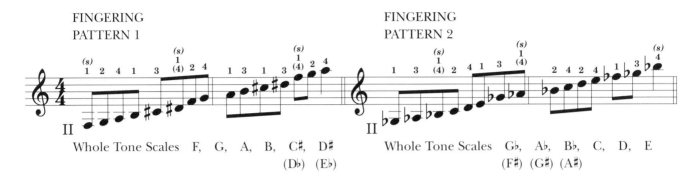

FINGERING PATTERN 1

II — Whole Tone Scales   F,   G,   A,   B,   C♯,   D♯
(D♭)   (E♭)

FINGERING PATTERN 2

II — Whole Tone Scales   G♭,   A♭,   B♭,   C,   D,   E
(F♯)   (G♯)   (A♯)

Practice ascending and descending from each finger. (First-finger stretches are the most practical, but eventually include all possibilities.)

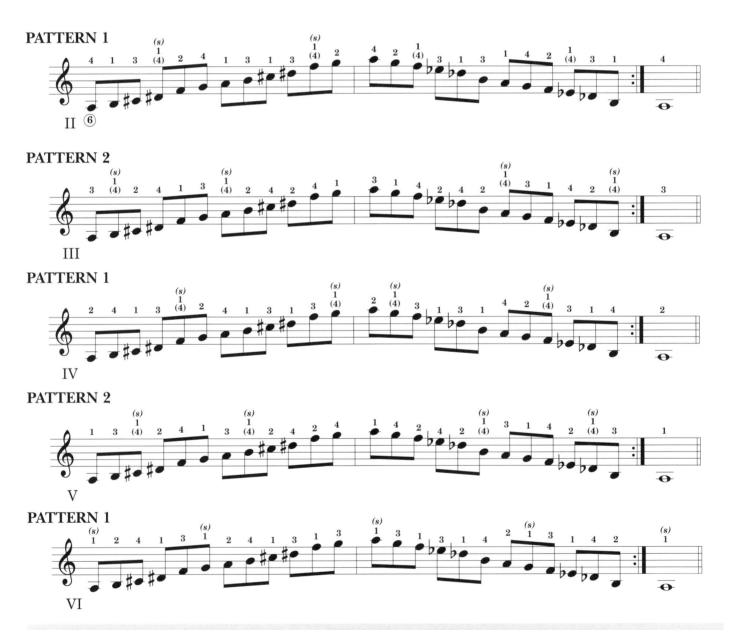

PATTERN 1

II ⑥

PATTERN 2

III

PATTERN 1

IV

PATTERN 2

V

PATTERN 1

VI

Memorize the fingering patterns. Practice both whole tone scales, in all positions.

The principal use of whole tone scales in improvisation is over augmented triads, and (augmented) dominant 7 chords (where the ninth is unaltered, or can be assumed to be unaltered).

EXAMPLE

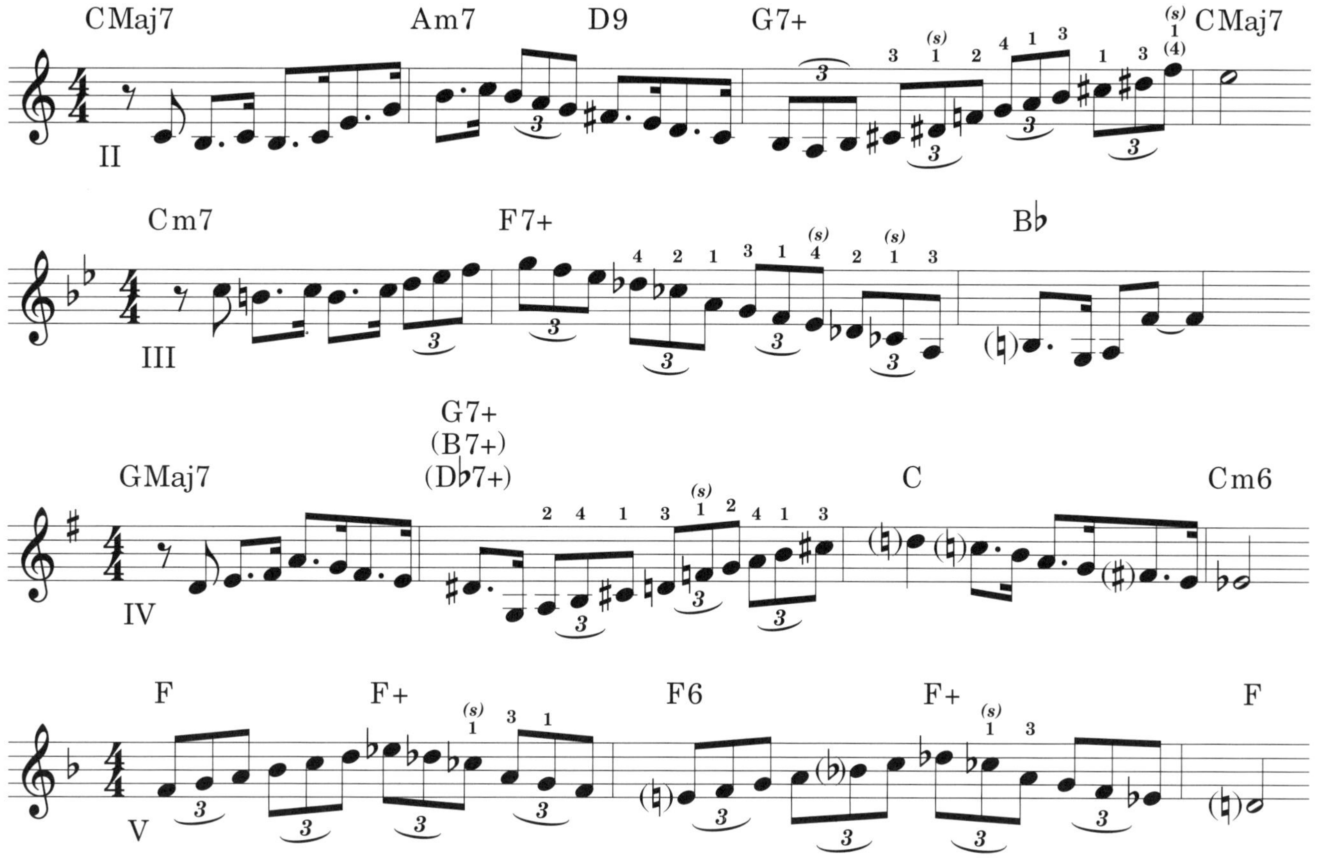

The following example employs both whole tone scales (same position).

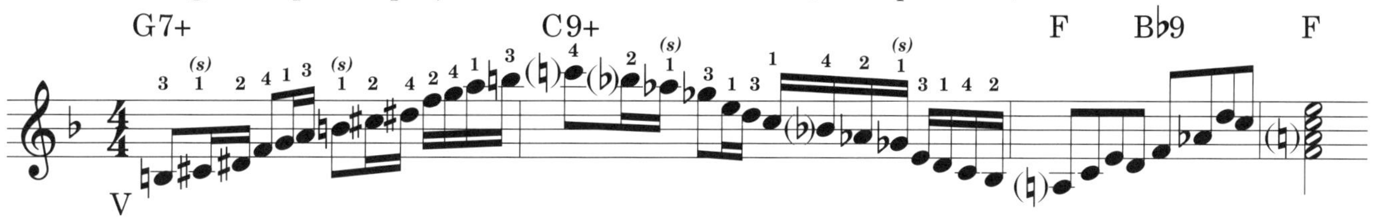

Additional Whole Tone Scale Fingerings with Position Changes:

1.) Across and down the fingerboard as scale ascends (two octaves).

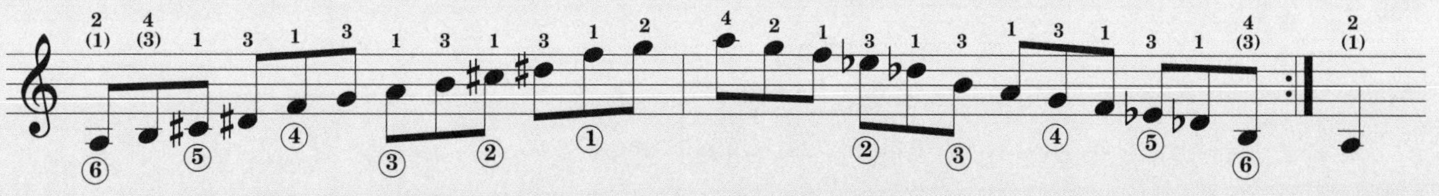

2.) Constant fingering-position change every string (three octaves).

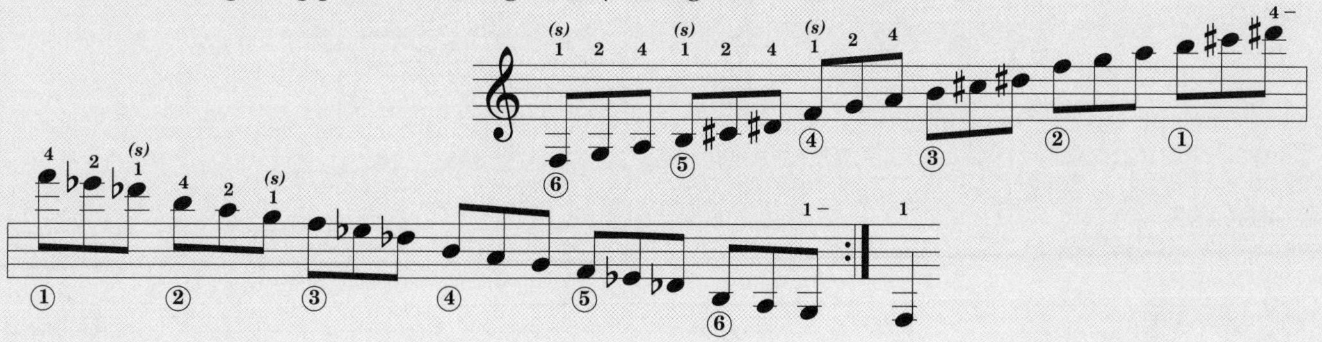

❀ These additional fingerings are less practical for general use.

Rhythm Guitar—The Right Hand (Bossa Nova)

Basic Stroke 1

Bass note or muffled bass strings

Orchestral

■ **EXERCISE**

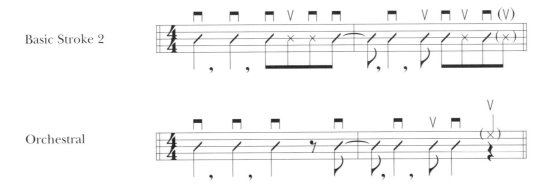

Observe notation. Practice with basic and orchestral strokes.

Basic Stroke 2

Orchestral

■ **EXERCISE**

Practice with each Basic Stroke 2.

Variation 1
Orchestral

■ Tap the foot in "2."

■ **EXERCISE**

Tap the foot in "2."

■ EXERCISE

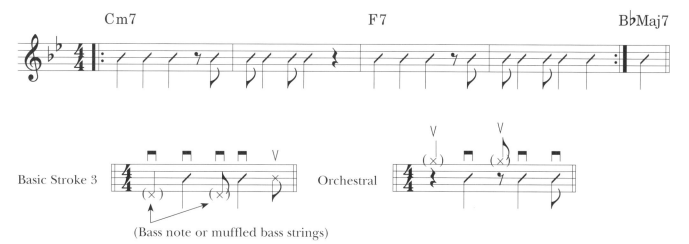

Cm7   F7   B♭Maj7

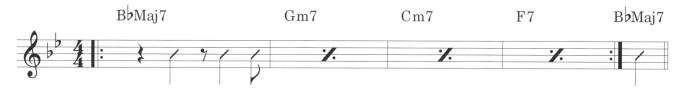

Basic Stroke 3   Orchestral

(Bass note or muffled bass strings)

■ EXERCISE

B♭Maj7   Gm7   Cm7   F7   B♭Maj7

■ Practice this exercise with each Bossa Nova basic stroke #3.

Two-Octave Arpeggios
B♭, F♯, and D Augmented Triads
From the root, 3rd, and augmented 5th—Across and up the fingerboard.

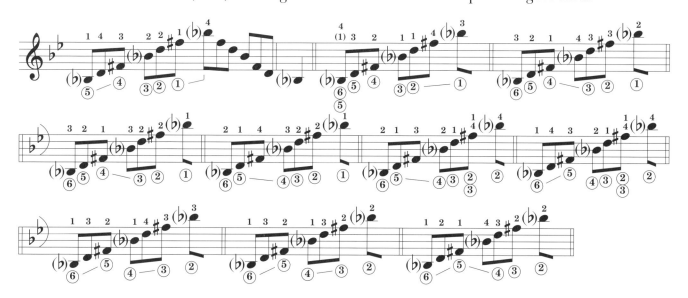

Using the preceding forms, practice and learn augmented triad arpeggios from all notes possible.

Theory: Chord-Scale Relationships

For improvisation.

Nondiatonic Minor 6 and (Unaltered*) Dominant 7 Chords

1.) The tonic and subdominant (I and IV) chords in a major key are often found temporarily altered to minor 6 structures (Im6 and IVm6). Use the real melodic minor scale built from the chord name for Im6 and IVm6 in major keys. Be careful of minor 6 chords. Be sure they are actually functioning as Im6 or IVm6 before employing the above. They are often misnamed minor 7(♭5) chords (the diatonic VIIm7(♭5) of a major key) or ninth chords (V7(9) renamed to indicate bass motion).

2.) These same Im6 and IVm6 chords will also appear (harmonically extended) as dominant 7 chords on the 4th and lowered 7th scale degrees (IV7 and ♭VII7). These dominant 7 structures include chord degrees 9, 11+, and 13. Use the real melodic minor scale from the 5th chordal degree of IV7 and ♭VII7.

EXAMPLE

Chord	C	Cm6	C	C7	F	Fm6	C G7	C
Scale	CMaj	C Real Mel. Min.	CMaj	FMaj	CMaj or FMaj	F Real Mel. Min.	CMaj	→

Chord	C	F9	C	C7	F	B♭9	C G7	C
Scale	CMaj	C Real Mel. Min.	CMaj	FMaj	CMaj or FMaj	F Real Mel. Min.	CMaj	→

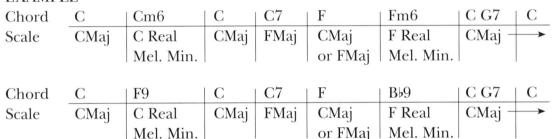

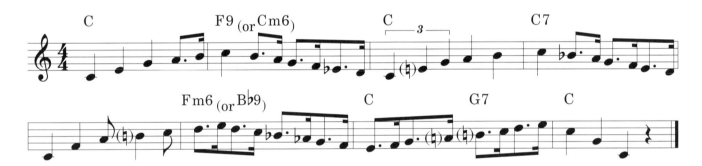

3.) Any unaltered dominant 7 chord with a nondiatonic root (not preceded by a modulating IIm7) tends to sound like ♭VIIm7 of whatever key it is the lowered 7th degree of. All dominant 7 chords with nondiatonic roots include chord degrees 9, 11+, and 13. Use the real melodic minor scale from the 5th chordal degree of the dominant 7 with nondiatonic root.

EXAMPLE

Chord	C	E♭9	Am7	A♭13	Dm9	D♭9	C	B♭9	C
Scale	CMaj	B♭ Real Mel. Min.	CMaj	E♭ Real Mel. Min.	CMaj	A♭ Real Mel. Min.	CMaj	F Real Mel. Min.	CMaj

✲ Unaltered in this instance means no ♭9, +9, ♭5, or +5.

4.) We do not (as yet) have the necessary "scale tools" to properly handle all dominant 7 chords with diatonic roots. Therefore I suggest that, for now, you use the major or real melodic minor scale derived from the **intended tonic*** chord for all dominant 7 chords with scale tone roots, except IV7. (See previous page.)

*Intended tonic: Where the chord would normally resolve to, e.g., B7 to E, E7 to A, A7 to D, etc.

(E Major Scale)   (E Real Melodic Minor)

The real melodic minor constructed from the 5th chordal degree may be used on any (unaltered) dominant 7 chord at any time. But, because most dominant 7 chords with scale tone roots have 9 and/or 13 altered by the surrounding key sound, this chord-scale relationship is imperfect. I recommend that you avoid this for now.

* * * * * * * * * *

You must hear the sound of related scales with chords. Have someone play the changes for you (or use a tape recorder) and experiment with them. Much depends upon your command of the scales, mentally and physically, and upon correct chord names.

It is a very long process to learn (never mind to use!) the chord-scale relationships covering all harmonic situations. Only diligence, perseverance, and considerable experimentation (including thinking, playing, and listening) will make it possible.

I have only scratched the surface of chord and scale relationships in this book. We will pursue this much further in *Volume III*.

Solo in D

Slowly (Rubato)

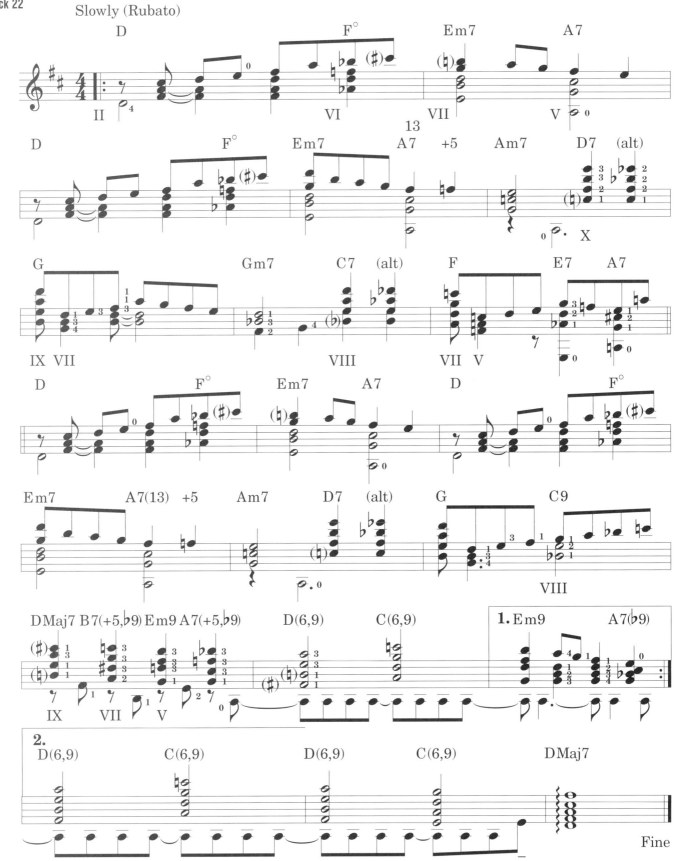

Index

A
MODERN
METHOD
FOR
GUITAR

william leavitt

volume

3

Introduction

This book is a continuation of *A Modern Method for Guitar, Volumes I and II.* Most of the terms and techniques are directly evolved from material presented in those books. Fingerings for two-octave scales and arpeggios are developed to the ultimate, in that any other patterns that you may discover will consist of nothing more than combinations of two or more of those presented here. Three-octave patterns will be shown in later volumes, but many can be worked out with the aid of the position-to-position fingerings on pp. 76 and 77.

With regard to chords and harmony, diagrams are totally dispensed of, and everything is worked out from a knowledge of chord spelling and the construction of voicings. There will be further development later in this area of study.

Mastery of the "Right-Hand Rhythms" pages should enable you to perform any rhythmic combinations that may confront you at any time, assuming, of course, that you have the ability to swing. (If this property is lacking, then perhaps you had better throw the pick away!)

Should you be fortunate enough to possess a creative soul, I'm sure that the pages devoted to chord and scale relationships will be a rather large help. In any event this knowledge can certainly keep you out of trouble when you have some on-the-spot filling to do.

As in the preceding volumes, all music is original and has been created especially for the presentation and perfection of the lesson material.

Once again, all the best and good luck.

Wm. G. Leavitt

It is important that you cover the following material in consecutive order. The index on pg. 158 is for reference purposes only and will prove valuable for review or concentration on specific techniques.

Contents

Evolution of Major Scale Fingering Patterns

Type I fingerings evolve through cycle 5 (down a 5th). Using the second position as a sample, we start with C major, fingering Type 1, then proceed to F major (Type 1A), B♭ major (Type 1B), E♭ major (Type 1C), and A♭ major (Type 1D). Observe that each new key requires additional first-finger stretches. Also note the optional fourth-finger stretch shown on the 2nd string of Type 1D. This will occasionally be necessary for certain melodic patterns, such as 3rds.

Type I

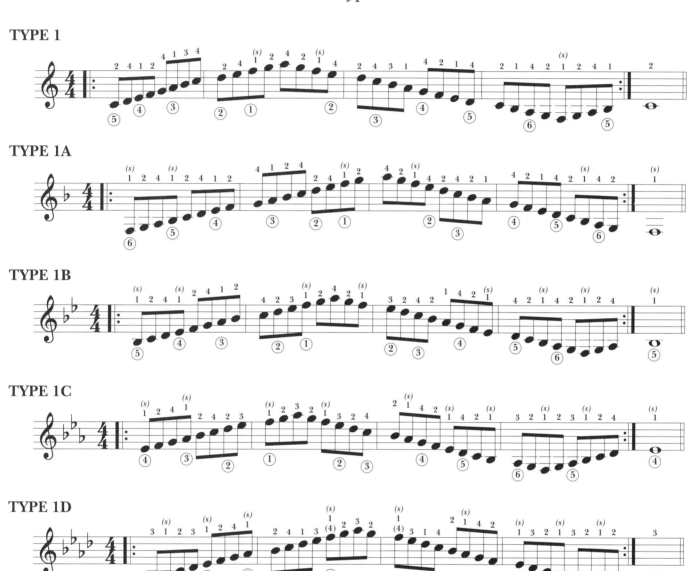

1

Type II

TYPE 2

▌ No derivative fingerings

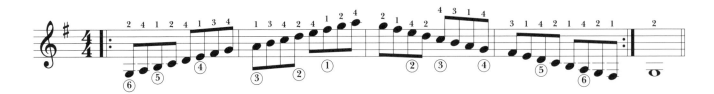

Type III

TYPE 3

▌ No derivative fingerings

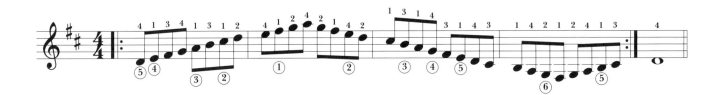

Type IV

TYPE 4

▌ Type 4 fingerings evolve through negative cycle 5 (up a 5th). Using the second position as a sample, we start with A major, fingering Type 4, then proceed to E major (Type 4A), B or C♭ major (Type 4B), F♯ or G♭ major (Type 4C), and C♯ or D♭ major (Type 4D). Observe that each new key requires additional fourth-finger stretches.

▌ Also note that fingering Type 4D is shown with optional first-finger stretches, which actually represent a combination of Types 1 and 4. The combined pattern is usually best.

TYPE 4

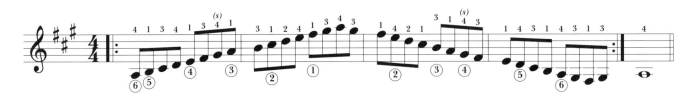

TYPE 4A

TYPE 4B

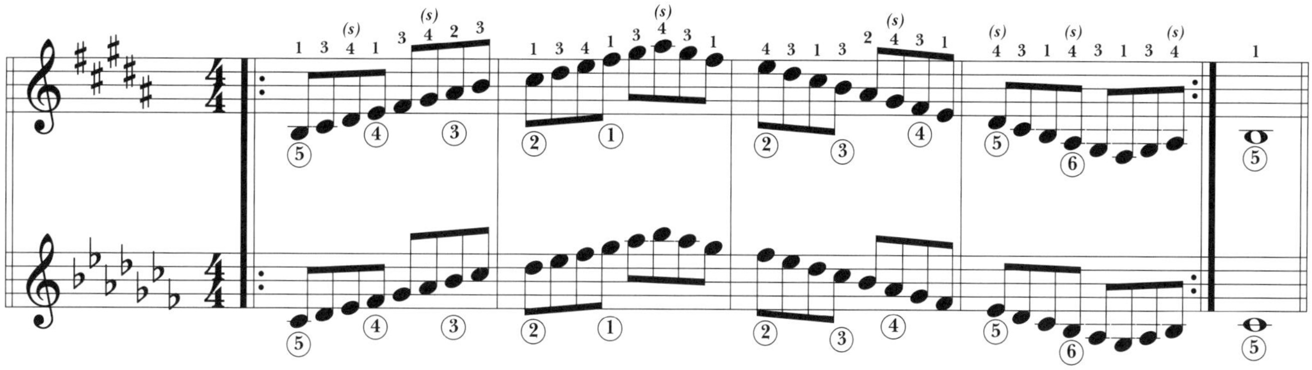

TYPE 4C

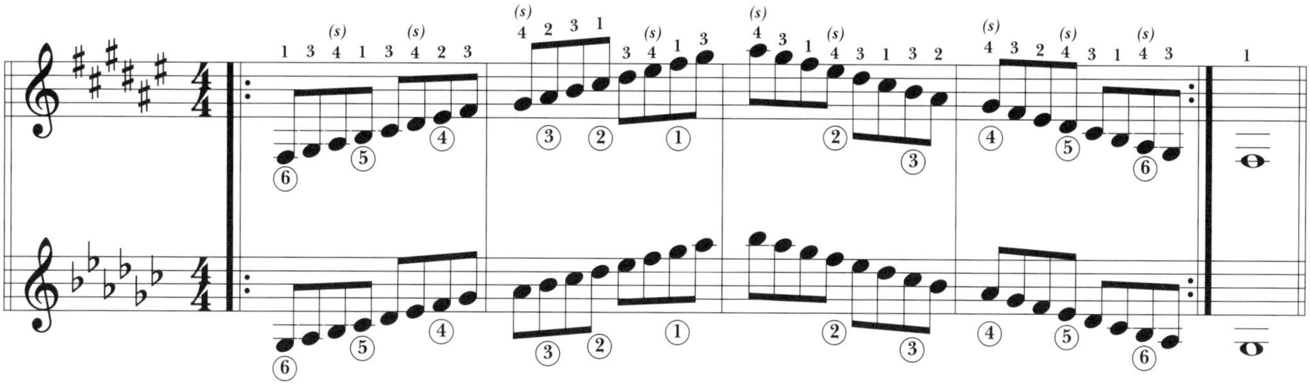

TYPE 4D*

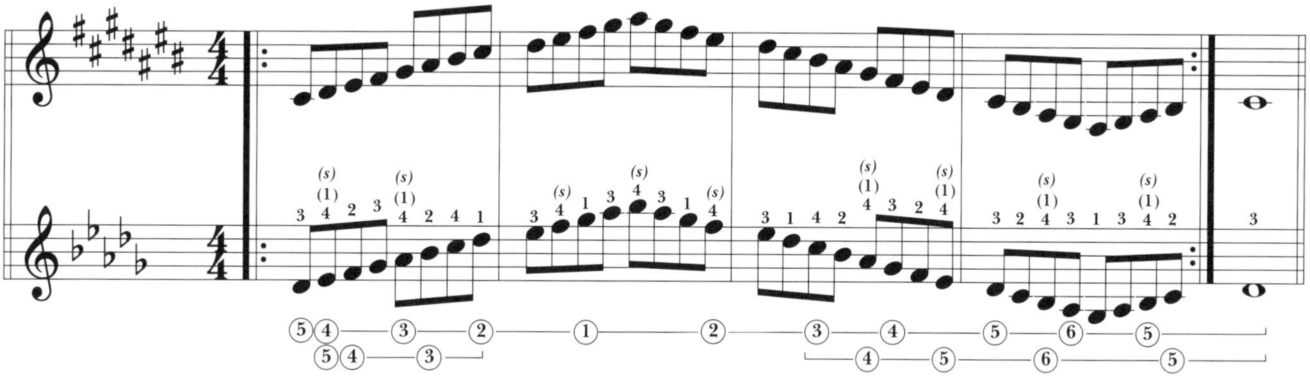

❉ Although this fingering has evolved from Type 4, it is best played in combination with Type 1. On the following pages only this mixed fingering will be shown. (It will be referred to as 1D/4D.)

Familiarity with all twelve major scale fingerings is valuable, especially when reading something for the first time. All forms do not, however, convert to really practical minor scale fingerings. On the following pages, only the nine best minor forms resulting from the conversion of the preceding major patterns will be emphasized. Eventually, all possibilities will be shown.

A Refined Definition of Position
Now that we have encountered many finger stretches with all the fingering possibilities,
let's refine the definition of position. Let's now say: *one fret below the placement
of the second finger determines the position.*

Speed Study
Tempo must be constant throughout.

Change the signature and practice in other keys in this position. Possible keys include C through
all sharps and up to four flats. Later, convert to minor keys.

Solo in B♭

In the following arrangement, strings are indicated by numbers in circles to aid in positioning the chord voicings.

Rhythm Guitar—The Right Hand

Rhumba: Basic and Orchestral

This is difficult but very good for the right hand. It may help to count the eighth notes: 1, 2, 3–1, 2, 3–1, 2 while learning.

■ **EXERCISE**

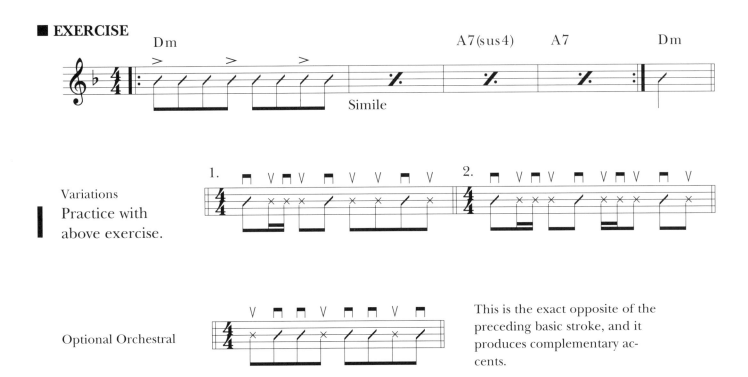

Variations
Practice with above exercise.

Optional Orchestral

This is the exact opposite of the preceding basic stroke, and it produces complementary accents.

■ **EXERCISE**

Variations
Practice with above exercise.

(Also see "Orchestral Beguine," *Vol. II*, pg. 93.)

Each note in a chord is called a "voice." These voices are numbered from the top down. The top note is always called the first voice. The note immediately below it is the second voice. The next note down is the third voice, and so on, depending on the number of notes in the chord. This is always the same, regardless of whether the chord appears in close or open harmony.

Triad Studies: Chords in C Major

The following triad studies are primarily to train the fingers to move from chord to chord, with emphasis on related (or economical) finger movement. *Pay strict attention to fingerings.*

CLOSE VOICINGS

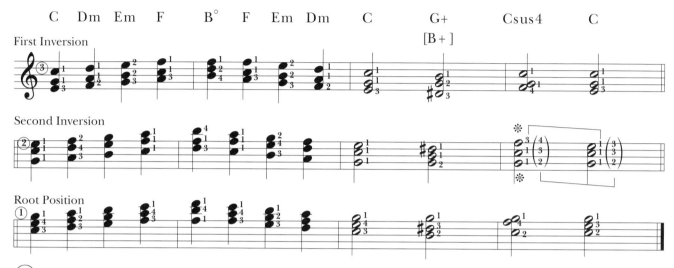

✸ These brackets represent related fingerings. Do not mix them.

OPEN VOICINGS

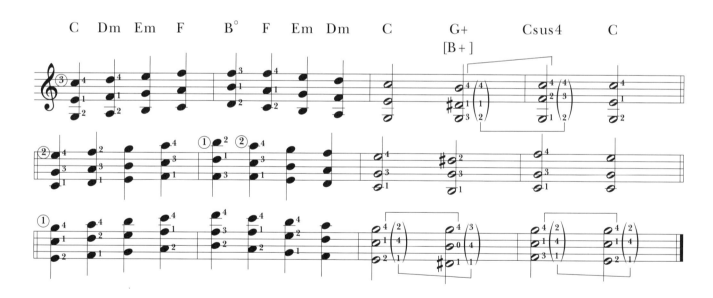

In the preceding open-voiced triads, the chords on the first stave have the 5th degree on the bottom. Chords on the second stave have the root on the bottom. These are the strongest chord degrees and therefore are the best "bass" notes. The open voicings on the third stave have the 3rd degree on the bottom, but because they do not (and cannot) sound in the "real bass" range, special handling is not necessary. (See *Vol. II*, pg. 84.)

Adjacent Strings—Common Finger Exercises

"Roll" the fingertip from string to string so the notes flow from one to the next without running into each other.

In the following exercise, roll the finger from the tip to the first joint. Do not let the notes ring together as a chord.

Major Scales—Position II

Twelve keys—ascending chromatically.

FINGERING TYPE

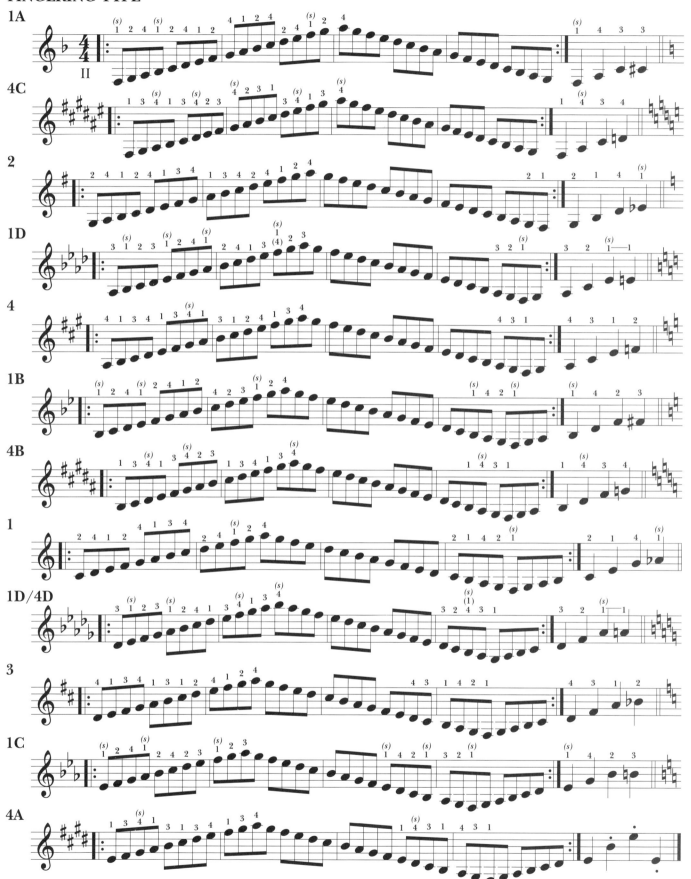

Principal Real Melodic Minor Scales*—Position II
Nine Practical Fingerings

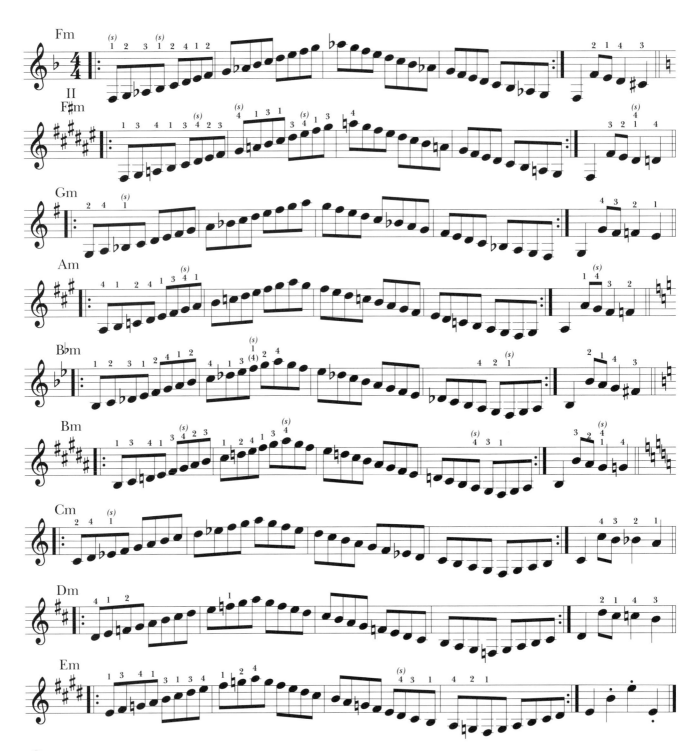

✳ Real melodic minor scale is derived from tonic major scale with ♭3.

Triad Studies—Chords in G Major

Pay strict attention to fingerings.

CLOSE VOICINGS

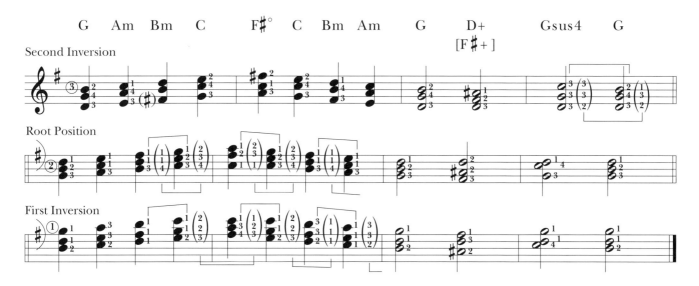

OPEN VOICINGS

❀ The augmented 5th is a weak bass note unless used in passing. Treat ♯5 the same as the 3rd in the bass. (See *Vol. II*, pg. 84.)

Arpeggios—Three-Note Chords

All major triads (Position V) presented chromatically.

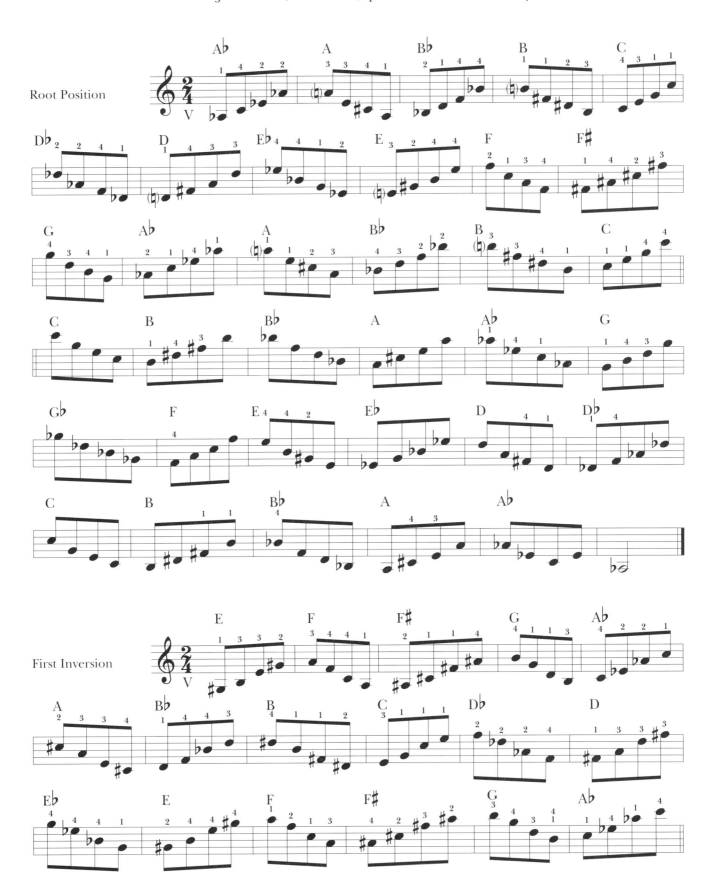

Second Inversion

13

Arpeggios—Three-Note Chords

All minor triads (Position V) presented chromatically.

Second Inversion

15

About Chord Symbols

Chord symbols are a form of musical shorthand to indicate chord structures. They can sometimes be so explicit as to indicate both the harmonic content as well as the voicing and melodic potential. The following facts may help clear up some of the discrepancies that exist in their interpretation.

Any chord symbol involving the number 7 or higher (9, 11, 13) and containing no descriptive term or special mark (maj, min, –, dim, °, etc.) always represents a dominant 7 structure.

The abbreviation "alt" (for altered) means to play the indicated chord degree chromatically altered up and/or down. This term is used exclusively with the 5th degree of major chords and minor 7 chords, and with the 5th and 9th degrees of dominant 7 chords. When the term alt appears with no specific chord degree indicated—and this only happens with dominant 7 chords—then chromatically alter both the 5th and 9th degrees (in either or both directions) in the same structure.

REFERENCE CHART FOR MAJOR SCALE FINGERING TYPES

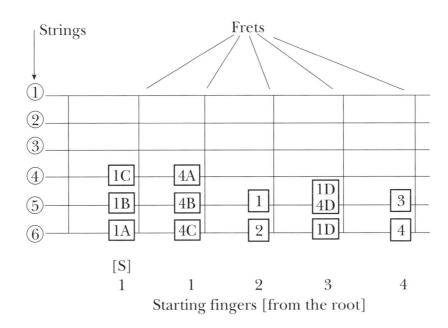

EXAMPLE: Notated in Position V (All notes are roots.)

Major Scales—Position III

Twelve keys—descending chromatically.

Melodic Rhythm Study No. 8 (duet)

Easy Swing Tempo

About Practicing

Because the guitar is a percussive instrument, it is easy and natural to play staccato phrasing. Therefore emphasis should be placed on legato practice of all studies—a smooth performance of connected notes (with absolutely minimal silences between attacks). This type of phrasing is considerably more difficult and consequently more beneficial. A slow, strict tempo is best for legato practice, as the slightest inaccuracy is far more apparent.

The amount of time involved in practice varies with the individual, as concentration spans vary from person to person. For most students, I suggest that instead of one long session, the maximum benefit is derived from two or three shorter periods of daily practice.

Triad Studies—Chords in F Major

Pay strict attention to fingerings.

CLOSE VOICINGS

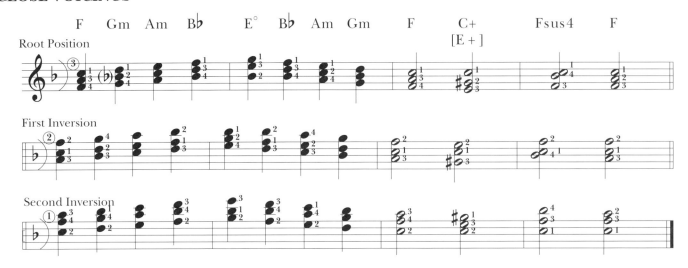

OPEN VOICINGS

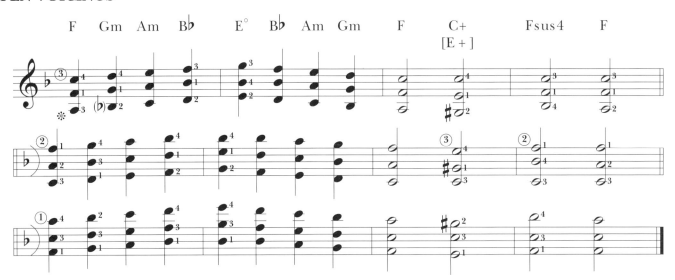

❊ All voicings in this sequence have the 3rd in the bass. (See *Vol. II*, pg. 84.)

Technical Study

Practice with all possible fingerings, picking each note and also picking on the first note of each triplet group and slurring the rest.

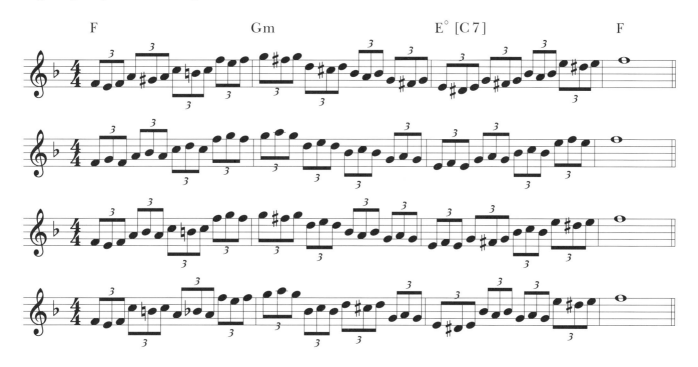

About Chord Construction

Chords are built upwards in 3rds. On the following pages, all chord degrees are to be derived from major scales.

❋ The 11th is (or should be) called sus4 on major and dominant 7 chords.

❋❋ The 6th often replaces the major 7th with tonic and subdominant chords.

❋❋❋ The 13th (same note as the 6th) can only exist with dominant chords.

21

Major Scales—Position IV

Twelve keys—through cycle 5.

FINGERING TYPE

Principal Real Melodic Minor Scales—Position IV
Nine Practical Fingerings

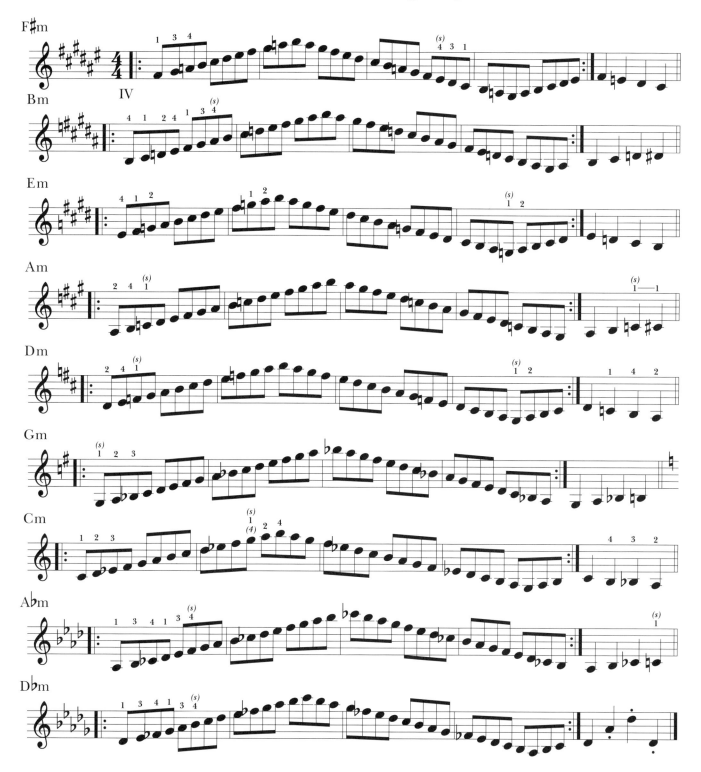

Chord Construction—Four-Part Harmony

All chords are constructed from major scale degrees.

▌ Major scale degrees appear below each staff.

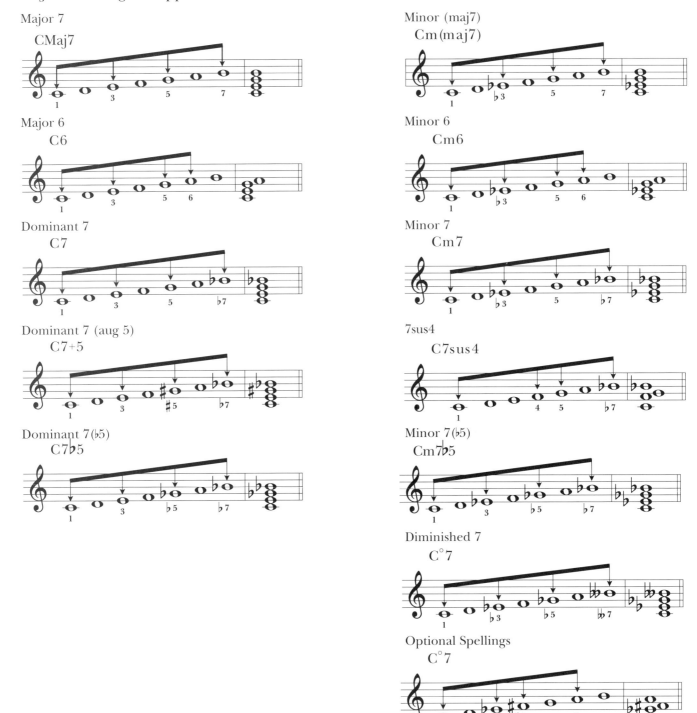

As it is impossible to play most close-voiced structures as chords, we must learn their spelling by practicing them as arpeggios. This must be done so thoroughly that chord spelling becomes automatic. Fingerings are derived from the twelve major scales. Practice them until they require very little, if any, conscious effort.

✳ See special pp. 96 and 97 for information on diminished 7 and dominant 7(♭5) chords.

Arpeggios—Four-Note C Chords
Chord Spelling

Fingering for all four-note chords is shown in the fifth position, with temporary changes to adjacent positions when necessary. After learning the spelling and fingering for each group of arpeggios as written, you must learn to spell and play all structures from all letter names existing from position II through position X. (I suggest doing this transposition on the guitar without writing it out.)

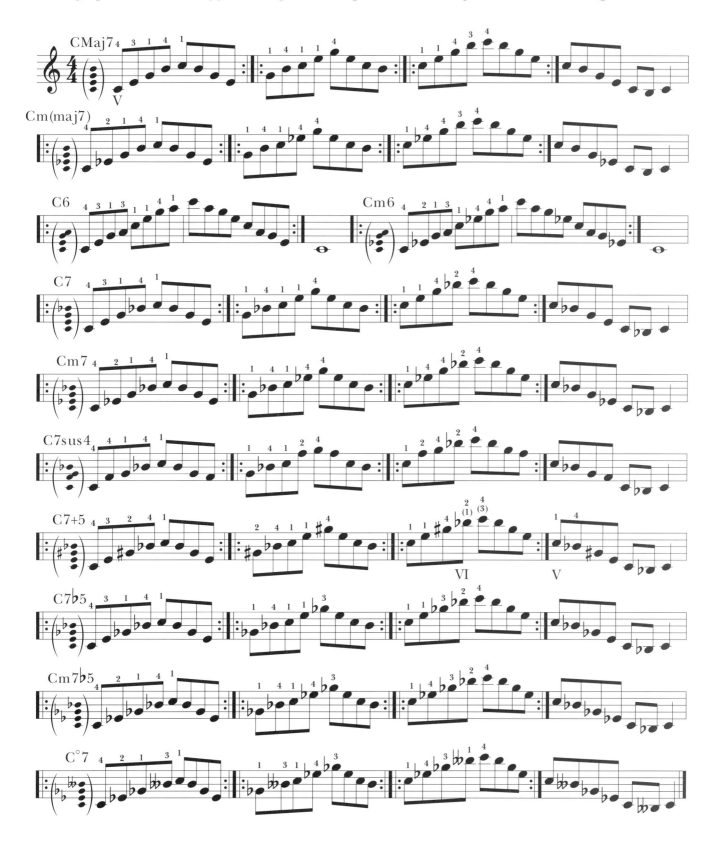

Rhythm Guitar—The Right Hand

Tango 1
Moderately slow
to slow

▌ Practice with each preceding tango beat.

■ **EXERCISE**

Tango 2

Tango 3

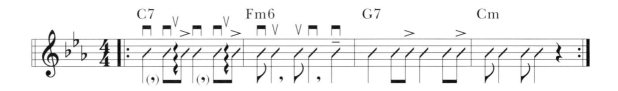

Merengue 1
Fast in 2

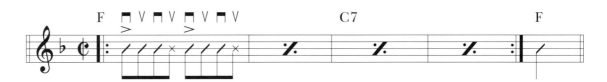

Merengue 2

Merengue 3

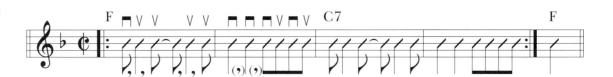

C Major Scale (Twelve Positions)

FINGERING TYPE

Natural Minor Scales

The natural minor scale has the same key signature and exactly the same notes as its relative major scale. Start on the 6th degree of any major scale. Consider this note as the tonic (1st degree) of the natural minor scale. Renumber the notes (1 through 7 upwards) from this new tonic for the degrees of the relative natural minor scale.

C Major Scale Degrees

A Natural Minor Scale Degrees

Another way to construct the relative natural minor scale is to take the notes a *diatonic 3rd below those of the major scale. (Take the note one line below a note on a line, or one space below a note on a space; do not change the key signature.)

✽ Diatonic: Confined to the notes of the key signature, with no alterations.

F Major

D Natural Minor

TABLE OF RELATIVE MAJOR-MINOR KEYS

C major	D major	E♭ major	F major	G major	A major	B♭ major
A minor	B minor	C minor	D minor	E minor	F♯ minor	G minor

When you play a major scale from its 6th degree, this is called the natural minor or Aeolian mode.

No exercises in natural minor scales are given here, as the fingerings are exactly the same as the relative major scales shown before. (For reading practice, see modal transposition in the next section.)

Modes: A Brief Discussion

There are names to indicate the playing of a scale from each of the seven notes. These are called modes. They are as follows:

Ionian   From the tonic (or 1)
Dorian   From the 2nd
Phrygian   From the 3rd
Lydian   From the 4th
Mixolydian   From the 5th
Aeolian   From the 6th
Locrian   From the 7th

There are two ways in which these modal terms are expressed:
- **Dorian mode, key of C**, means the C scale starting on the second note (D).
- **C Dorian**, means to start on the note C and play the scale of which C is the 2nd degree, i.e., the B♭ scale, starting from C.

Automatic Modal Transpositions: Playing the notes as written on the staff, but with a different key signature from the original.

Addition of 2 flats to a key signature produces the Dorian mode.
Addition of 4 flats to a key signature produces the Phrygian mode.
Addition of 1 sharp to a key signature produces the Lydian mode.
Addition of 1 flat to a key signature produces the Mixolydian mode.
Addition of 3 flats to a key signature produces the Aeolian mode.
Addition of 5 flats to a key signature produces the Locrian mode.

Note: When you add flats to a signature containing sharps, each flat cancels out one sharp.
Example: Adding two flats to the key of D major = C major; adding two flats to G major = F major.

To familiarize your ear with the sounds of these modes (and for extra reading practice from music you already own), refer to reading studies, speed studies, or any completely diatonic music in *Volumes I* and *II*. Transpose first into the Aeolian mode (add of three flats to the signature), as it has the most natural sound to our ears. Then later (in this order), transpose to Phrygian, Dorian, Lydian, Mixolydian, and Locrian modes.

Harmonic Minor Scales

The harmonic minor scale has the same key signature as its relative major scale and all notes but one are the same. Follow the same procedure as with natural minor, except raise the 7th degree one half step. This raised 7th degree becomes the leading tone of the harmonic minor scale.

EXAMPLE:

						1	2	3	4	5	6
Degrees	1	2	3	4	5	6	7	(8)	(9)	(10)	(11)	(12)	(13)
Major Scale →	C	D	E	F	G	A	B	C	D	E	F	G	A
Minor Scale →						a	b	c	d	e	f	g♯	a
					Degrees	1	2	3	4	5	6	7	(8)

The fingerings of a harmonic minor scale are easily mastered when you realize that it is nothing more than the relative major scale with one note raised. Therefore, all playing positions and fingering types coincide. Learn harmonic minor by converting from relative major to minor. Use any major scale fingering pattern. Sharp the 5th scale degree of the major, and you are playing the relative harmonic minor scale. Or, use the natural minor scale and give it a **leading tone** by raising its 7th degree.

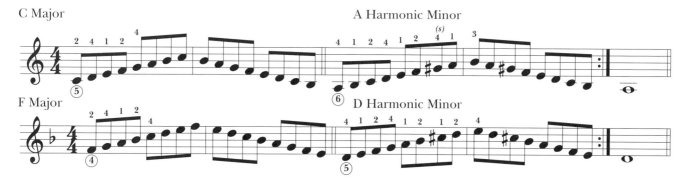

C Major — A Harmonic Minor
F Major — D Harmonic Minor

Note: Harmonic minor is the only scale that contains an interval of an augmented 2nd. It occurs between the 6th and 7th scale degrees.

A Harmonic Minor (Nine Positions)

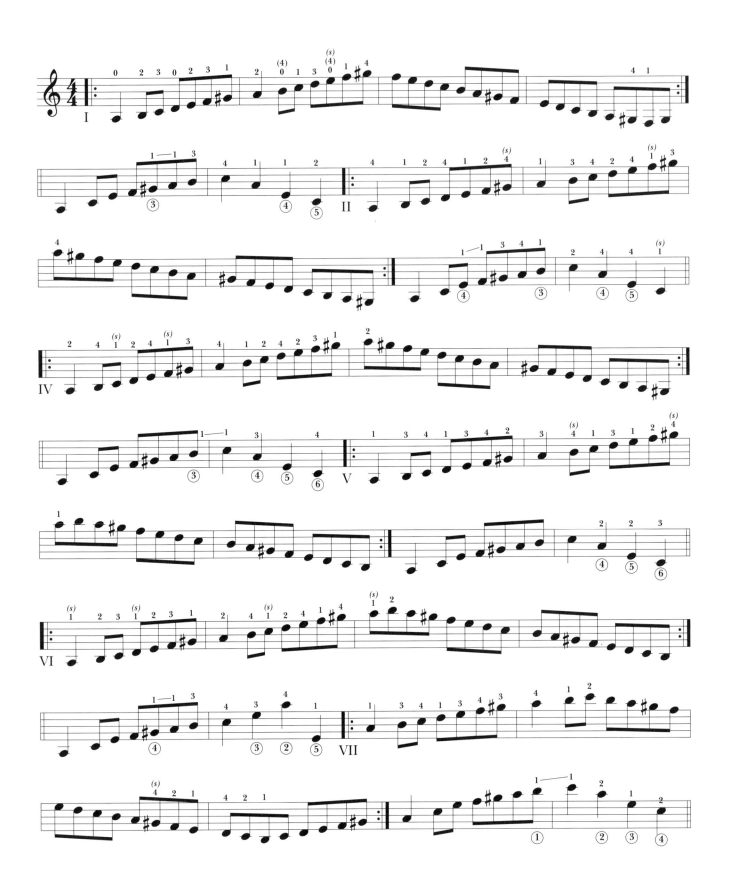

A Minor Etude (solo)

31

The guitar is a very difficult instrument on which to see exactly what you are playing. There are multiple choices for playing single notes and many chord voicings in the same octave. The strings are not tuned with constant intervals between them (like the violin, viola, or cello), so the relative location and fingering for the same group of notes varies from one set of strings to another.

The fact that the guitar is not a very visual instrument can prove to be quite a problem at times, especially when dealing with the study of harmony. Position marks are a great help, but they don't begin to clarify the layout of sounds like the physical appearance of the other harmonic instruments: the black and white keys of the piano, harpsichord, and accordion, the staggered bars of the xylophone and vibes, even the colored strings of the harp.

With regard to all this, and because I feel it is very important to be able to apply directly to the guitar (without any intermediate steps), in the following studies involving chord construction, melodic analysis, etc., we shall concentrate on three-note chord voicings.

Melodization of Triads

Melodization of triads is accomplished by replacing the top note of a triad (the root, 3rd, or 5th, depending on the inversion) with a higher degree of the scale from which the chord is formed. These notes (other than 1, 3, or 5) are referred to as tension notes, tensions, or high degrees.

MELODIC TENSIONS POSSIBLE FOR TONIC MAJOR CHORDS

Root Position			First Inversion		Second Inversion	
5	6	maj7	1	9	3	sus4*
3	3	3	5	5	1	1
1	1	1	3	3	5	5

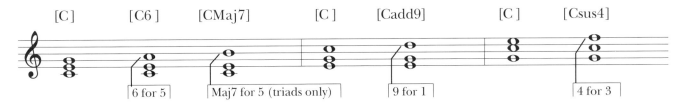

General Rule: A melodic tension replaces the first triadic tone directly below it in pitch (usually found on the same string).

Note that the 3rd is present in all voicings (except sus4*). The 3rd is the most important chord degree, as it alone indicates whether the chord structure is major or minor.

Tensions are also used as inside voices of chords, but because these are more difficult to "see," we shall not emphasize them until later.

(✳) The symbol sus is an abbreviation for "suspension." It is a dissonant note that eventually resolves into the same chord. It usually moves downward to a lower chordal degree, or into a different chord that contains the same note.

Recognition of Melodic Degrees

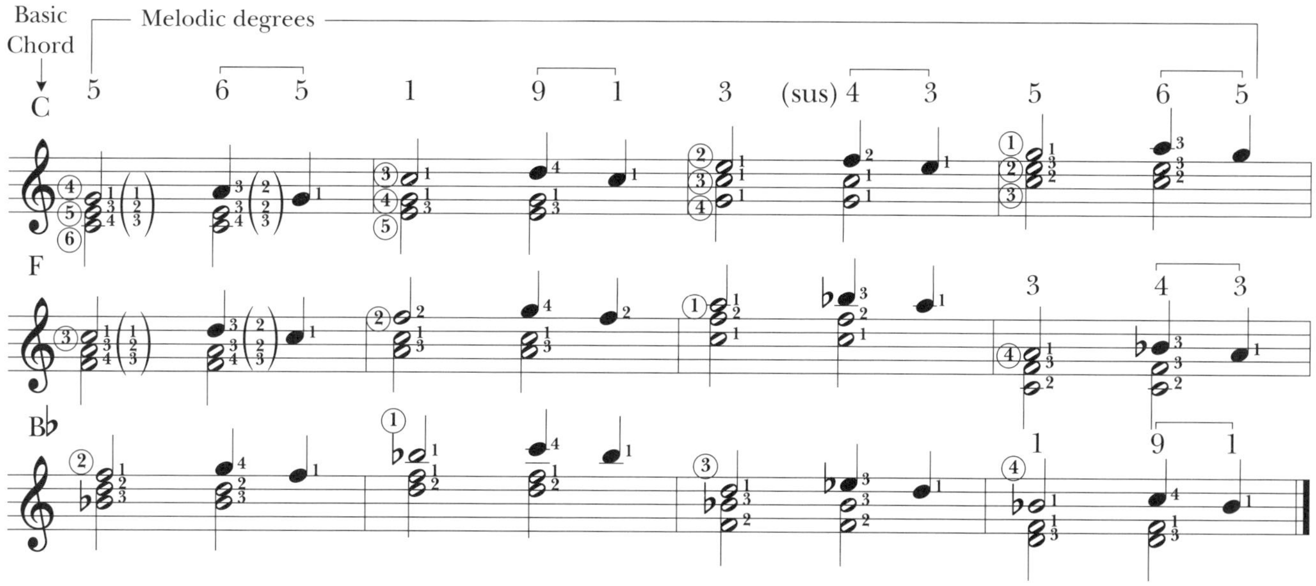

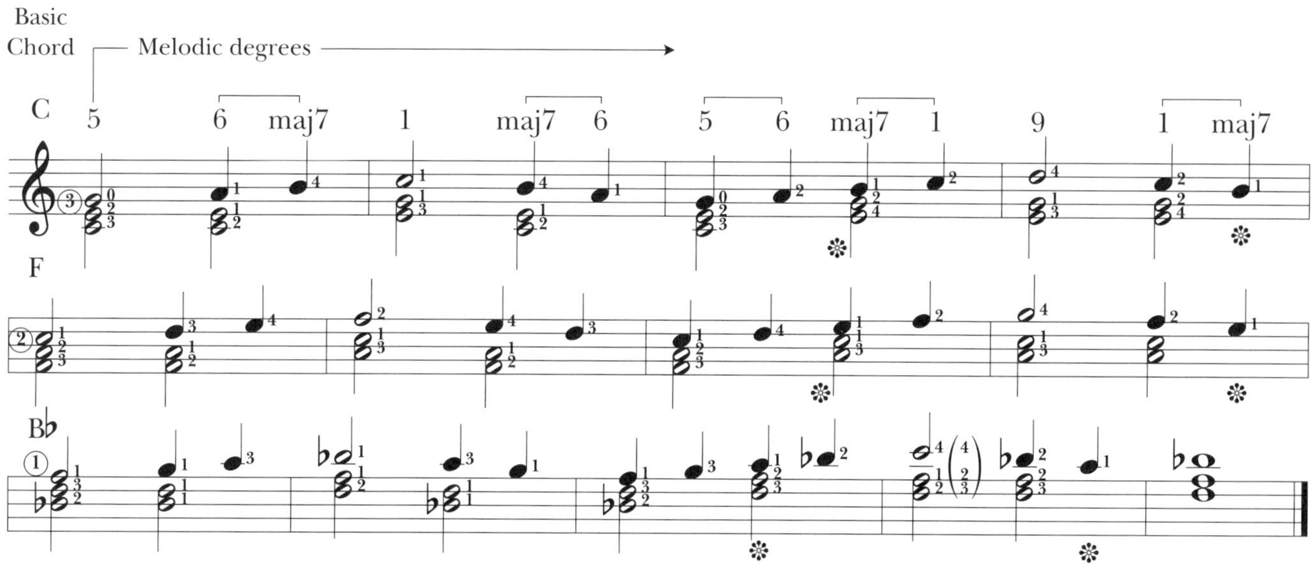

❁ The 7th degree offers an exception to the general rule for tensions on three-part voicings, in that it may replace the 1st triadic tone above it, i.e., maj7 for 1 (usually located on the same string).

Melodic degrees:
#5 to ♭5

The abbreviation alt (for altered), when used with chord symbols, means to chromatically raise and/or lower the indicated degree.

#4 to 5 (♭5)

✱ #4 (like 7) may replace the first triadic tone above it, i.e. #4 for 5. This is because the #4 is the enharmonic equivalent of ♭5. (Enharmonic = two different letter or number designations for the same tone.)

Note: #4 is a diatonic tension on subdominant (IV) chords.

About Chord Voicings

On the guitar, it is usually impossible to play all notes in chords containing tensions or double alterations. The lack of mobility of five (or more) note structures and the sounding range involved in voicings with double alterations prohibits their use even when they are physically possible—which is seldom. However, any and all chord degrees that are present in a voicing must conform to the instructions contained in the chord symbol. Remember: Additions to chord structures are dangerous (major 7ths, 6ths, etc.), at least until after you have heard what is sounding around you. Alterations not indicated are madness; deletions are the norm, smart, sensible, and usually the most musical.

Because of all this, it is important to remember that the root and 5th are the most dispensable degrees of almost all types of chord structures. The 3rd is the most necessary. Like the frosting on a cake, more than one tension is nice if physically available, but it is certainly not a requisite.

Arpeggios—Four-Note F Chords
Chord Spelling

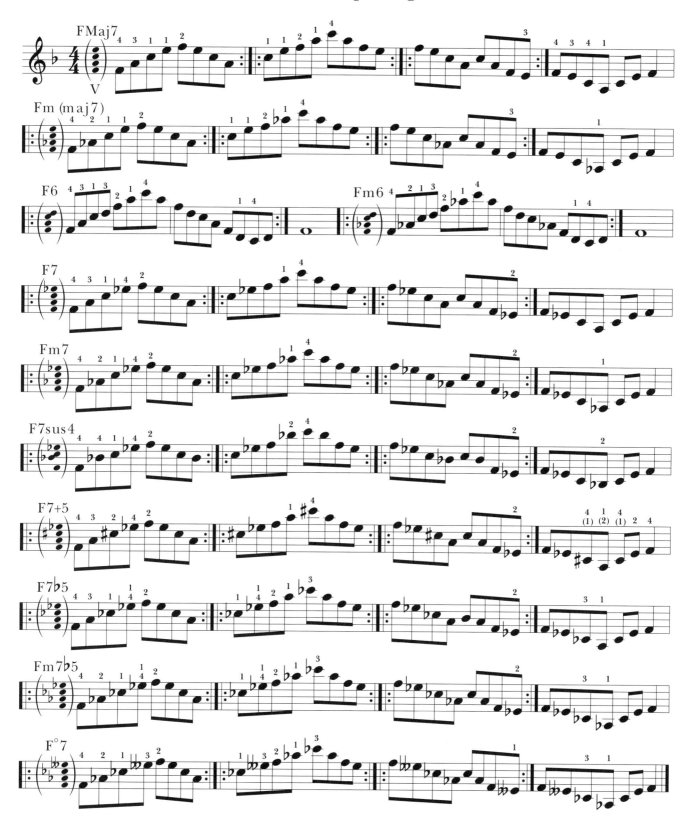

Arpeggios—Four-Note G Chords
Chord Spelling

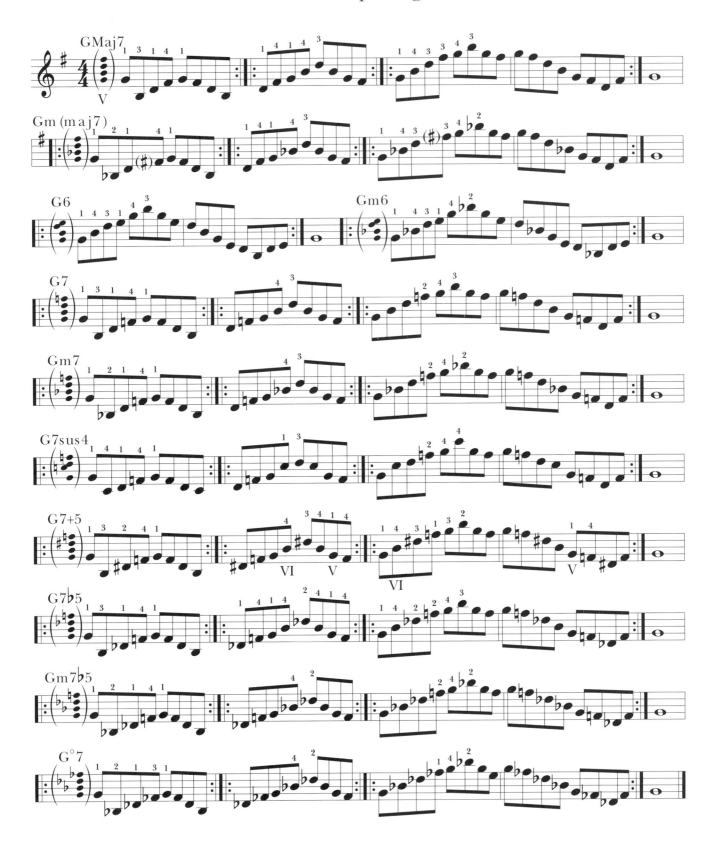

Chord-Scale Relationships—Dominant 7 Chords

For improvisation.

The Basic Idea: Chord-scale relationships are the result of alterations forced on the preceding scale sound by the actual construction of the chord itself.

An E7 chord occurring in the key of C major forces the G♮ to become G♯. Therefore until the occurrence of the next chord, you are functioning in the scale of A harmonic minor. An E7 chord occurring in F major alters the existing G♮ to G♯ and forces the B♭ to become B♮. Therefore, once again the scale for the duration of the E7 chord is A harmonic minor. An E7 chord occurring in the key of G raises the G to G♯, as in the previous examples, but when this G♯ is added to the F♯ that already exists in the scale, the sound that results is A real melodic minor.

EXAMPLES: Scales are named below each sequence of chords.

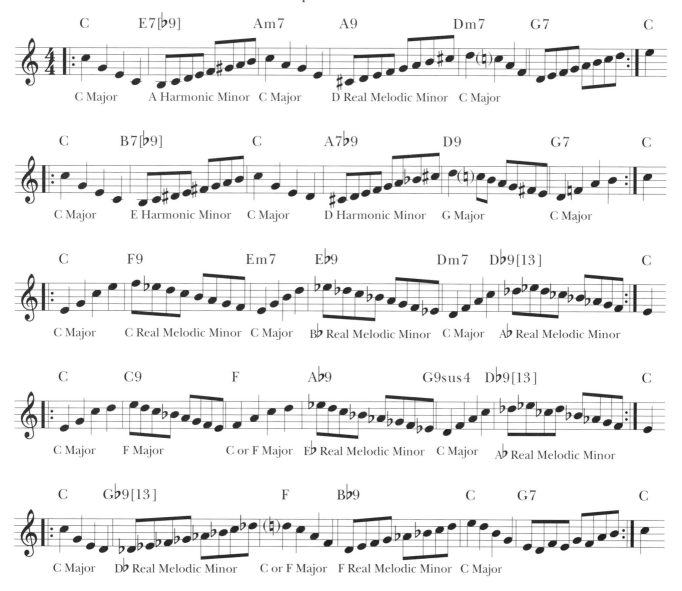

A more in-depth look at dominant 7 chord-scale relationships follows later.

Major Scales—Position V

Twelve keys—descending chromatically.

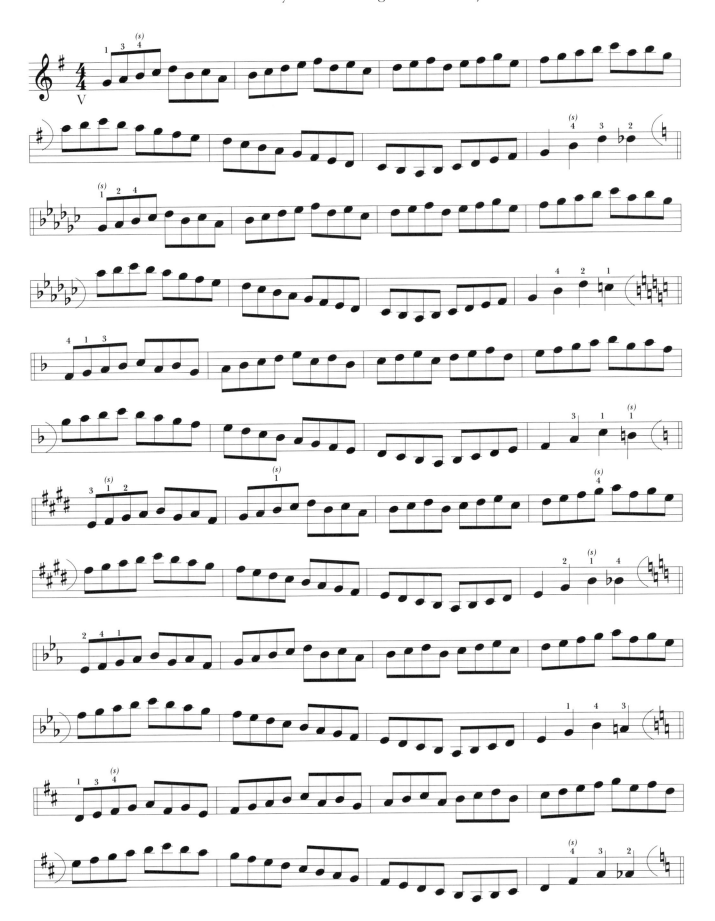

38

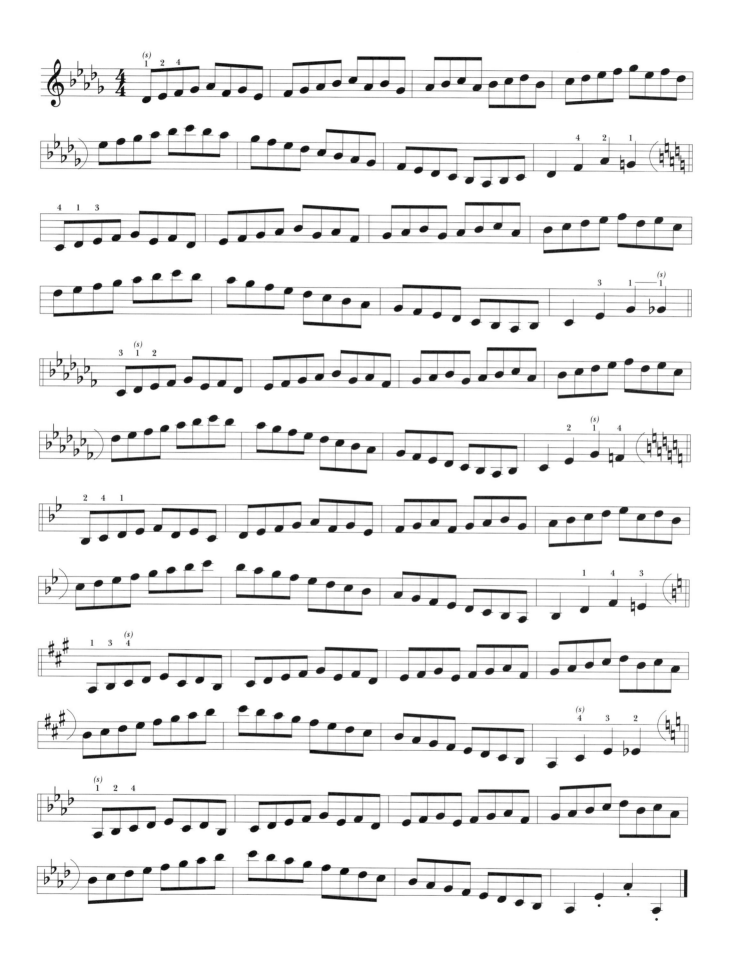

Principal Real Melodic Minor Scales—Position V

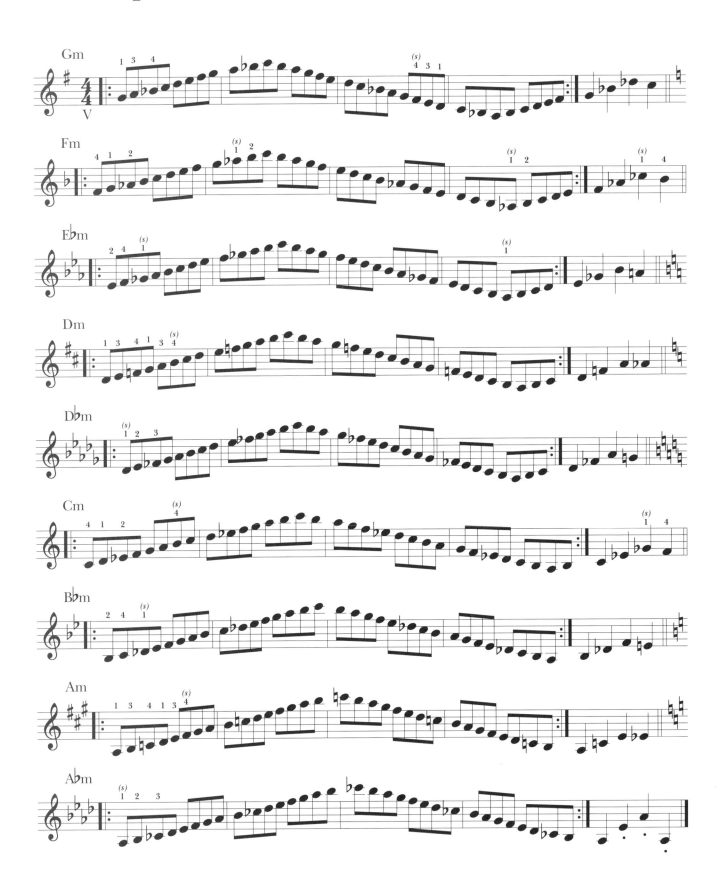

40

Chord Construction—Three-Note Voicings
Melodization of Tonic Major Chords

Melodic degrees

To melodize the above as subdominant (IV) chords, sharp the 4th degree.

Melodization of Tonic and Subdominant Minor 6 Chords

Melodic degrees

Diminished Scales—In Position

The diminished scale is made up of intervals 2, 1, 2, 1, 2, 1, 2, 1, 2, etc. Practice very carefully, as this uniformity produces a rather strange sound. Each fingering pattern contains at least one double stretch, indicated by ⌐1 2 3 4⌐ or ⌐4 3 2 1⌐. This extending of the 1st and 4th fingers may feel awkard at first, but it will prove very valuable for future scale situations. Remember: Stretch the fingers; don't move the hand.

The primary use of diminished scales in improvisation is over diminished 7 chords. When descending, it sounds better if you start on a high degree (or non-chord tone) of the diminished chord. When ascending, start from any note of the scale.

G°/B♭°/D♭°/E°
FINGERING PATTERN 1

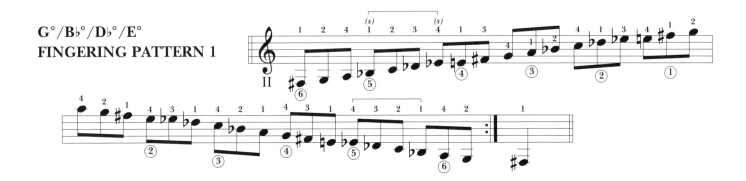

FINGERING PATTERN 2

Fingering pattern 2 employs the double stretch on strings 4 and 2.

G°/B♭°/D♭°/E°

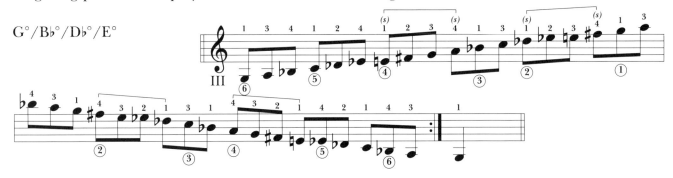

FINGERING PATTERN 3

Fingering pattern 3 employs the double stretch on strings 6 and 1.

G°/B♭°/D♭°/E°

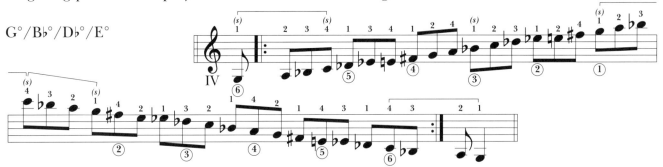

Memorize the fingering patterns. Practice all diminished scales, in all positions.

❙ Practice as follows:

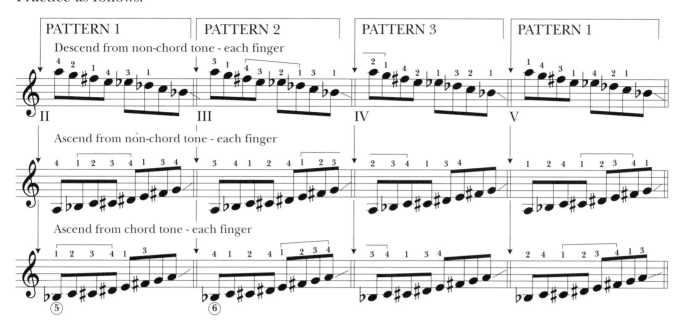

EXAMPLES OF APPLICATION FOR IMPROVISATION:

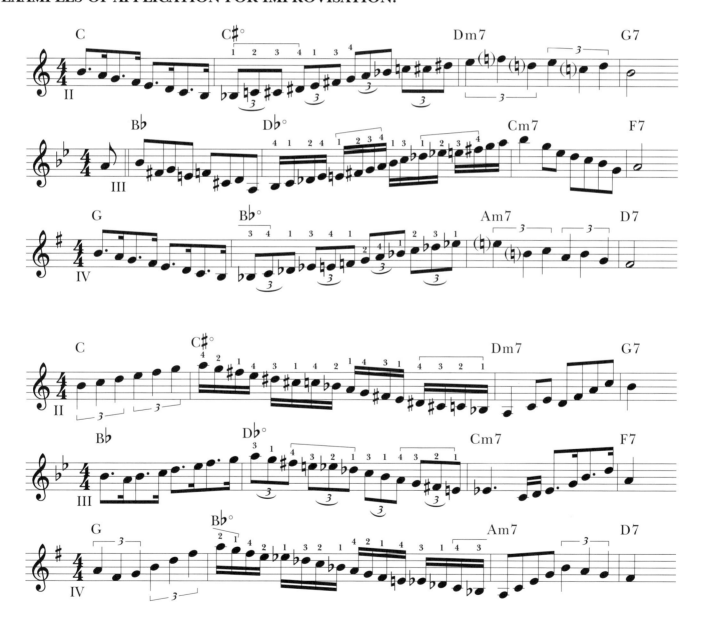

ANOTHER EXAMPLE OF APPLICATION:

▌ Treating (cycle 5) dominant 7 progressions like a chromatic sequence of diminished 7 chords.

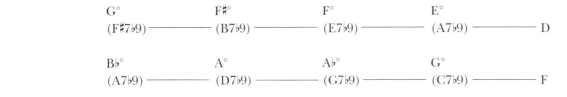

ADDITIONAL DIMINISHED SCALE FINGERINGS:

▌ Constant fingering: one position change (two octaves; no stretches)

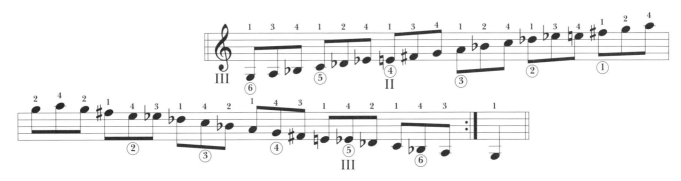

▌ Constant fingering: double stretch and position change on every string (three octaves)

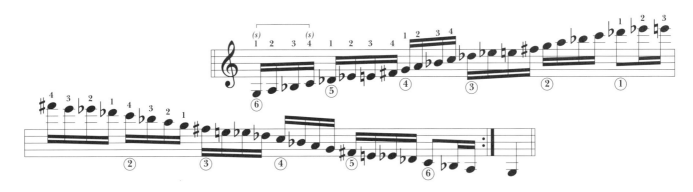

These additional fingerings are less practical for general use.

Chord Construction—Three-Note Voicings
Dominant 7 Chords

A complete dominant 7 chord contains four notes. To construct three-note voicings that accurately represent its sound, chord degrees 3 and ♭7 must be present. These two notes of the dominant 7 chord are called the tritone, as they are three whole steps apart. They form the unstable element that causes the restless sound and the need to resolve by moving on to another chord.

PREPARATION OF CLOSE VOICINGS

Recognition of Melodic Degrees—Dominant 7 Chords

Melodic degrees

Speed Study

▌ Play thirteen times as written, but each time with a new key signature.

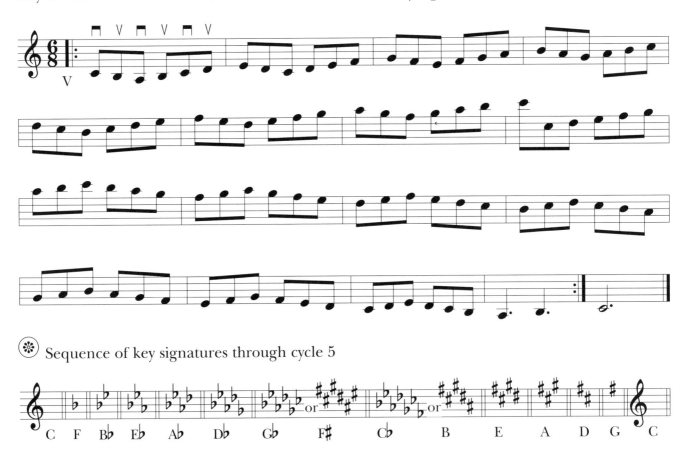

❊ Sequence of key signatures through cycle 5

C   F   B♭   E♭   A♭   D♭   G♭   F♯   C♭   B   E   A   D   G   C

Also practice with minor scales. Nine of each are possible now, but all will be possible later.
Real Melodic Minor: Start with A (major with ♭3), then D, G, etc, chrough D♭.
Harmonic Minor: Start with (G major) E natural minor and add leading tone.

Arpeggios—Four-Note B♭ Chords
Chord Spelling

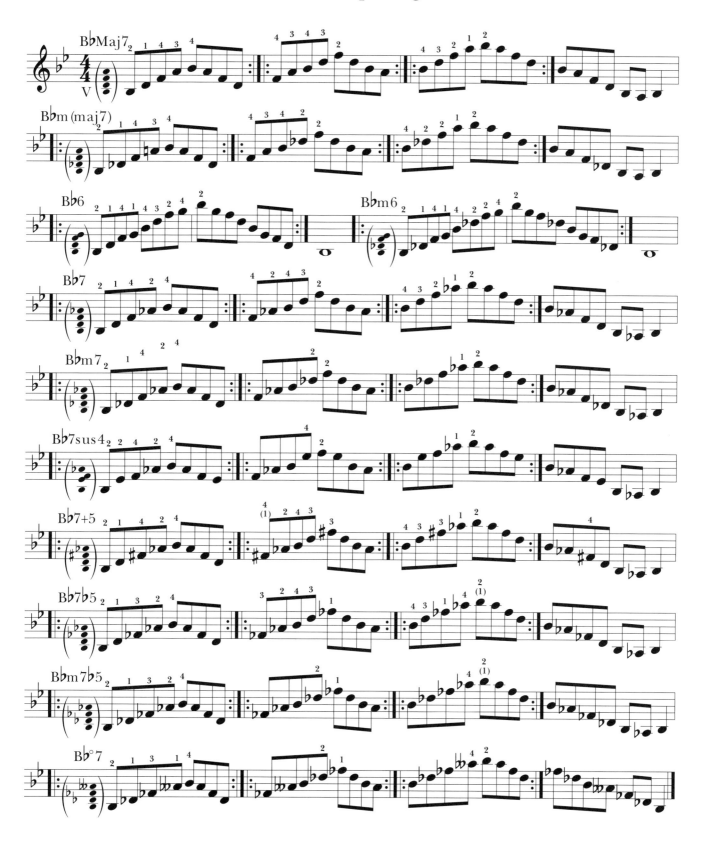

Arpeggios—Four-Note D Chords
Chord Spelling

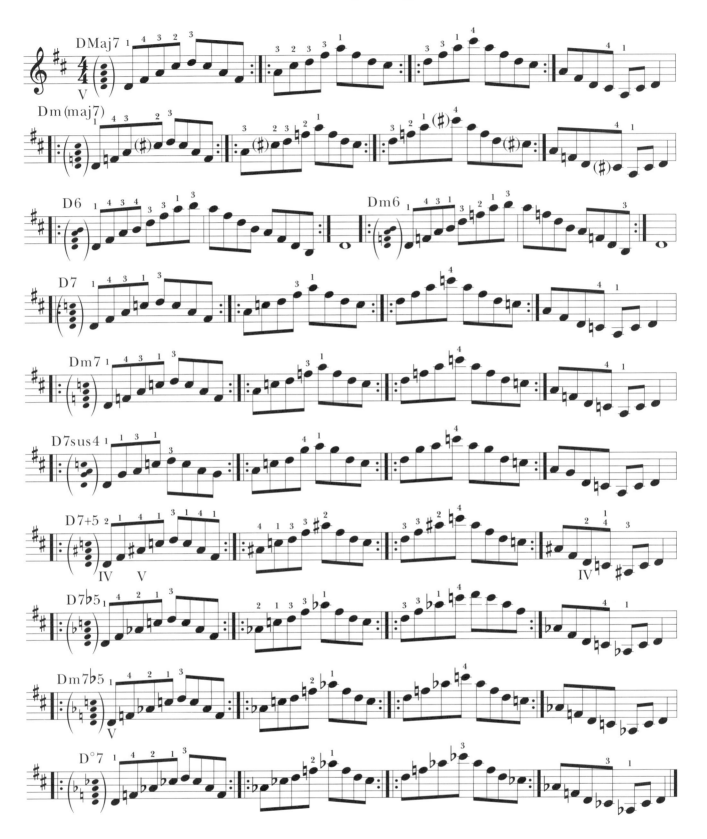

Melodic Rhythm Study No. 9 (duet)

Tracks 7–9

rit.

Rhythm Guitar—The Right Hand

Mambo
Fast in 2

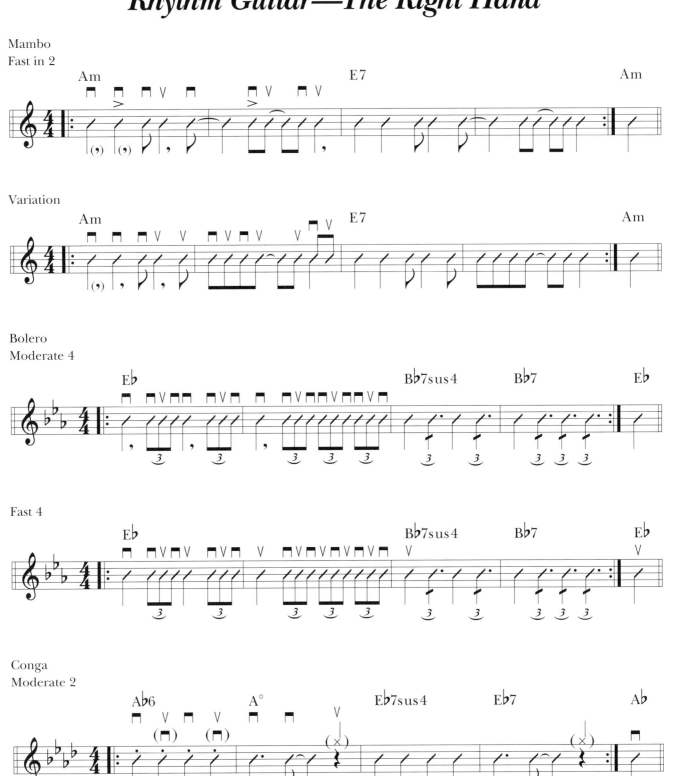

Legato-Staccato
(Portato)
Long and short marks combined

50

F Major Scale (Twelve Positions)

FINGERING TYPE

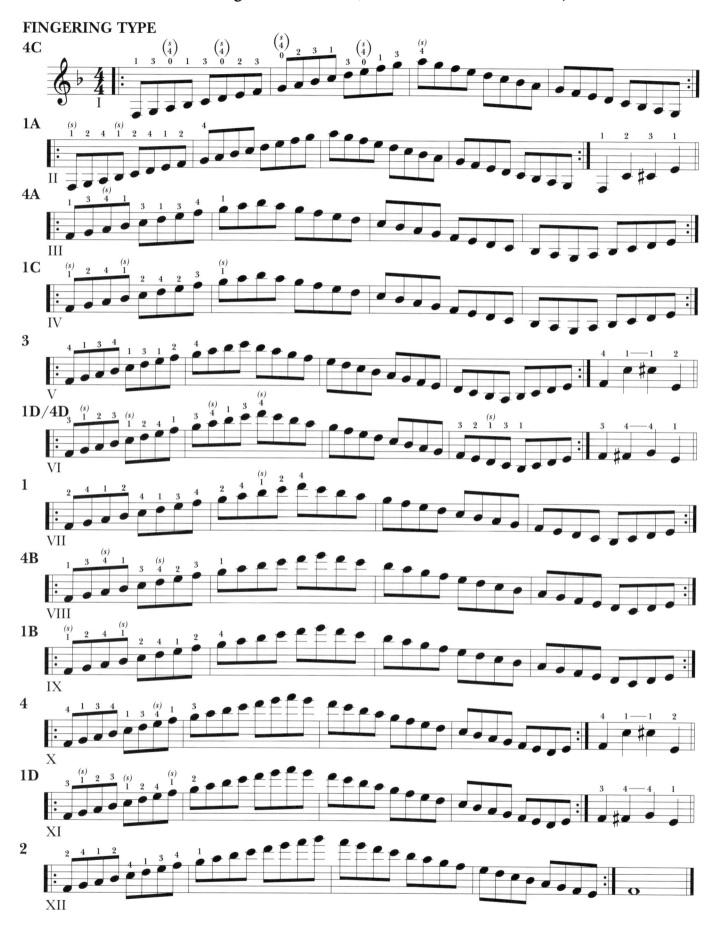

51

D Harmonic Minor (Nine Positions)

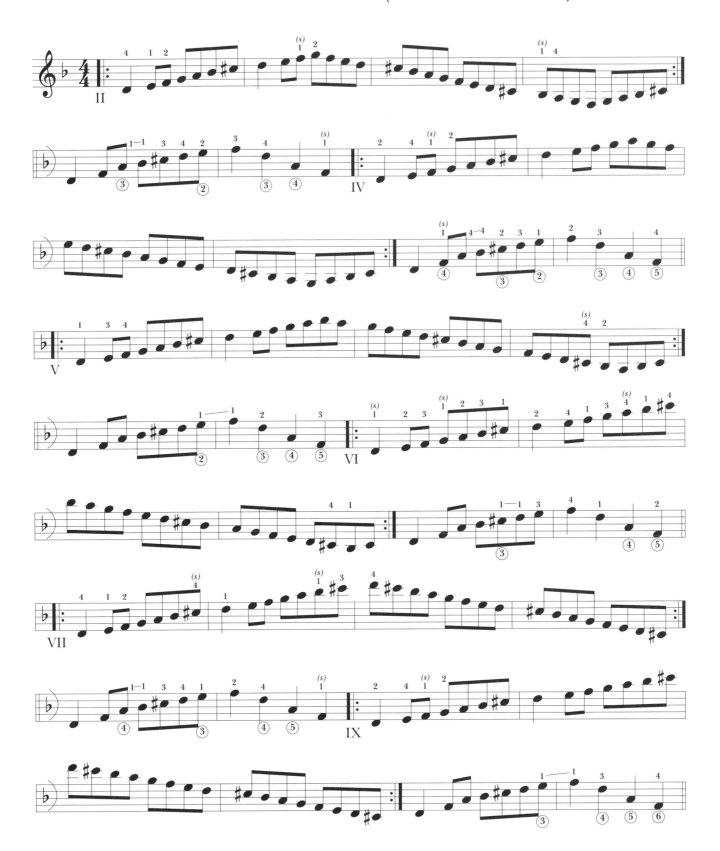

Etude in D Minor (solo)

Track 10

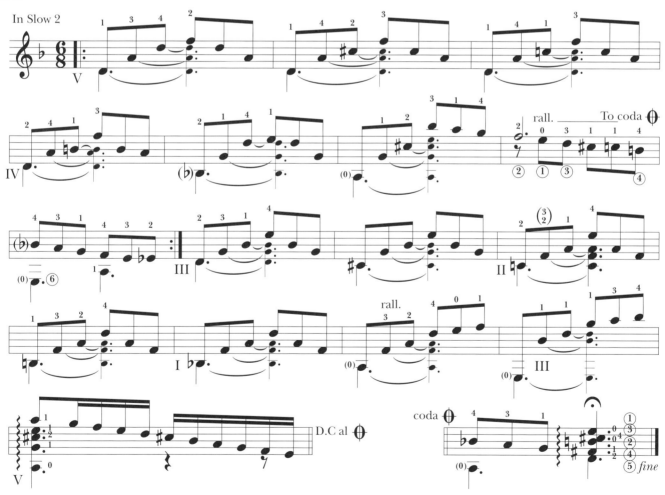

53

Melodic Embellishment

For improvisation.

The Appoggiatura: Temporary replacement of a note by a note that is one step above and/or below it.

The following exercises are based on three-note arpeggios. However, by extracting from all chords the smaller structures contained within them, the following has unlimited application.

Practice with all possible fingerings. Use finger stretches as often as possible; use slides only when absolutely necessary.

CHROMATIC APPROACH FROM BELOW: DIRECT RESOLUTION TO CHORD TONE

SCALE TONE APPROACH FROM ABOVE: DIRECT RESOLUTION TO CHORD TONE

INDIRECT CHROMATIC APPROACH: RESOLUTION DELAYED BY INSERTION OF SCALE TONE

INDIRECT SCALE TONE APPROACH: RESOLUTION DELAYED BY INSERTION OF CHROMATIC APPROACH

COMBINATION 1: ALTERNATING CHROMATIC AND SCALE TONE APPROACHES

COMBINATION 2: CHORD DEGREES NOT IN CONSECUTIVE ORDER; APPROACHES MIXED

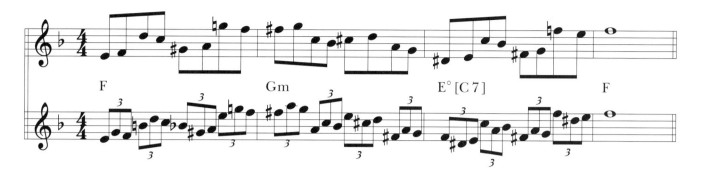

▋ Many other combinations await your discovery.

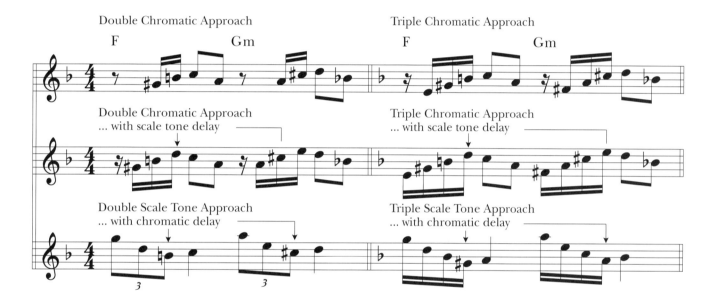

Rhythm Guitar—The Right Hand

5/4 Swing

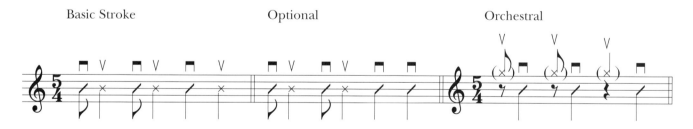

About Altered Chords and Chord Degrees

4th   The sus4 (suspended 4th) means that the 4th degree replaces the 3rd in all major and dominant 7 structures. The 3rd is available only as a melodic passing tone.

With minor chords, sus4 may replace or be used with ♭3. (See 11th, below.)

5th   When the 5th is specifically indicated as sharped or flatted on dominant 7 chords, you might assume that it is truly altered, but this is not so. Rather often the real meaning of a written ♭5 is +11, and ♯5 is ♭13. (See +11 and ♭13.)

When improvising, the player frequently can choose whether to raise or lower the 5th. Sometimes, it may be slightly imperfect theoretically, but ultimately it will be more musical.

For example, when the 5th is sharped, it may be treated melodically as a ♭13, and the normal 5th is used as a passing tone. When the 5th is flatted, it may be treated melodically as a +11, and the 5th is used as a passing tone.

With minor 7 chords, a specifically raised or lowered 5th does in fact represent a truly altered 5th degree.

9th   When the 9th is specifically flatted or sharped, it is truly altered harmonically and melodically. The ♯9 is sometimes melodically treated as ♭3. Alt 9 occurs with dominant 7 chords only.

11th   The 11th with dominant 7 structures is actually an enharmonically named sus4, but it indicates the possible presence of 9 and ♭7 in the voicing. An 11th chord therefore is a dominant 9sus4.

The 11th with minor chords represents the addition of another degree to the total structure, as it may be used with the ♭3 and/or 5, ♭7, and 9.

The augmented 11th (♯11, +11, 11+) exists only with major and dominant 7 chords. It is an added degree to the total structure (of 1, 3, 5, 7, 9) and is used with the 3rd. It does not necessarily replace any chord degree. It is often misleadingly called ♭5.

13th   The ♭13 is actually an enharmonically named ♯5. It cannot be used harmonically with a normal 5th, but it does not represent an altered 5th.

It is called ♭13 to indicate that the normal 5th is to be used as a melodic passing tone. The ♭13 is often misleadingly named ♯5. (13ths can occur only in dominant 7 chords.)

Whenever ♭13 seems to exist on a minor 7 chord, you are actually dealing with a I-for-IIIm7 situation. The appearance of an open voicing of the I chord with the 3rd in the bass, the root in the lead, and the sound brightened up with the 9th inside may mislead you into thinking otherwise. Probably the best name for this structure is minor 7 (add ♭6).

Arpeggios—Four-Note E♭ Chords
Chord Spelling

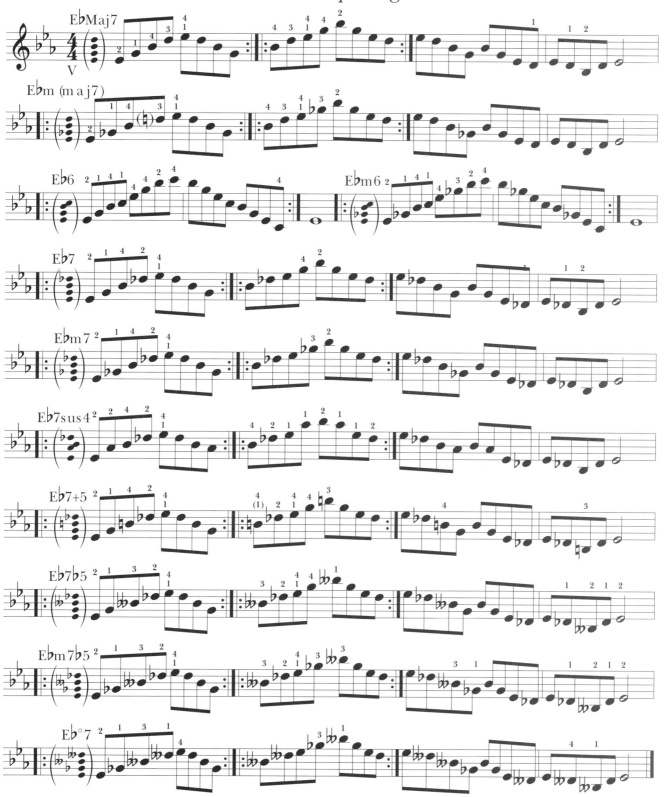

57

Arpeggios—Four-Note A Chords
Chord Spelling

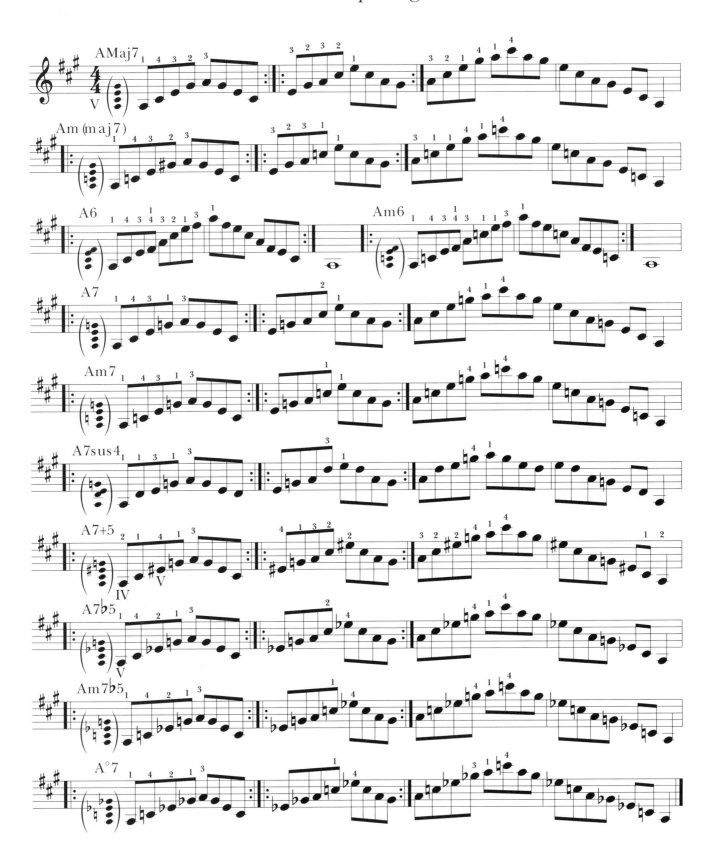

Chord Construction—Three-Note Voicings
Melodization of Dominant 7 Chords

Melodic degrees: Major scale from intended tonic

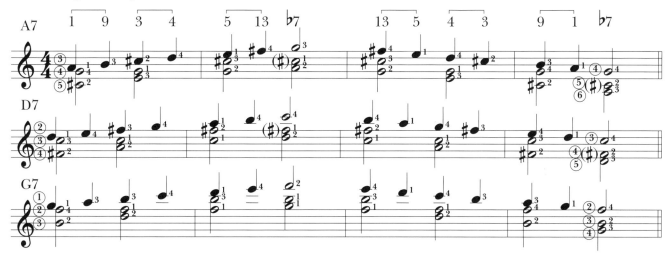

Once the dominant 7 sound has been established, voicings may be used in passing that do not contain the 3 and ♭7. The ear has a tendency to retain this sound.

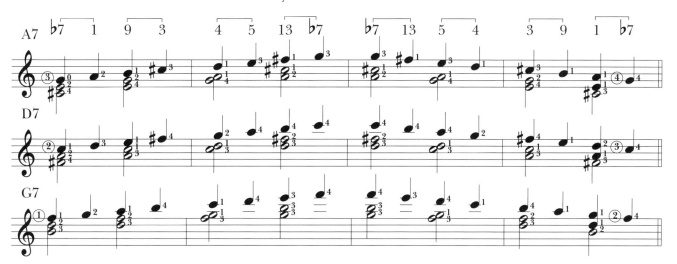

Important: Because of their mobility, three-note voicings are very valuable for chord melody playing, for harmonized fills, and for comping. They are shown melodized according to chord-scale relationships and can really open up the harmonic/melodic potential of the guitar.

Melodization of I Minor Chords with Harmonic Minor Scale

Melodic degrees: Harmonic minor scale from chord name

Arpeggio Study—Seventh Chords

▌ Play from all fingers, but stay in position throughout the entire sequence.

✸ Also play the first chord of each measure as a minor 7 chord.

Melodic Rhythm Study No. 10 (duet)

Major Scales—Position VII

Twelve keys—ascending chromatically.

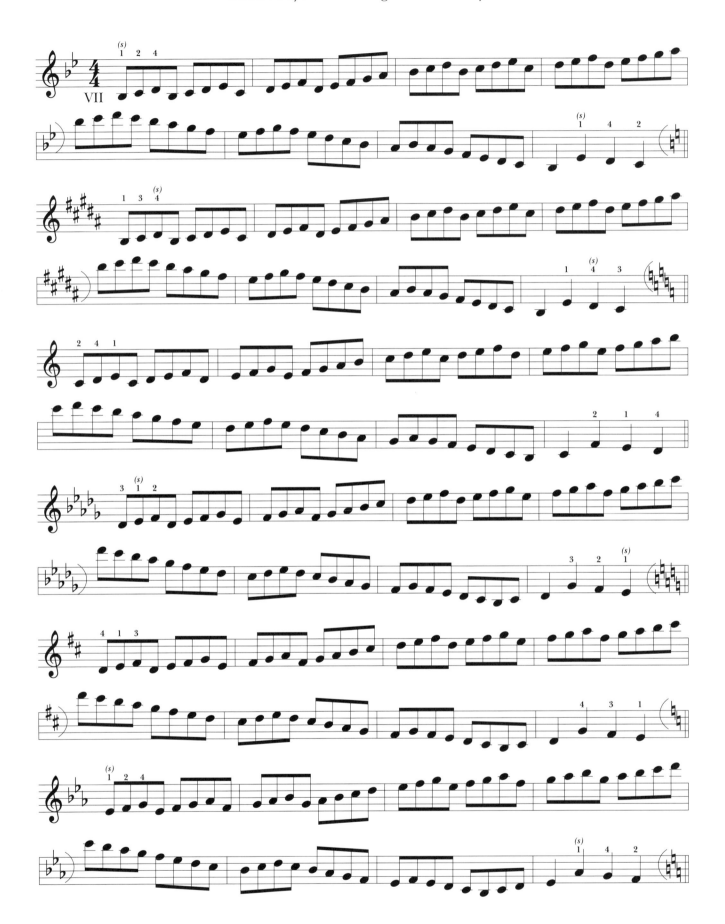

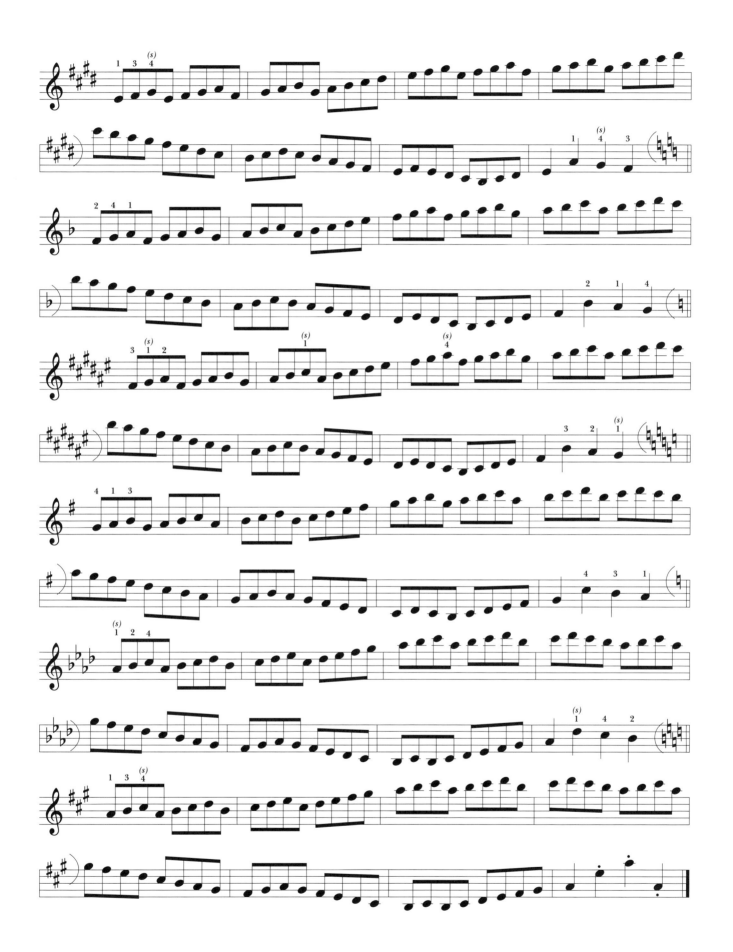

Principal Real Melodic Minor Scales—Position VII

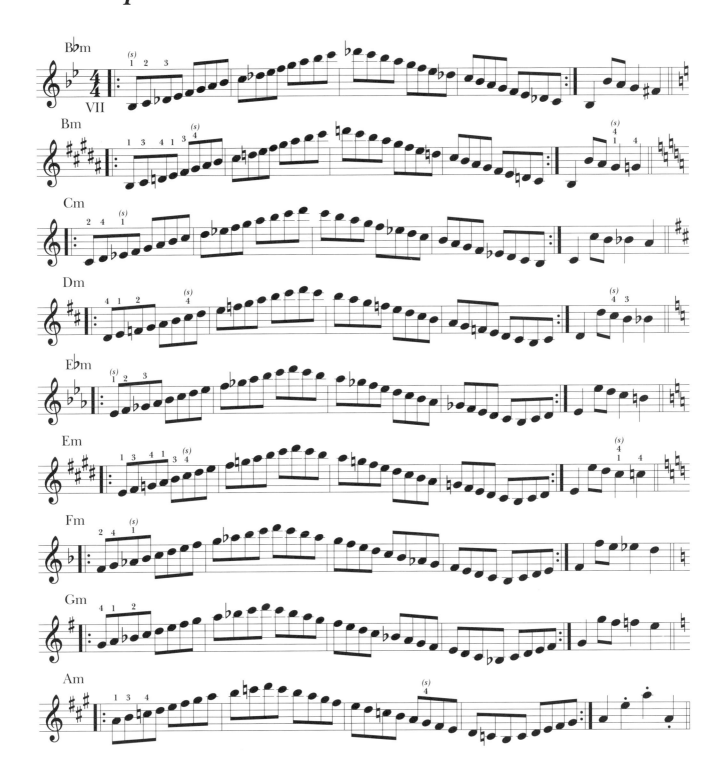

Chords—Three-Note Voicings
Melodization of Diminished Triads

Melodic degrees: Diminished scale (chord tones plus notes a whole step above and/or a half step below them).

▐ Fingering is constant if the sequence is played on the same set of strings.

Open Voicings

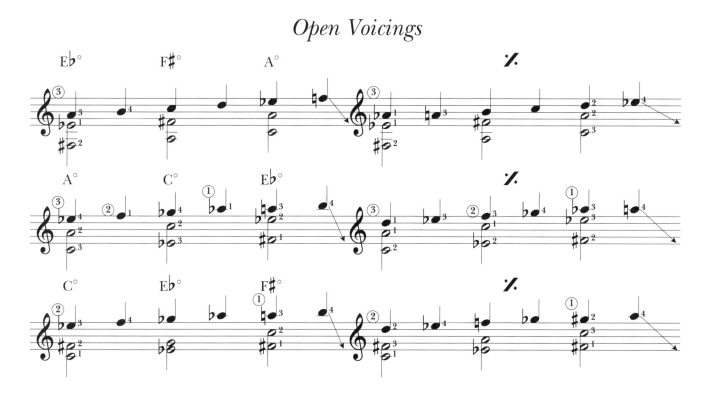

As we deal almost exclusively with diminished 7 chords, all of the preceding sequences may be played with any of the letter names that make up the four-note diminished 7 structure.

Melodization of Augmented Triads

Melodic degrees: Whole tone scale (chord tones plus notes a whole step above and/or below them—1, 9, 3, ♭5, +5, ♭7).

Fingering is constant if the sequence is played on the same set of strings. Note: These sequences also apply to dominant 7(+5) chords.

Open Voicings

As an augmented chord primarily represents the whole tone scale, the entire structure may move in whole steps.

Arpeggios—Four-Note A♭ Chords
Chord Spelling

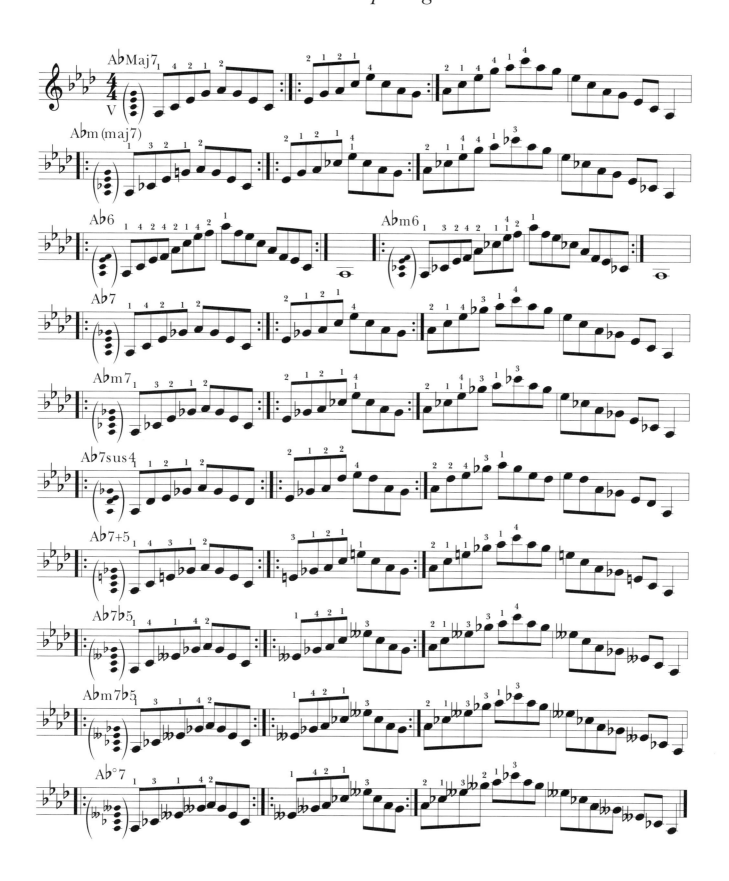

Arpeggios—Four-Note E Chords
Chord Spelling

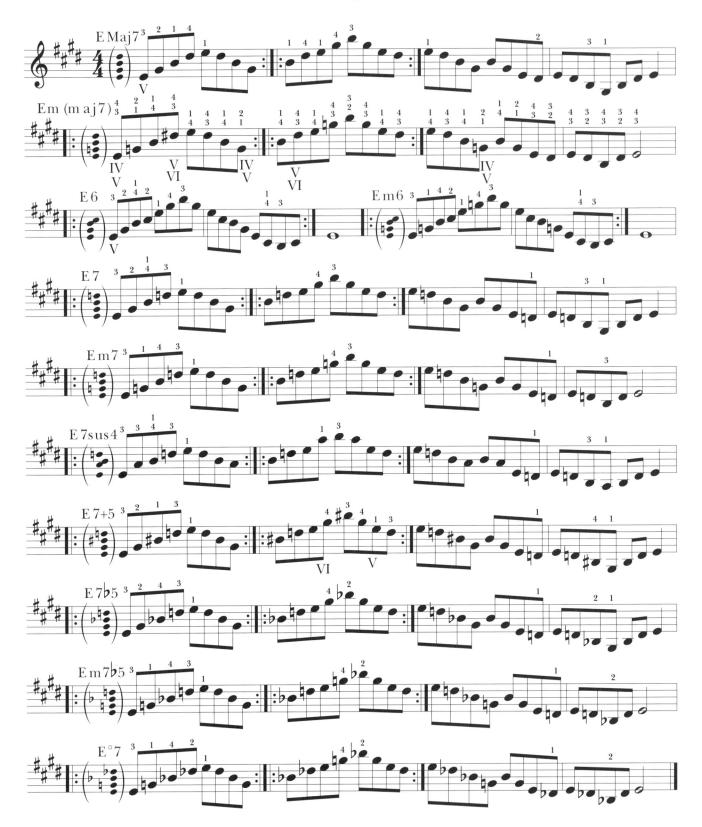

G Major Scale (Twelve Positions)

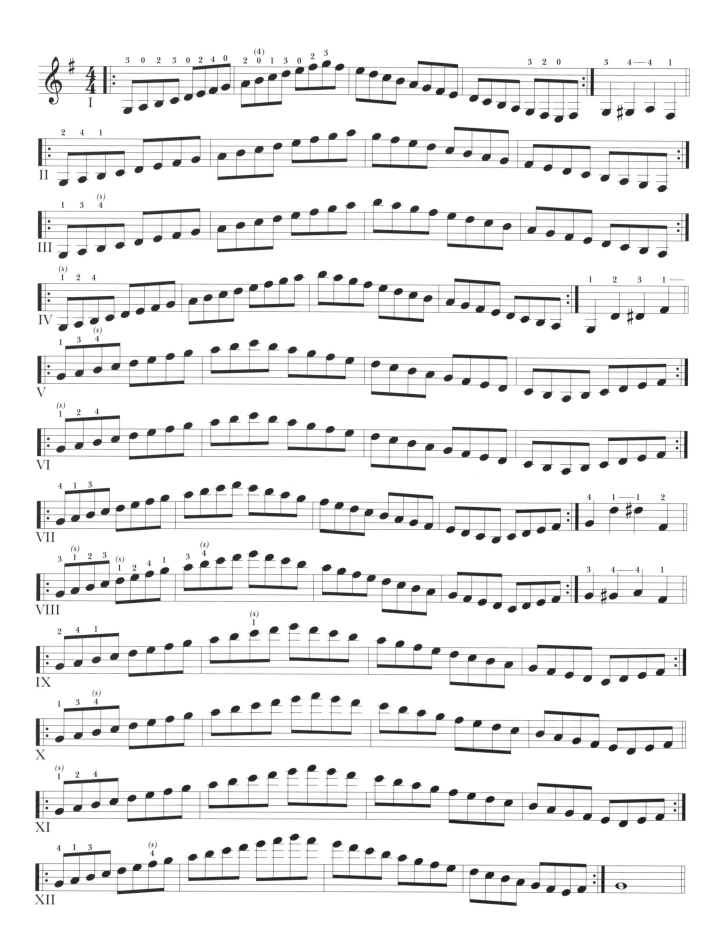

E Harmonic Minor—Nine Positions

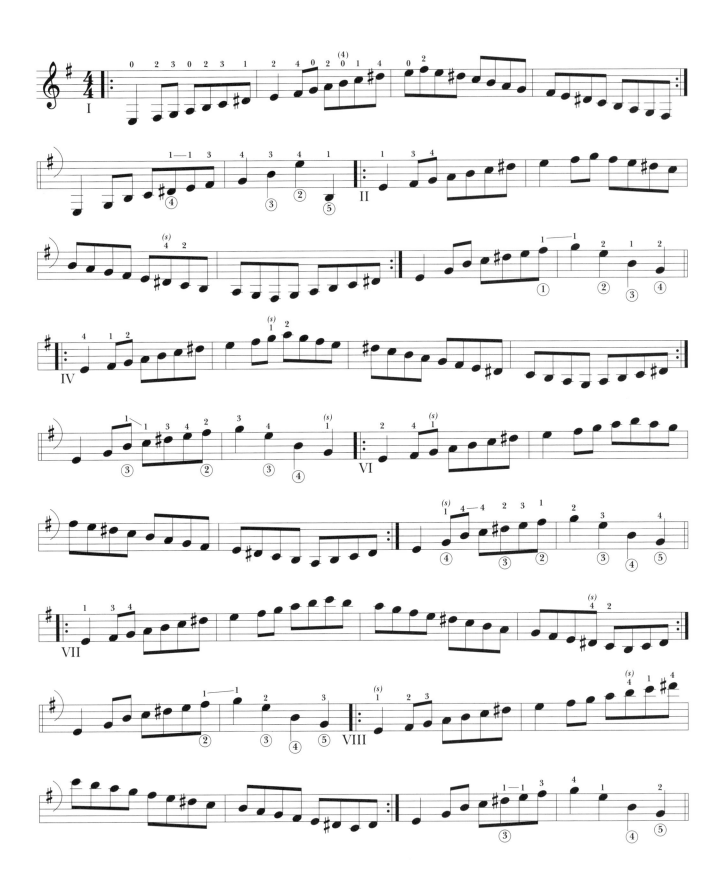

E Minor Etude (solo)

Chord-Scale Relationships—Dominant 7 Chords

For improvisation.

1. The condition of the three highest degrees (tensions 9, 11, 13) on all dominant 7 chords with scale tone roots is controlled by the preceding scale.

I7, II7, V7	1, 3, 5, ♭7, 9, (11), 13	Major scale from intended tonic
VI7	1, 3, 5, ♭7, 9, (11), (♭13)	Real melodic minor scale from intended tonic
III7, VII7	1, 3, 5, ♭7, ♭9, (11), (♭13)	Harmonic minor scale from intended tonic
IV7	1, 3, 5, ♭7, 9, +11, 13	Real melodic minor scale from 5th

✳ The III7 and VII7 chords have a "built-in" ♭9. When the 9 is flatted, it is truly altered and ♯9 is compatible with it. By treating the ♯9 melodically as ♭3, the natural minor scale is the result. This is a second choice of related scale. All eight notes of the combined harmonic and natural minor scales are also used.

2. These three high degrees on all dominant 7 chords with non-scale tone roots are constant (9, +11, 13) and they are all treated the same as the IV7 chord.

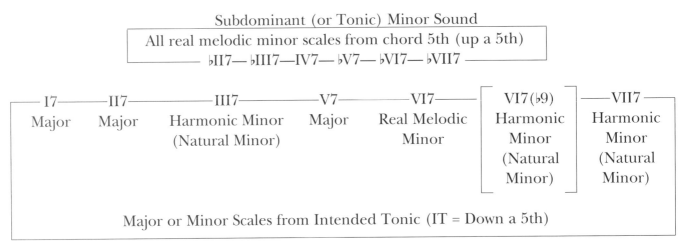

There is one structure containing an added alteration (not forced on it by the preceding scale sound): VI7(♭9). That chord has been included here, because it is encountered so often that we have become conditioned to hear it as the "norm." The VI7 with unaltered 9 is usually found only as a result of the melody being this note.

Have someone play the progressions for you (or use a tape recorder) and practice the proper scales over the following chord sequences.

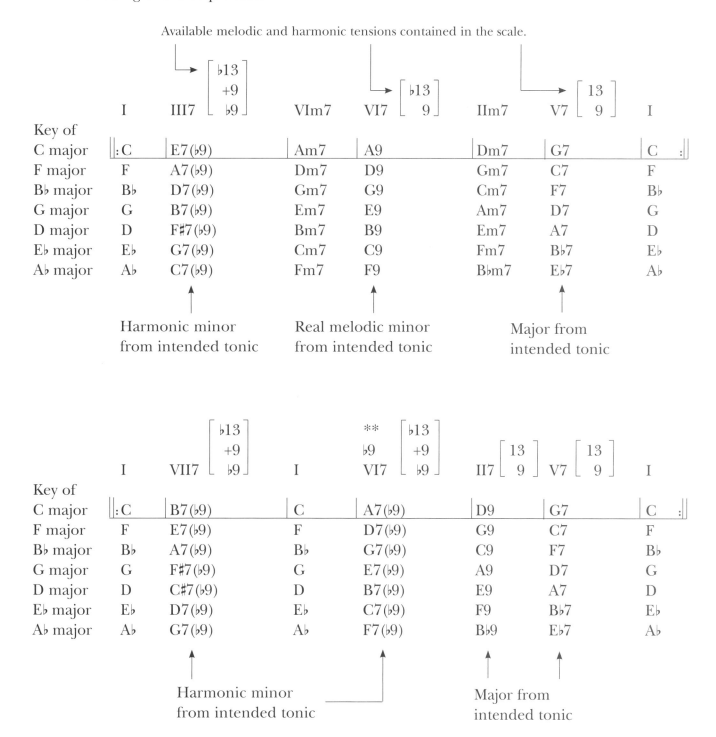

Available melodic and harmonic tensions contained in the scale.

	I	III7 $\begin{bmatrix} \flat13 \\ +9 \\ \flat9 \end{bmatrix}$	VIm7	VI7 $\begin{bmatrix} \flat13 \\ 9 \end{bmatrix}$	IIm7	V7 $\begin{bmatrix} 13 \\ 9 \end{bmatrix}$	I
Key of C major	‖: C	E7(♭9)	Am7	A9	Dm7	G7	C :‖
F major	F	A7(♭9)	Dm7	D9	Gm7	C7	F
B♭ major	B♭	D7(♭9)	Gm7	G9	Cm7	F7	B♭
G major	G	B7(♭9)	Em7	E9	Am7	D7	G
D major	D	F♯7(♭9)	Bm7	B9	Em7	A7	D
E♭ major	E♭	G7(♭9)	Cm7	C9	Fm7	B♭7	E♭
A♭ major	A♭	C7(♭9)	Fm7	F9	B♭m7	E♭7	A♭

Harmonic minor from intended tonic · Real melodic minor from intended tonic · Major from intended tonic

	I	VII7 $\begin{bmatrix} \flat13 \\ +9 \\ \flat9 \end{bmatrix}$	I	** VI7 $\begin{bmatrix} \flat13 \\ +9 \\ \flat9 \end{bmatrix}$ $\flat9$	II7 $\begin{bmatrix} 13 \\ 9 \end{bmatrix}$	V7 $\begin{bmatrix} 13 \\ 9 \end{bmatrix}$	I
Key of C major	‖: C	B7(♭9)	C	A7(♭9)	D9	G7	C :‖
F major	F	E7(♭9)	F	D7(♭9)	G9	C7	F
B♭ major	B♭	A7(♭9)	B♭	G7(♭9)	C9	F7	B♭
G major	G	F♯7(♭9)	G	E7(♭9)	A9	D7	G
D major	D	C♯7(♭9)	D	B7(♭9)	E9	A7	D
E♭ major	E♭	D7(♭9)	E♭	C7(♭9)	F9	B♭7	E♭
A♭ major	A♭	G7(♭9)	A♭	F7(♭9)	B♭9	E♭7	A♭

Harmonic minor from intended tonic · Major from intended tonic

	I	IV7 [13, +11, 9]	IIIm7	bIII7 [13, +11, 9]	IIm7	bII7 [13, +11, 9]	I
Key of C major	‖: C	F9	Em7	Eb9	Dm7	Db9	C :‖
F major	F	Bb9	Am7	Ab9	Gm7	Gb9	F
Bb major	Bb	Eb9	Dm7	Db9	Cm7	Cb9 (B9)	Bb
G major	G	C9	Bm7	Bb9	Am7	Ab9	G
D major	D	G9	F#m7	F9	Em7	Eb9	D
Eb major	Eb	Ab9	Gm7	Gb9	Fm7	Fb9 (E9)	Eb
Ab major	Ab	Db9	C7	Cb9 (B9)	Bbm7	A9	Ab

—— Real melodic minor from chord 5th ——

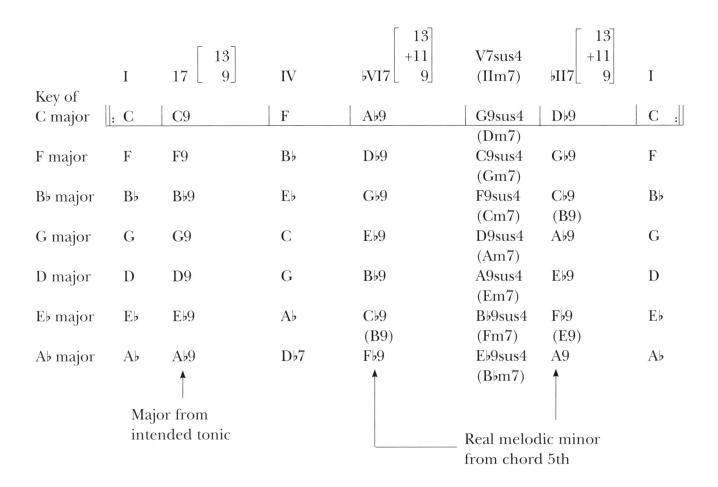

	I	17 [13, 9]	IV	bVI7 [13, +11, 9]	V7sus4 (IIm7)	bII7 [13, +11, 9]	I
Key of C major	‖: C	C9	F	Ab9	G9sus4 (Dm7)	Db9	C :‖
F major	F	F9	Bb	Db9	C9sus4 (Gm7)	Gb9	F
Bb major	Bb	Bb9	Eb	Gb9	F9sus4 (Cm7)	Cb9 (B9)	Bb
G major	G	G9	C	Eb9	D9sus4 (Am7)	Ab9	G
D major	D	D9	G	Bb9	A9sus4 (Em7)	Eb9	D
Eb major	Eb	Eb9	Ab	Cb9 (B9)	Bb9sus4 (Fm7)	Fb9 (E9)	Eb
Ab major	Ab	Ab9	Db7	Fb9	Eb9sus4 (Bbm7)	A9	Ab

Major from intended tonic

Real melodic minor from chord 5th

Key	I	♭V7	$\begin{bmatrix}13\\+11\\9\end{bmatrix}$	IV	♭VII7	$\begin{bmatrix}13\\+11\\9\end{bmatrix}$	I	B7 $\begin{bmatrix}13\\9\end{bmatrix}$	I
C major	‖: C	G♭9		F	B♭9		C	G7	C :‖
F major	F	C♭9 (B9)		B♭	E♭9		F	C7	F
B♭ major	B♭	F♭9 (E9)		E♭	A♭9		B♭	F7	B♭
G major	G	D♭9		C	F9		G	D7	G
D major	D	A♭9		G	C9		D	A7	D
E♭ major	E♭	A9		A♭	D♭9		E♭	B♭7	E♭
A♭ major	A♭	D9		D♭7	G♭9		A♭	E♭7	A♭

↑   ↑

Real melodic minor from chord 5th

It is necessary that you know (very well) the normal condition of tensions on all dominant 7 structures so you will instantly recognize any alterations that may be present. The effect of specially altered degrees on dominant 7 chord-scale relationships will be discussed later.

From this point on, all chord-scale pages consist of a great deal of information applicable to composition, spontaneous or otherwise, presented very concisely. As this concerted presentation can be confusing, the material must be worked out by the interested student very gradually over a considerable period of time.

Determine the scale for a chord by its effect on the scale preceding it.

Practical Fingerings for Moving from Position to Position

4-4 AND 1-1 FINGER SLIDES EMPLOYING THE HALF STEP

F Major Scale — C Harmonic Minor Scale

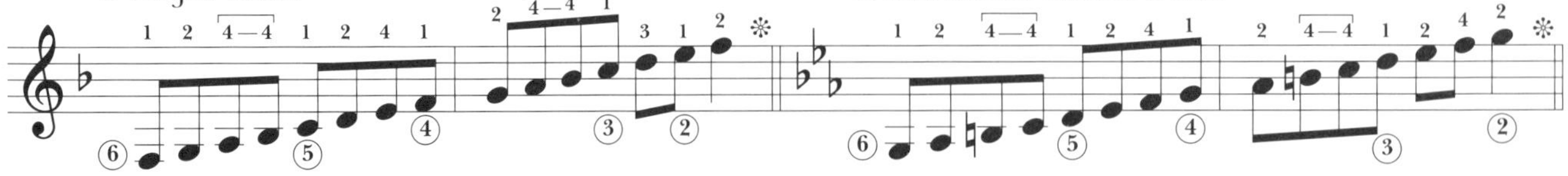

C Major Scale — G° Scale

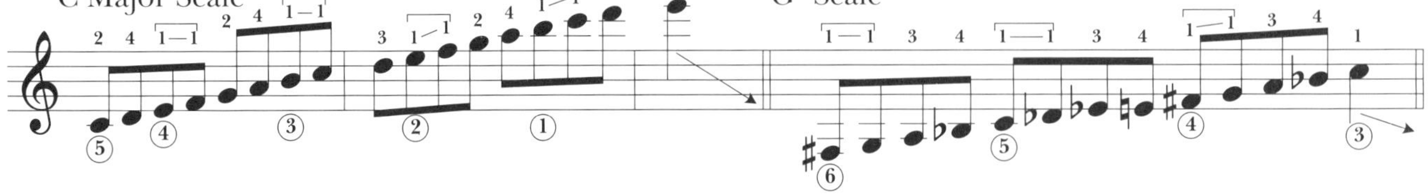

❊ No descent with 4th finger slides

The preceding 1st and 4th finger slides are also possible (and practical) for distances of from two to three frets.

B♭ Major Scale — A Harmonic Minor Scale

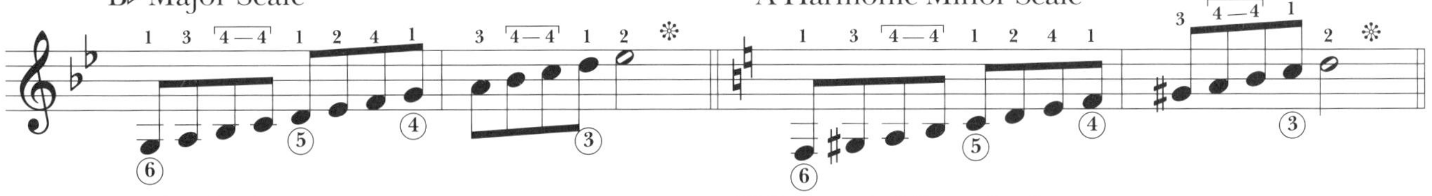

F Major Scale — C Harmonic Minor Scale

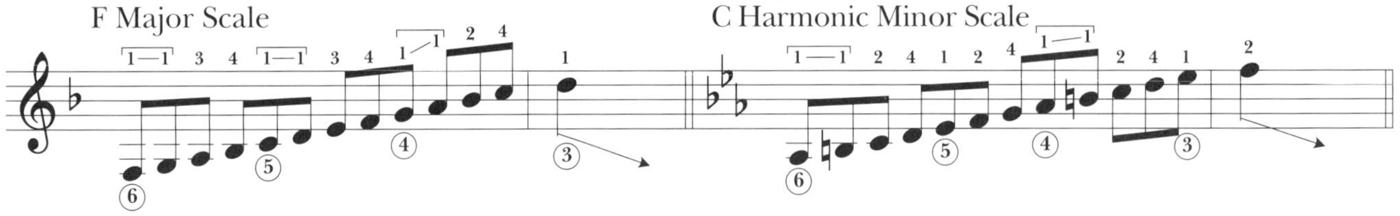

13-13 EMPLOYING THE HALF STEP 12-13, 12-12 VARIATIONS

C Major Scale — G Real Melodic Minor Scale

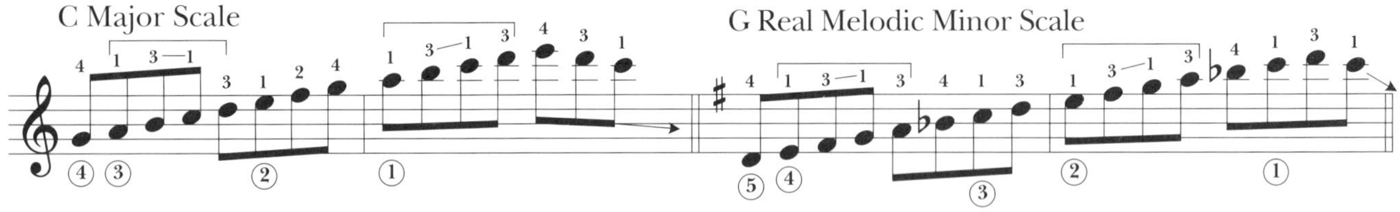

F Major Scale — D Harmonic Minor Scale

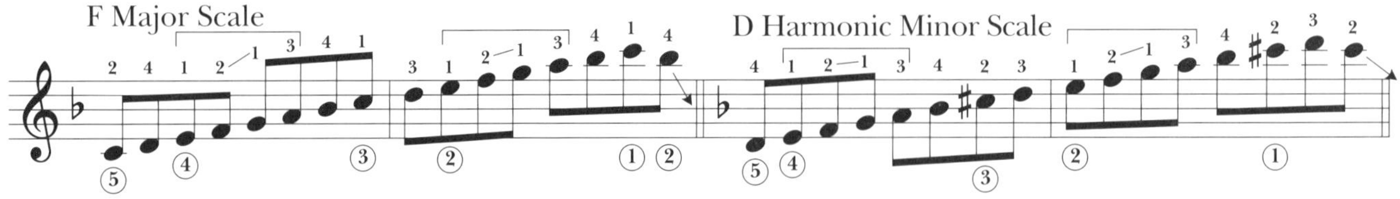

F Real Melodic Minor Scale — F° Scale

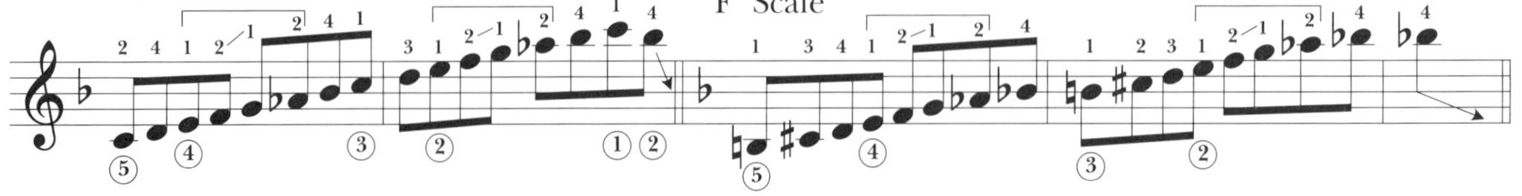

1-2 3-4 THE DOUBLE STRETCH—EMPLOYING THE HALF STEP

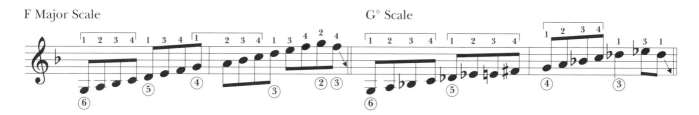

13-24 FINGER EXCHANGE—EMPLOYING THE HALF STEP

124-124 REPEATED FINGERING—SEPARATED BY A WHOLE STEP

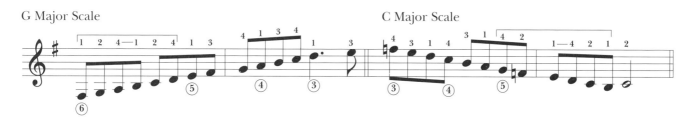

134-134 REPEATED FINGERING—SEPARATED BY A WHOLE STEP

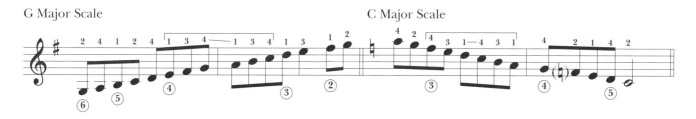

13-134 VARIATION OF ABOVE, 13-124 VARIATION OF ABOVE

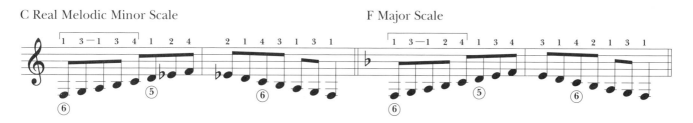

Analyze the intervals involved in the preceding position-to-position fingerings. You will find many other possibilities for application, especially when used in combinations.

All of the fingerings employing the half step are very reliable, as they do not require looking at the fingerboard. The others are sometimes dangerous when the music and/or conductor demand your full attention.

77

Chord Construction—Three-Note Voicings
Dominant 7 Chords—Preparation of Close and Open Voicings

The distance between the 3rd and ♭7th chord degrees of a dominant structure is called a tritone. This tritone interval (an augmented 4th or a diminished 5th) divides our twelve-tone (chromatic) scale exactly in half. Therefore, each tritone by itself represents the sound of two dominant 7 chords, their roots being separated by the same ♯4 or ♭5 interval. A third note must be added to a tritone to remove this ambiguity.

In a cycle 5 chord progression, tritones move chromatically downward. The ♭7 of the first chord moves to 3 of the next chord, which moves to ♭7 of the next, and so on.

In the following studies, root and 5th chordal degrees are added to chromatic tritone sequences (representing cycle 5 progressions as follows: 1) below, 2) above, and 3) between.

1

TRITONE ON 3RD AND 4TH STRINGS (♭7, 3 IN THE LEAD)

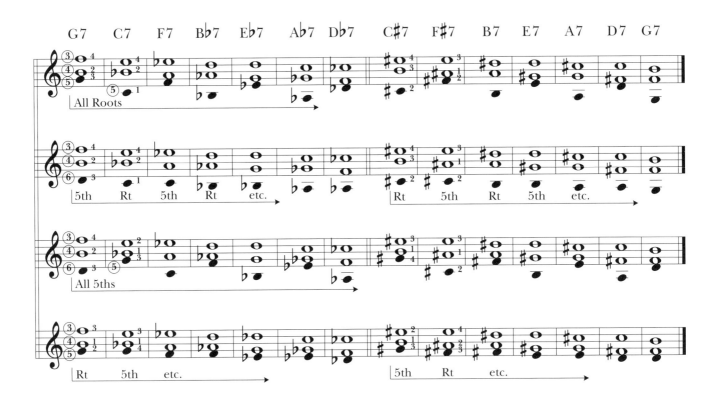

78

TRITONE ON 2ND AND 3RD STRINGS (♭7, 3 IN THE LEAD)

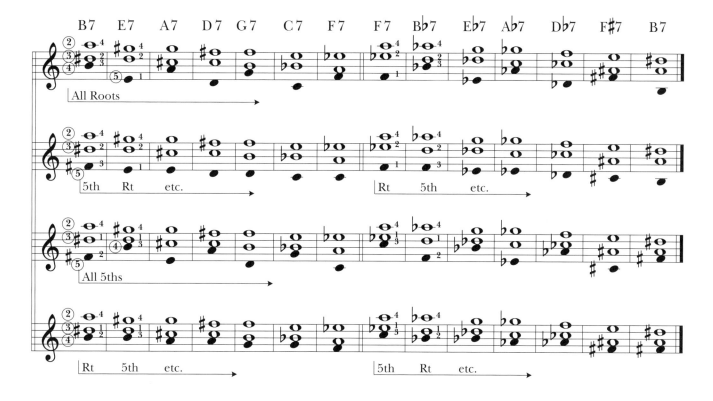

2

TRITONE ON 4TH AND 5TH STRINGS (ROOT, 5 IN THE LEAD)

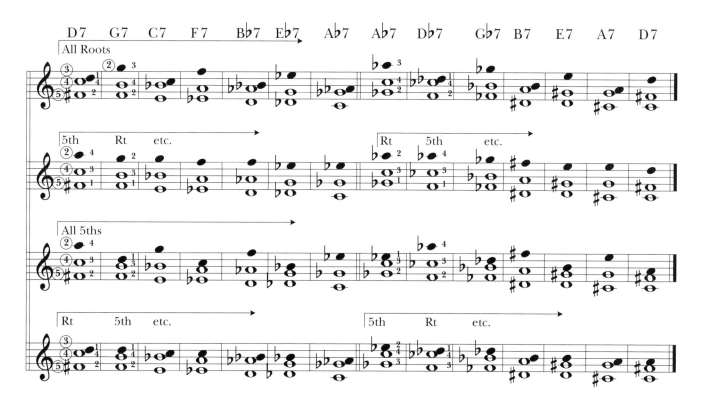

TRITONE ON 3RD AND 4TH STRINGS (ROOT, 5 IN THE LEAD)

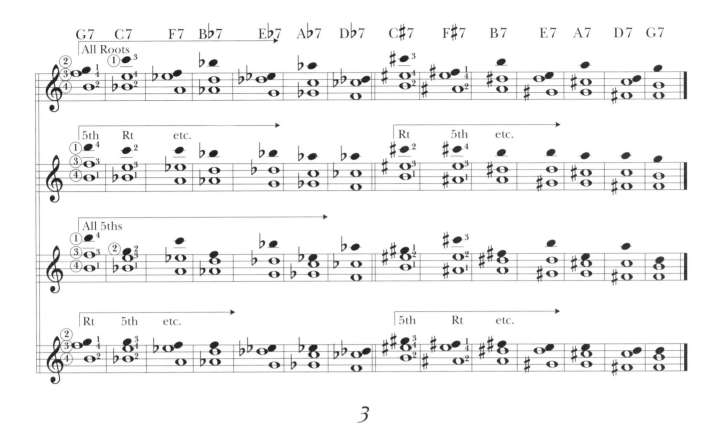

3

TRITONE ON 2ND AND 4TH STRINGS (3, ♭7 IN THE LEAD)

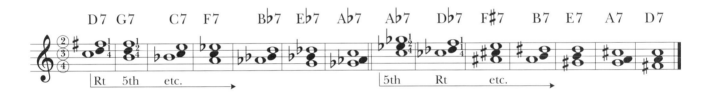

TRITONE ON 3RD AND 4TH STRINGS (3, ♭7 IN THE LEAD)

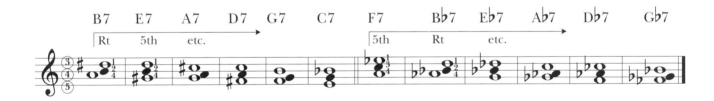

The tritone (interval of ♯4 or ♭5) should not be used below B–F as found on the 5th and 4th strings, respectively. The sound becomes cloudy in pitch from this point on down.

Arpeggios—Four-Note D♭ Chords
Chord Spelling

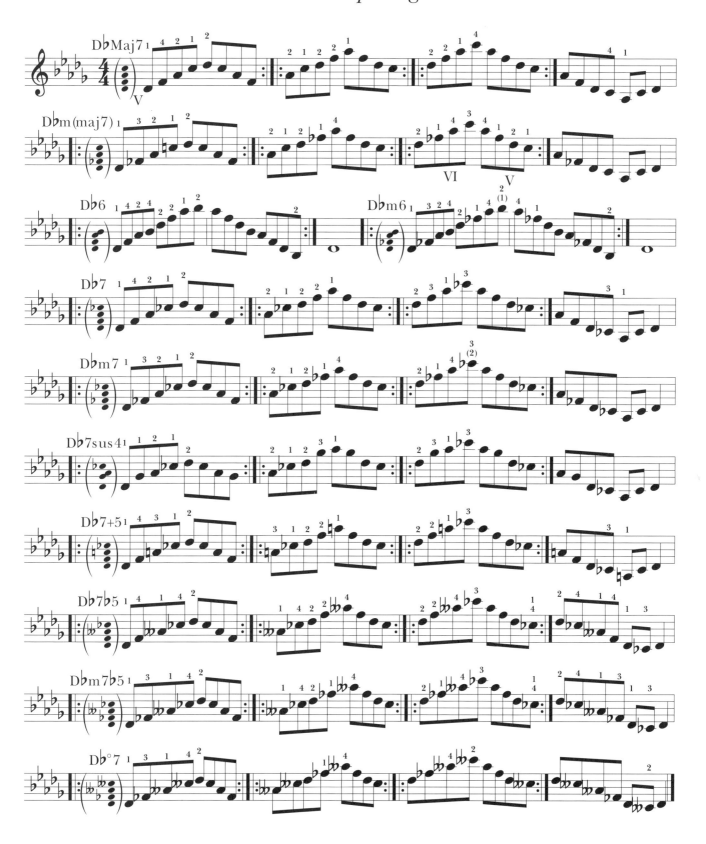

Arpeggios—Four-Note B Chords
Chord Spelling

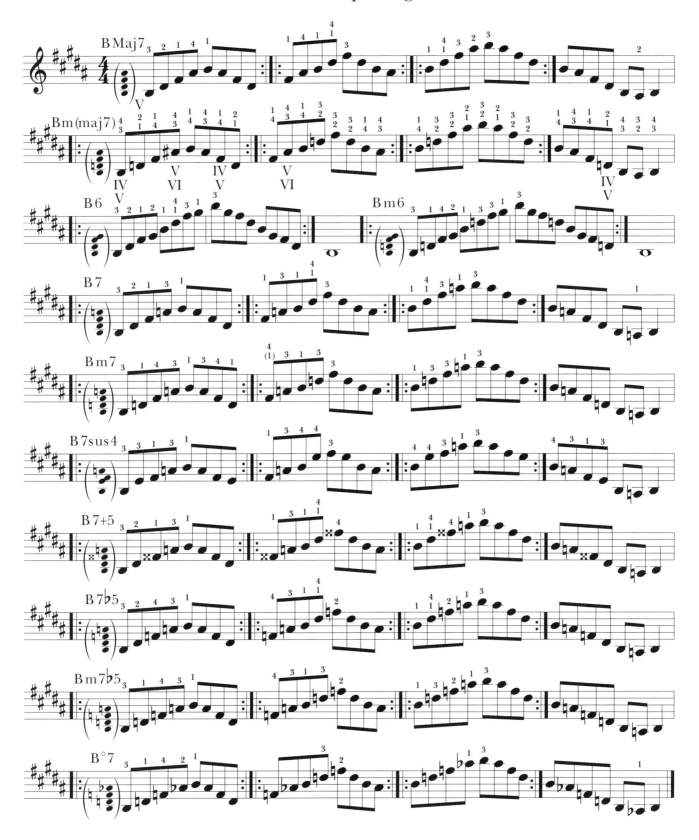

Rhythm Guitar—The Right Hand

Polka Dot (Polka-Duet)

Major Scales—Position VIII
Twelve Keys—Through Cycle 5

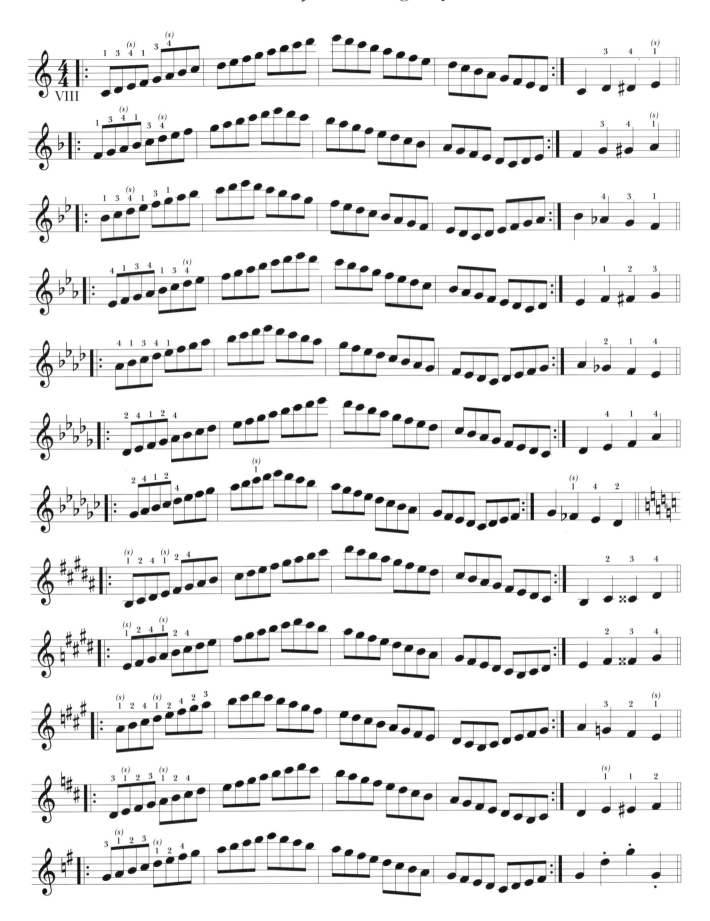

Chords—Three-Note Voicings
Melodization of Tonic Major Chords

Melodic degrees: Major scale from chord name

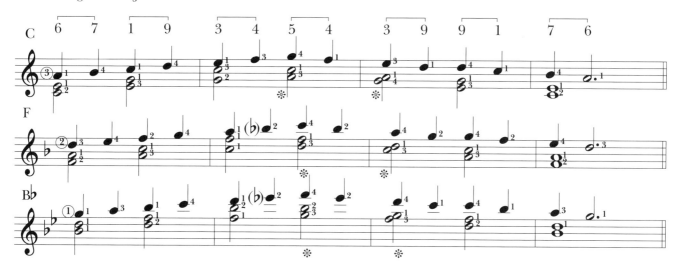

✱ 6th degree necessary as an undervoice

Melodization of Minor 7 Chords as VIm7

Melodic degrees: Major scale from ♭3 of chord

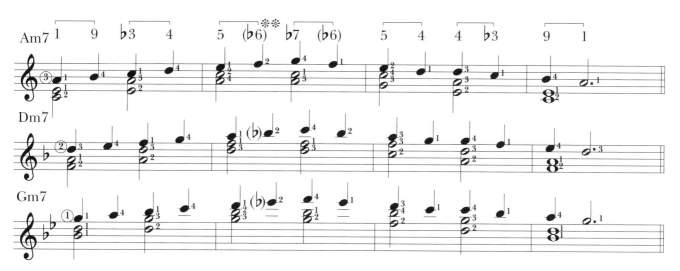

✱ ✱ Melodic degrees shown in parentheses must be used only in passing.

As the preceding I major and VIm7 chords produce the same tonic major sound, their voicings are interchangeable (C = Am7, F = Dm7, B♭ = Gm7). This is called **diatonic substitution**, or the replacement of one chord with another that represents the sound of the same scale and chord function (tonic, subdominant, and dominant) and whose chord tones are derived from higher or lower scale degrees.

Melodization of Subdominant Major Chords

Melodic degrees: Major scale from 5th of chord

✽ ♯4 is a diatonic tension on IV chords.

Melodization of Minor 7 Chords as IIm7

Melodic degrees: Major scale from ♭7 of chord

As the preceding IVmaj and IIm7 chords produce the same subdominant sound, their voicings are interchangeable (A♭ = Fm7, C = Am7, F = Dm7).

Arpeggios—Four-Note F♯ Chords
Chord Spelling

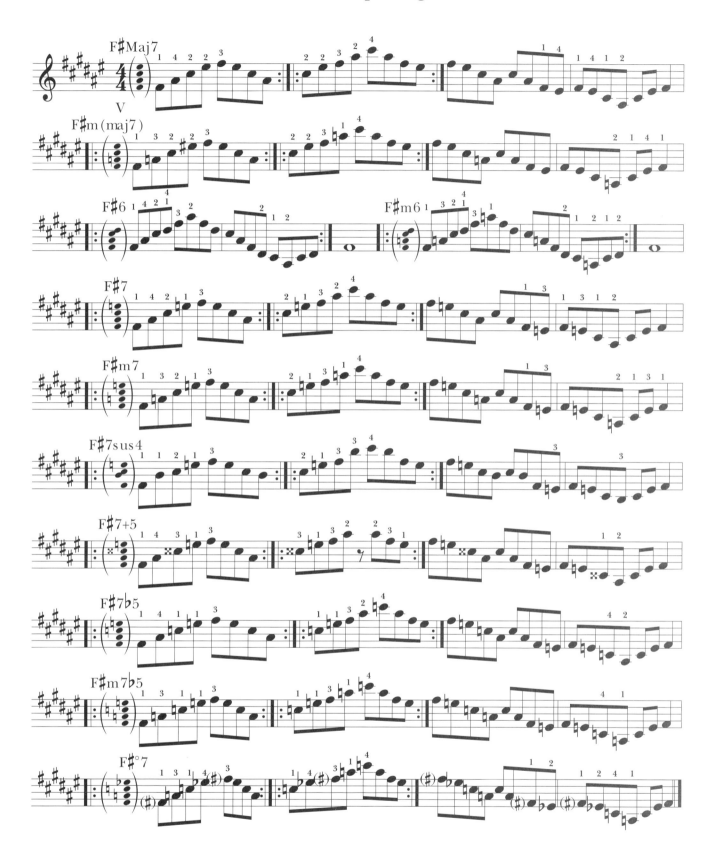

Arpeggios—Four-Note G♭ Chords
Chord Spelling
All fingering from preceding F♯ arpeggios.

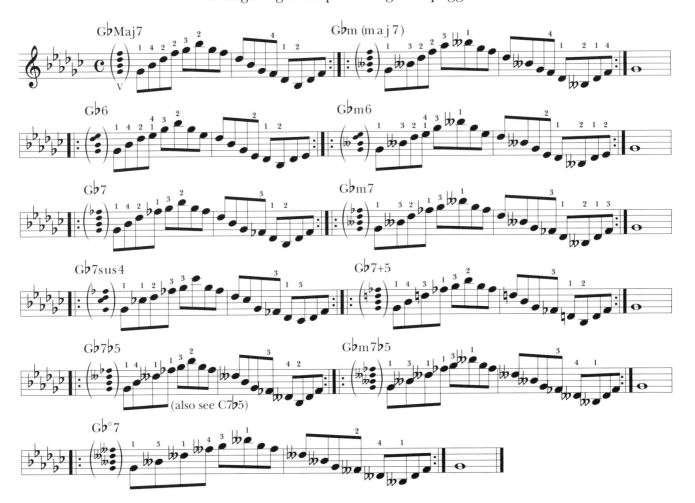

Four-Note C♯ Chords
Fingering from preceding D♭ arpeggios.

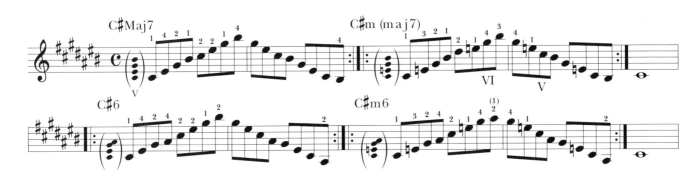

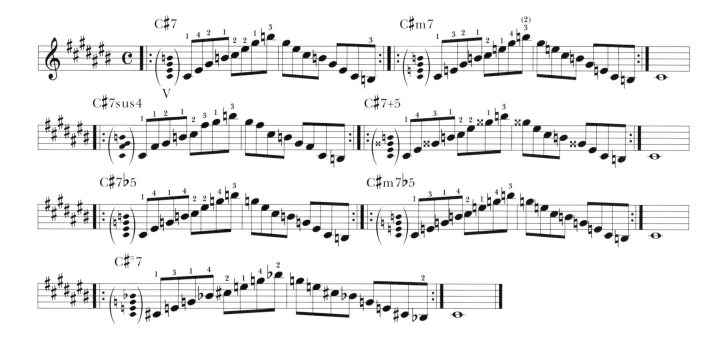

Four-Note C♭ Chords

Fingering from preceding B arpeggios.

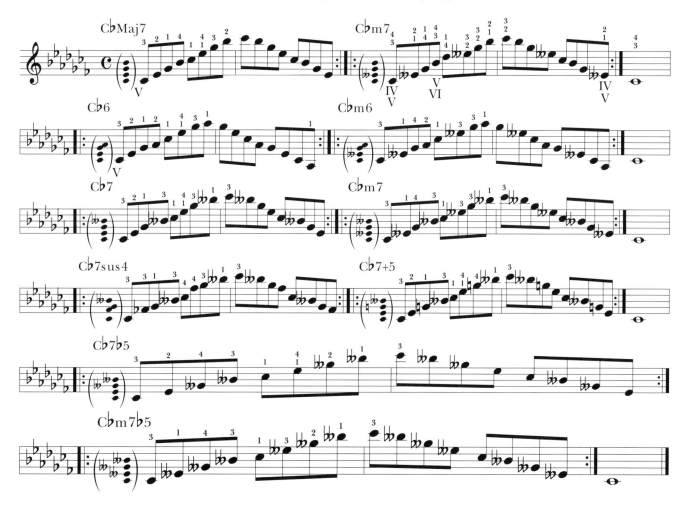

Chords—Three-Note Voicings
Dominant 7 Chords—Open Voicings, All Inversions

▌ Chord voicings notated here as (●) should be used only in passing for the following reasons:
  • Incomplete structure (indefinite sound)
  • Weak degree in the "bass"

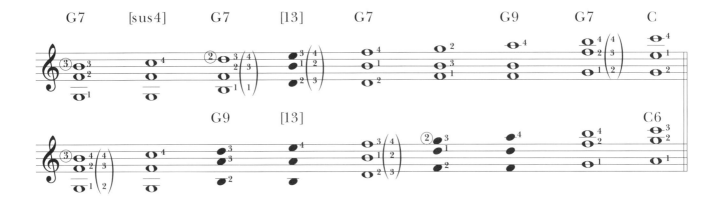

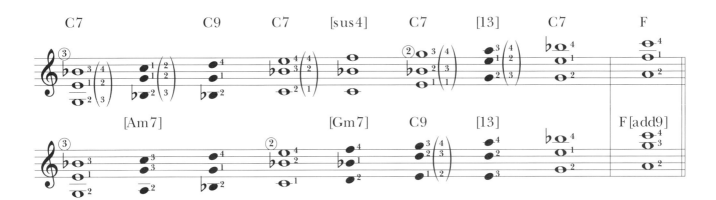

Most three-part chord voicings without the root do not have a well-defined sound, unless 1) they follow a strong voicing (including the root) of the same chord, or 2) they are the second chord of a strong cadence, closely voice led from the first chord (which has set the tonality), or 3) they are a spread voicing with the 5th degree on the bottom, sounding in the low register.

Bb Major Scale (Twelve Positions)

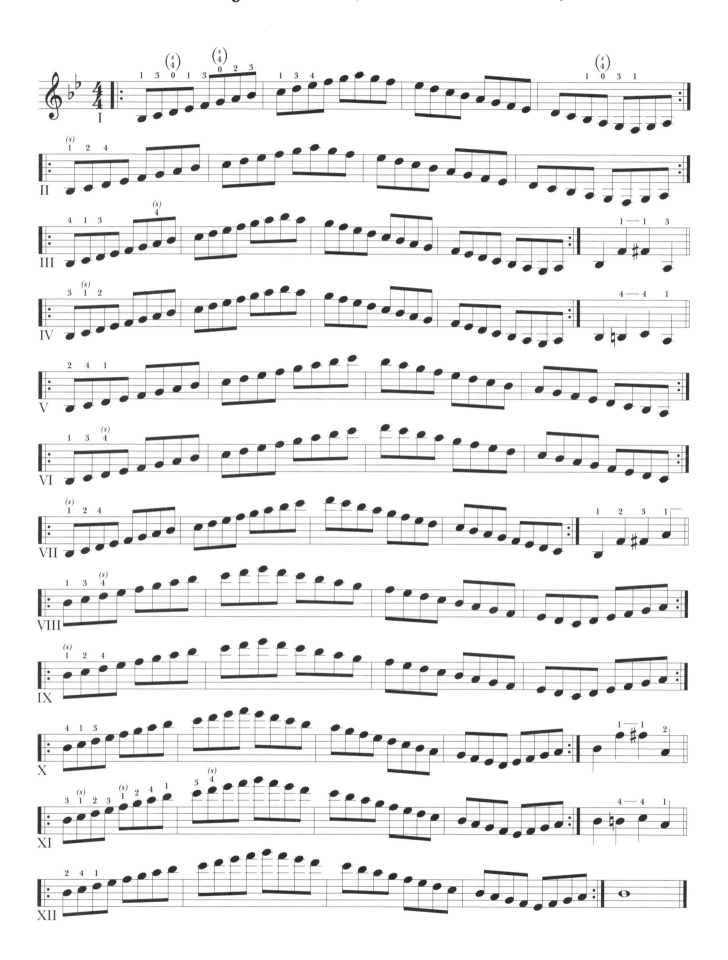

G Harmonic Minor (Nine Positions)

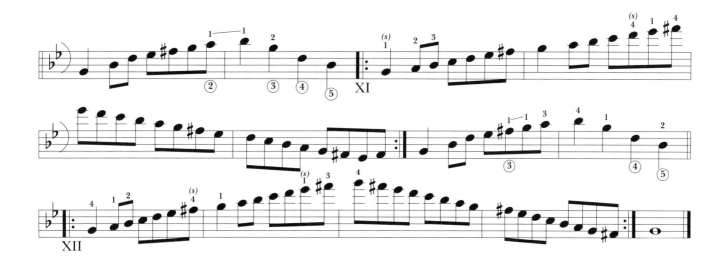

Etude in G Minor (solo)

Track 18

Arpeggios—Diminished 7 Chords
Chord Spelling Most Used

Because the notes of the diminished 7 chord divide the chromatic scale into four equal parts (all minor 3rd intervals), any chord tone may be considered the root. To eliminate the use of double flats in notation, chord spelling varies. Diminished 7 chords are often notated as if they were constructed from major scale degrees 1, ♭3, ♭5/♯4, and 6, as well as 1, ♭3, ♭5, ♭♭7. The number 7 is not usually used with diminished chord symbols. The 7th chordal degree is always assumed (unless a three-note structure is specified by the word "triad").

Scale degrees from chord name.

Arpeggios—Dominant 7(♭5) Chords

Because the notes of the dominant 7(♭5) chord divide the chromatic scale into two like parts (each consisting of four half steps and two half steps), the structure can be named from the ♭5 as well as the root.

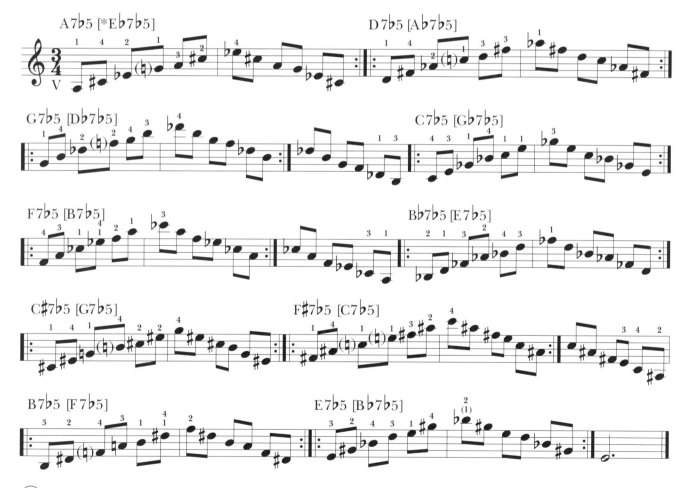

✳ Enharmonic spelling: same sound but different notation.

Theory: Diatonic 7th Chords—Harmonic Minor

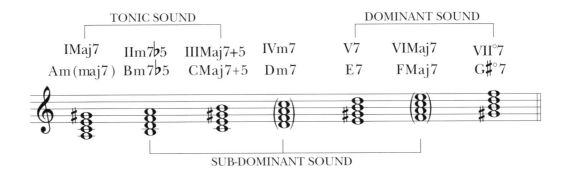

- Note the following:
  - The tonic chord is usually a minor triad. However it is sometimes found brightened up with the 6th degree borrowed from the melodic minor scale.
  - The II chord is always a minor 7(♭5).
  - IIm7(♭5) is often (and misleadingly) referred to as IVm6 (Bm7(♭5) = Dm6).
  - The 9th degree on V7 is always ♭9.
  - IVm7 and VIMaj7 usually occur as passing chords, for they tend to suggest the sound of the relative major (or natural minor).

Expect anything to happen in minor keys, from the most basic diatonic harmonic minor relationships to a conglomeration of (temporary) sounds borrowed from real or traditional melodic and natural minor scales.

Arpeggio and Scale Study

- Play in all possible areas of the fingerboard.

Play the entire sequence without changing position; don't "baby" your fingers.

Chords—Three-Note Voicings
Melodization of Subdominant Minor 6 Chords

Melodic degrees: Real melodic minor scale from chord name.

Melodization of Minor 7(♭5) as Altered IIm7 Chords

Melodic degrees: Real melodic minor scale from ♭3 of chord.

As the preceding IVm6 and IIm7(♭5) chords produce the same subdominant minor sound,
their voicings are interchangeable (A♭m = Fm7(♭5), etc.).

Melodization of Dominant 7 Chords as IV7 and ♭VII7

Melodic degrees: Real melodic minor scale from 5th degree of chord.

Melodization of Dominant 7 Chords as VI7

Melodic degrees: Real melodic minor scale from intended tonic.

Major Scales—Position X

Twelve keys—through cycle 5.

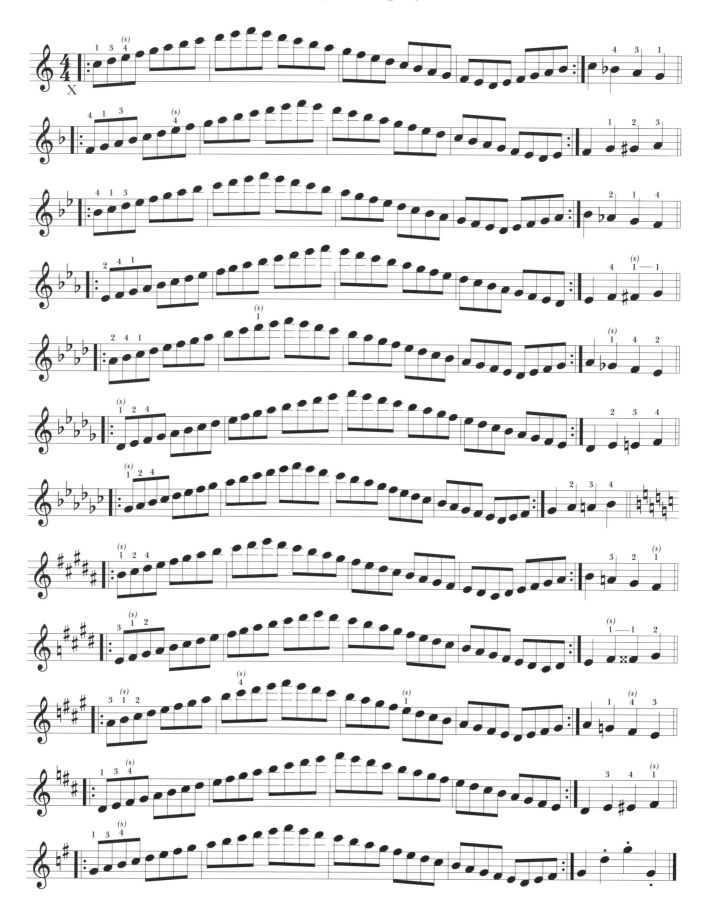

Principal Real Melodic Minor Scales—Position X

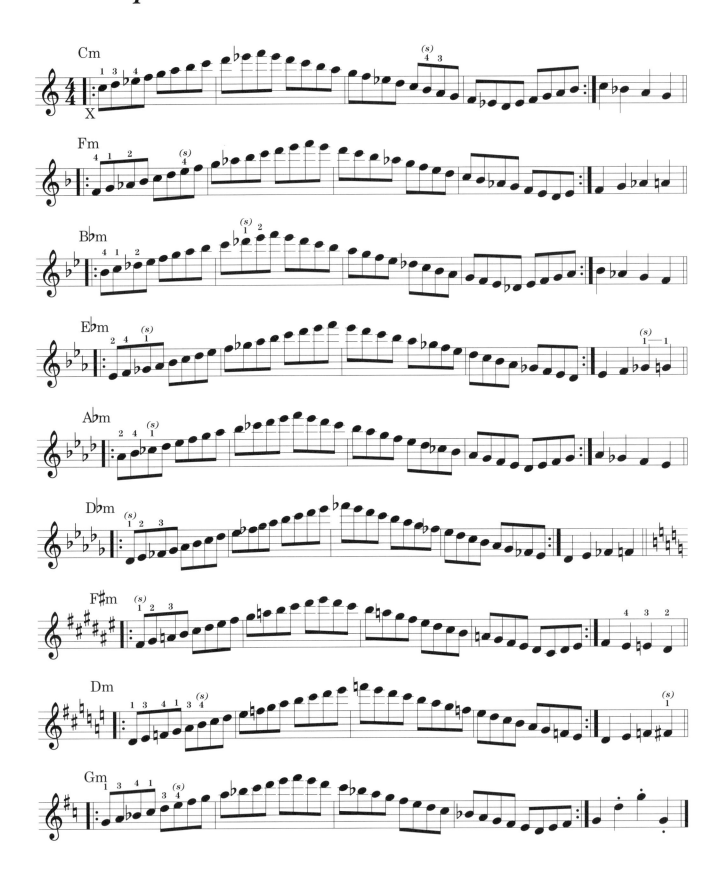

102

Chords—Three-Note Voicings
Major 6th Chords—Close and Open Voicings

6TH AND 3RD IN THE LEAD

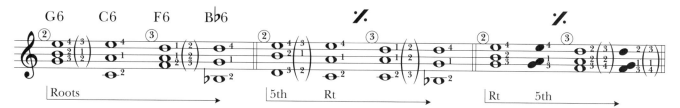

**3RD AND 6TH IN THE LEAD
(ROOT, 5TH, INSIDE VOICE)**

ROOT AND 5TH IN THE LEAD

Major 7th Chords

3RD AND MAJOR 7TH IN THE LEAD

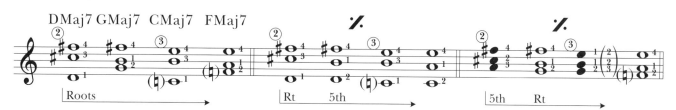

**3RD AND MAJOR 7TH IN THE LEAD
(ROOT, 5TH, INSIDE VOICE)**

NO ROOT, LEAD WITH MAJOR 7TH

5TH IN THE LEAD

Major 6 and 7 Chords—Open Voicings, All Inversions

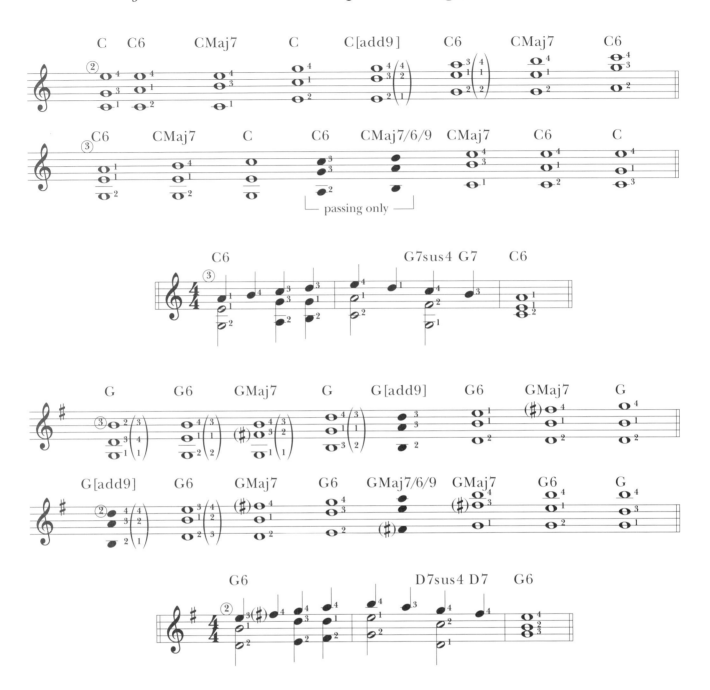

Chord Construction—Five-Part Harmony

▌ A 9th chord (five notes) is built by adding another note a 3rd above the four-part structure.

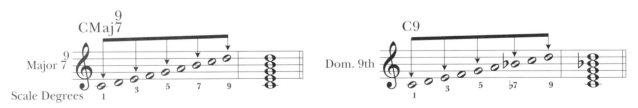

Only dominant 7 and sus4 chords will accept an alteration of a half step up or down to this added 9th, i.e. C7(♭9), C7(♯9), or +9.

Five-Note Arpeggios
Major 7 (9) and Dominant 9 Chords—Chord Spelling

Fingering for all five-note chords is shown in the fifth position with temporary changes to adjacent positions when necessary. After learning as written, transpose and play all structures from all letter names existing from position II through position X.

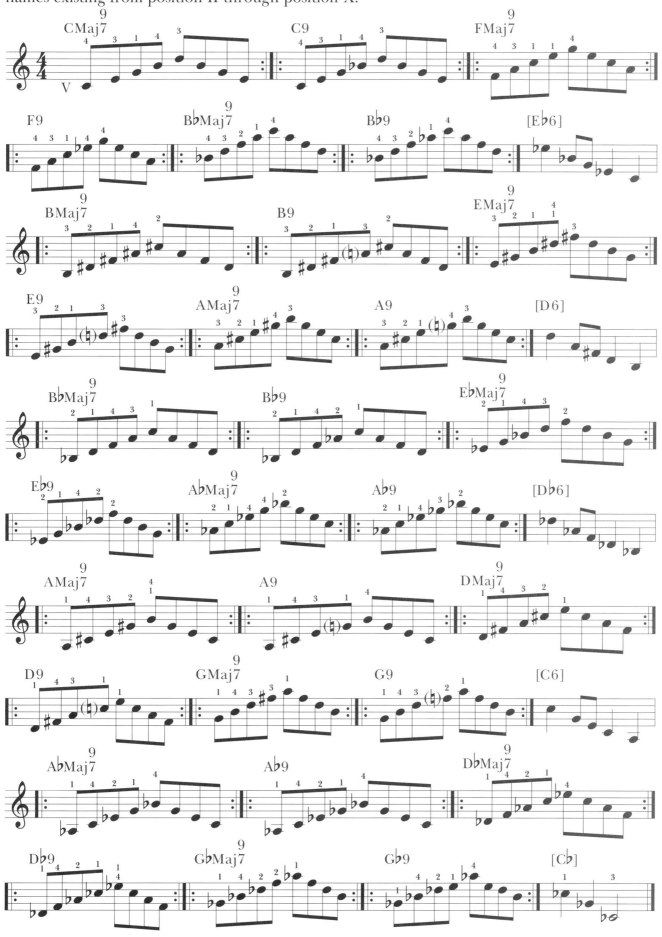

Tracks 19–21

Daydreams (duet)

Slow 4

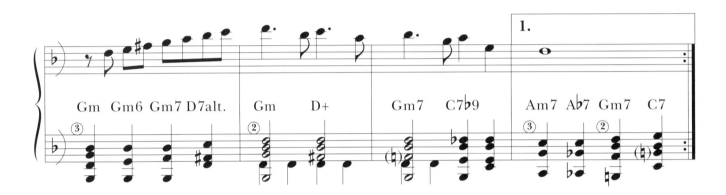

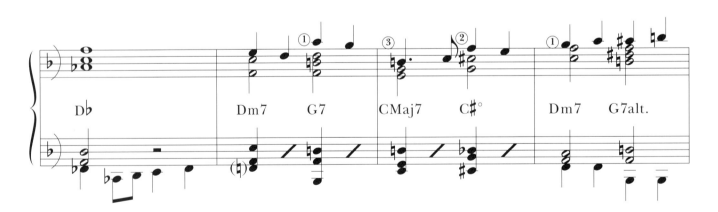

✻ Observe strings indicated for top note of chord voicings

Five-Note Arpeggios
Minor 9 and Diminished 9 Chords—Chord Spelling

The diminished 9 chord symbol used below does not indicate the lowering of the 9th chordal degree. Instead, it represents the four-part diminished 7 chord with the major 9th added. This is logical when you compare it with the meaning of minor 9 chord symbols, i.e. minor 7 with 9 added.

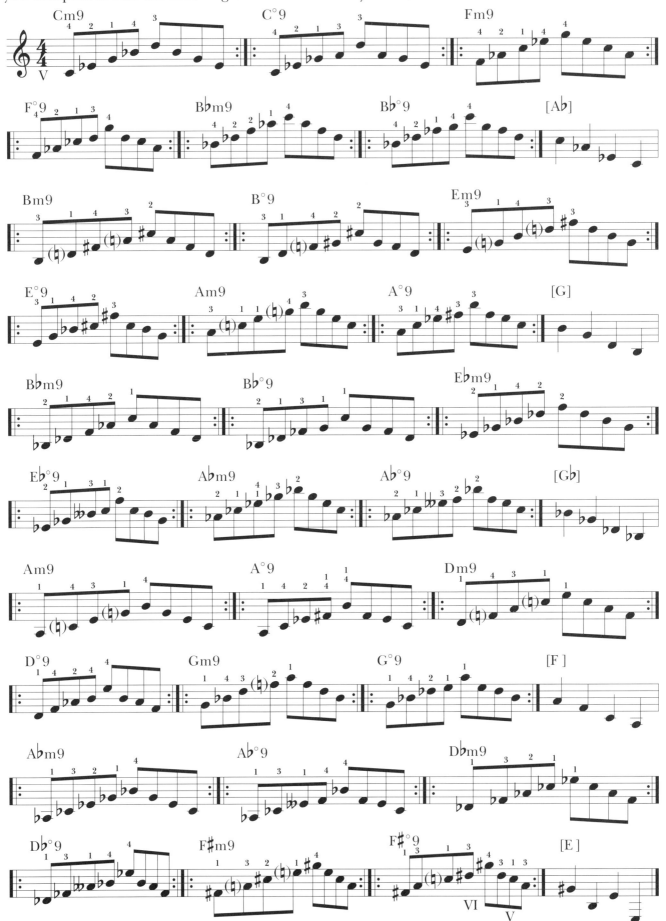

D Major Scale (Twelve Positions)

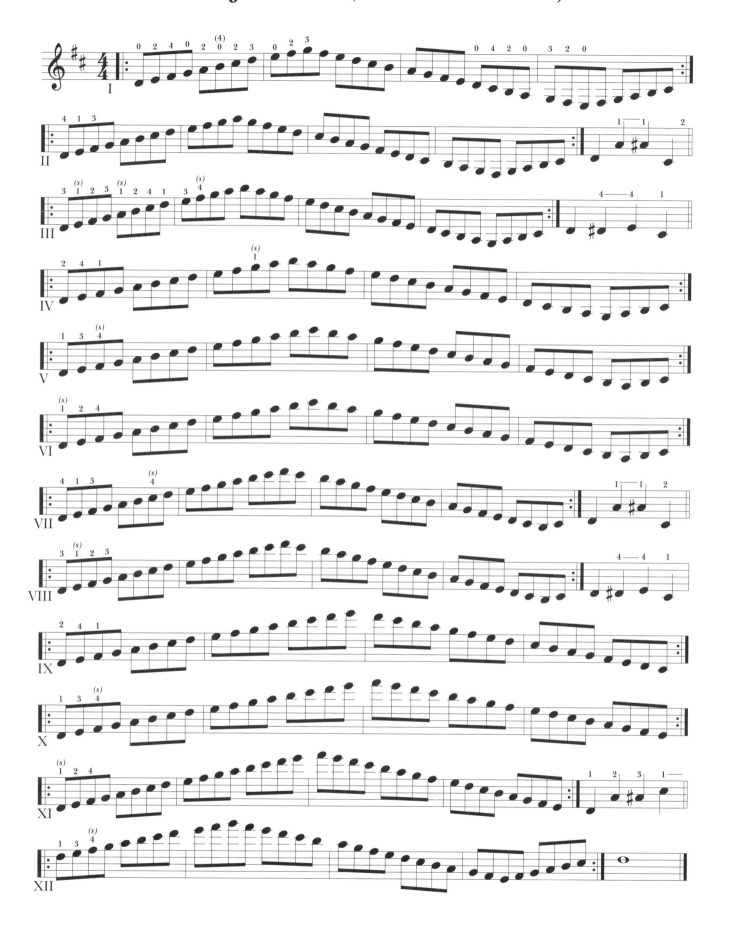

109

B Harmonic Minor (Nine Positions)

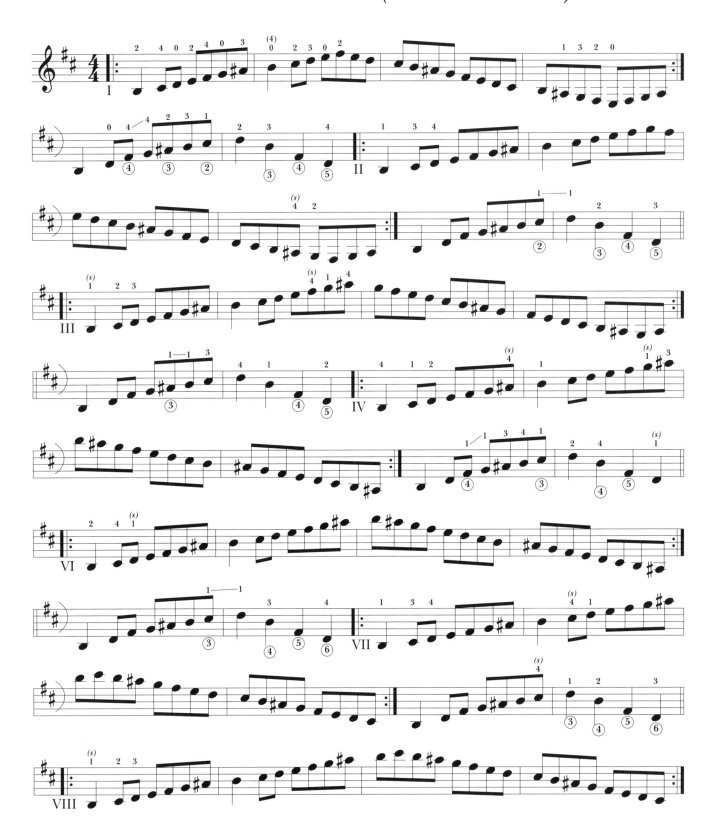

110

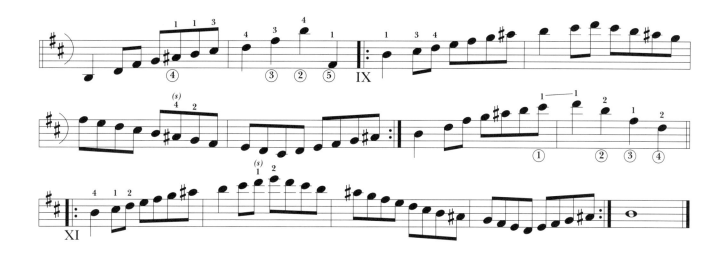

Track 22

B Minor Etude (solo)

Chords—Three-Note Voicings
Dominant 7 Chord Study with ♭5 (Chromatic Approach) in the Bass

Remember: ♭5 is a strong bass note.

About Chord Progressions (Cycle 5)

To aid in determining the true name of a chord structure, and therefore the related scale and function it represents, be aware that the strongest and most common chord movement is down a 5th (cycle 5). Investigate all possible names for the chord in question, and the one that makes the strongest cadence to the following chord will be the real name.

Examples:

Gm6 to F	= C9 to F	Gm6 to A7	= Em7(♭5) to A7
A° or F♯° to Gm7	= D7(♭9) to Gm7	A7 to F6	= A7 to Dm7
G° or E° to F	= C7(♭9) to F	Gm7(♭5) or B♭m6 to D9	= *A7alt or E♭9 to D9

*When a dominant 7 chord is completely altered (both 9 and 5 chromatically raised and/or lowered), it takes on all the characteristics of the other dominant 7 chords containing the same tritone. This substitute dominant 7 (with tensions 9, +11, 13) is constructed from the ♭5 of the altered V7 chord. The chromatic approach (from above) created by this substitute dominant 7 constitutes a very strong progression, second only to cycle 5. To help in the investigation of multiple names for chord structures, study the information on the next page.

Note: Look ahead to the next chord to analyze a progression.
Look back to the preceding chord to determine the related scale.

Theory: Interchangeable Chord Structures

The following chord structures could be referred to as diatonic substitutions, in that they represent (in the proper setting) the exact same scale sound.

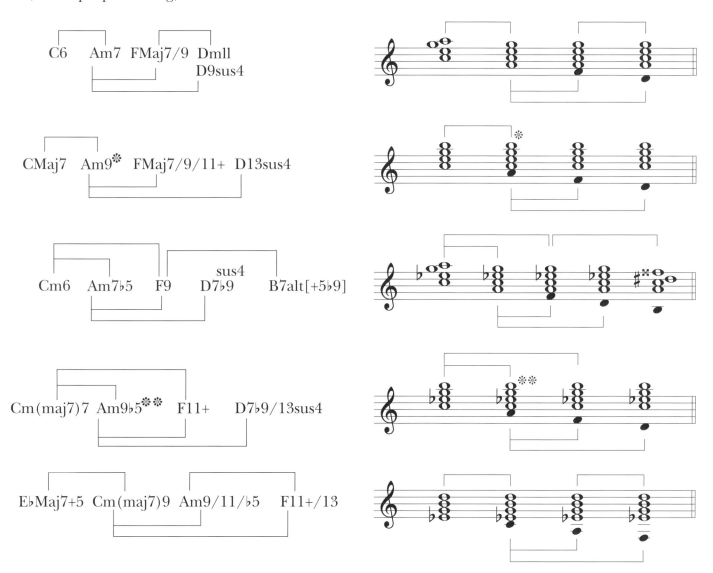

C6   Am7   FMaj7/9   Dm11
                              D9sus4

CMaj7   Am9✳   FMaj7/9/11+   D13sus4

Cm6   Am7♭5   F9   D7♭9   B7alt[+5♭9]

Cm(maj7)7   Am9♭5✳✳   F11+   D7♭9/13sus4

E♭Maj7+5   Cm(maj7)9   Am9/11/♭5   F11+/13

✳ Am9 can also be considered C6/7

✳✳ Am9(♭5) can be considered Cm6/7.

C°   B7♭9   A°   G♯7♭9   G♭°   F7♭9   E♭°   D7♭9

All four names of diminished 7 chords and their related dominant 7(♭9) chords are completely interchangeable.

Rhythm Guitar—The Right Hand

Joropo and Nanigo
Moderately fast to fast

Basic Strokes

Basic and Orchestral

Orchestral

Arpeggio Study—7th Chords

▮ Play from all fingers, but stay in position throughout the entire sequence.

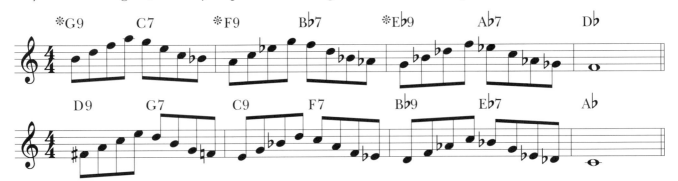

❋ Also play first chord of each measure as a minor 9 and as a dominant 7(♭9).

Chords—Three-Note Voicings
Melodization of Minor 7 Chords as IIIm7

Melodic degrees: Major scale a 3rd below chord name.

✻ Passing tones only. (Note: ♭9 can be a chord tone of dominant 7 only.)

IIIm7 can be used as a diatonic substitution for I (Am7 = Fmaj7). But stay out of the low register when doing this. The 5th of the IIIm7 chord is the major 7 of the I chord, and the major 7th chord degree should not occur below the note D on the first space below the staff.

Melodization of Minor 7(♭5) Chords as VIIm7(♭5)

Melodic degrees: Major scale a half step above chord name.

VIIm7(♭5) can be used as a diatonic substitution for V7 (Am7(♭5) = F9). But as with IIIm7 for I, this is not good in the low register.

Chromatic Melodization of Dominant 7 Chords

Eleven of the twelve chromatic tones can be considered chord degrees of a dominant 7 structure. The exception is the major 7.

CLOSE VOICINGS

※ 9 for 1, inside voice.

Also possible with root, but somewhat more difficult physically.

EXAMPLE

OPEN VOICINGS

Melodic Rhythm Study No. 11

Five-Note Arpeggios
Minor (6, 9), Major (6, 9), Dominant 9sus4, and Dominant 7(♭9) Chords
Chord Spelling

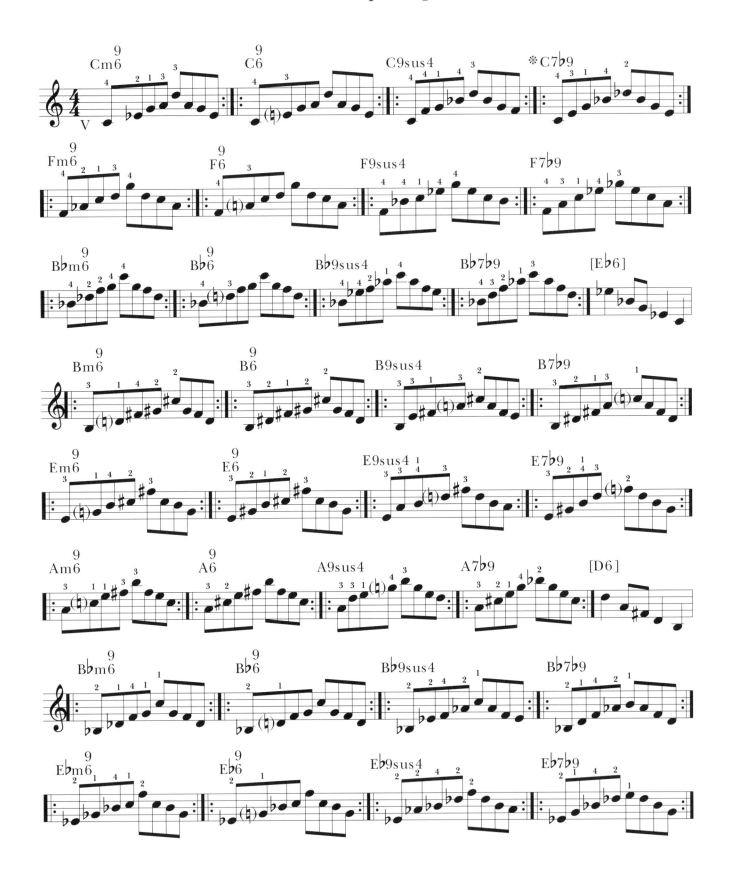

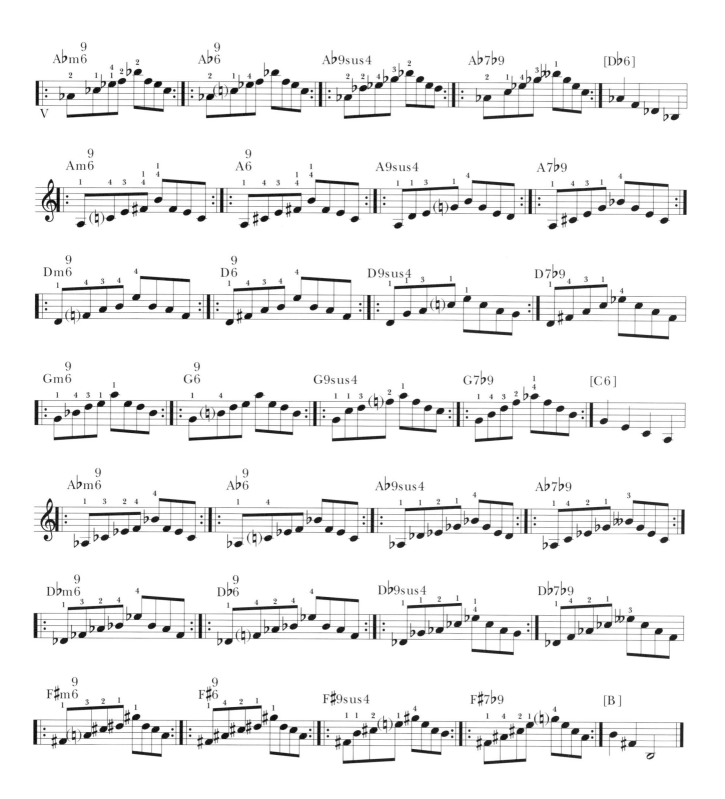

✳ Only dominant 7 and dominant 7sus4 chords will accept an alteration of a half step up or down to this added 9th chord degree.

Chords—Three-Note Voicings
Minor 7 Chords—Close and Open Voicings

♭3RD AND ♭7TH IN THE LEAD

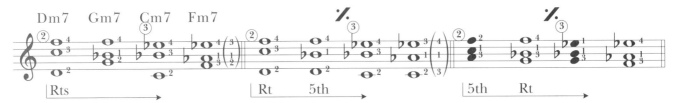

♭3RD AND ♭7TH IN THE LEAD
ROOT AND 5TH, INSIDE VOICE

ROOT AND 5TH IN THE LEAD

Minor 6 Chords

6TH AND ♭3RD IN THE LEAD

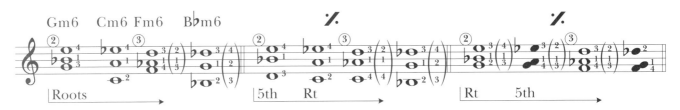

♭3RD AND 6TH IN THE LEAD
ROOT AND 5TH, INSIDE VOICE

ROOT AND 5TH IN THE LEAD

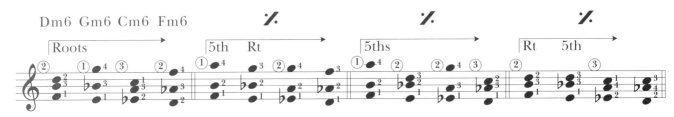

Minor 7 Chords—Open Voicings, All Inversions

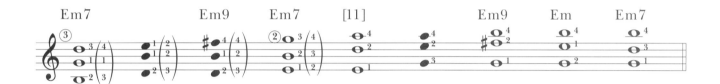

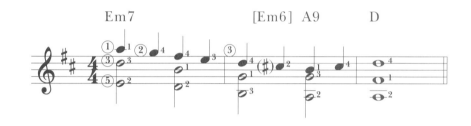

IIm7–V7–I Chord Study

Chord-Scale Relationships

For improvisation.

SPECIAL ALTERATIONS ON DOMINANT 7 CHORDS
WITH SCALE TONE ROOTS (EXCEPT IV7)

sus4	The subdominant sound of IIm7 (or IV6); treat accordingly
sus4(alt 9)	Subdominant minor sound of IIm7(♭5) (IV6); treat accordingly
	Note: 3rd degree of sus4 chords must be a melodic passing tone only.
Alt 5	On dominant 7 chords that contain an unaltered 9th, I7, II7, V7, VI7 = Whole tone scale from any chord tone.
	The specified ♯5 can often be treated as ♭13, and specified ♭5 can be treated as +11.
	See below, ♭13 and +11.
Alt 5 and 9	Real melodic minor scale from ♭9 of chord.
	Sometimes the alt 9 is not specified and must be remembered as already being present. Ex: III7 and VII7.
	For optional melodic treatment of ♯5 (alt 9) see below, ♭13(alt 9).
	For optional melodic treatment of ♭5 (alt 9) see below, +11(alt 9).
Alt 9	On V7, II7, I7, use real melodic minor from ♭7 of chord. Or, major scale with ♭6 from intended tonic.
	Also, you may combine both scales, real melodic minor with added ♯4.
	Harmonic or natural minor from intended tonic.
Alt 9 on VI7	Real melodic minor from intended tonic.
Unaltered 9 on III7 and VII7	Sus4 on dominant 7.
11	(See sus4.)
	On all dominant 7 chords, use real melodic minor from chord 5th.
Aug 11 ♯11, +11	The 9th is considered unaltered with +11 unless specified alt.
	Diminished scale from chord degrees 3, 5, ♭7, ♭9.
+11(alt 9)	On dominant 7 chords with scale tone roots (except IV7), use the major scale from the intended tonic.
13	The 9th is considered unaltered and the 11th natural with these 13th chords unless otherwise specified.

13(alt 9)	Same as alt 9 on V7.
13(+11)	Same as augmented 11.
13 (+11, ♭9)	Same as +11(alt 9).
♭13	On dominant 7 chords with unaltered 9ths, I7, II7, V7, (VI7) use real melodic minor from intended tonic.
♭13 (alt 9)	Harmonic (or natural) minor from intended tonic.
	Remember ♭13 and alt 9 are already contained in III7 and VII7 and therefore do not constitute any alteration on them.

SPECIAL ALTERATIONS ON IV7 AND DOMINANT 7 CHORDS WITH NON-SCALE TONE ROOTS

sus4	The sound of IIm7 (or IV6); treat accordingly.
Alt 5	Whole tone scale from any chord tone.
♭5	No alteration; ♭5 is already present as +11.
♯5	Same as alt 5 because ♭5 is already present as +11.
Alt 9	Diminished scale from chord degrees 3, 5, ♭7, ♭9.
Alt 5 and 9	Real melodic minor scale from ♭9 of chord.
11	See sus4.
Aug 11	No alteration (already contained in chord).
+11(alt 9)	Same as alt 9.
13	No alteration.
13(alt 9)	Same as alt 9.
♭13	Same as alt 5 (♭13 must be considered ♯5 here).
♭13 (alt 9)	Same as alt 5 and 9.

Pretty Please (duet)

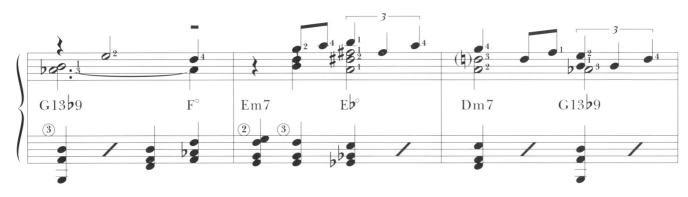

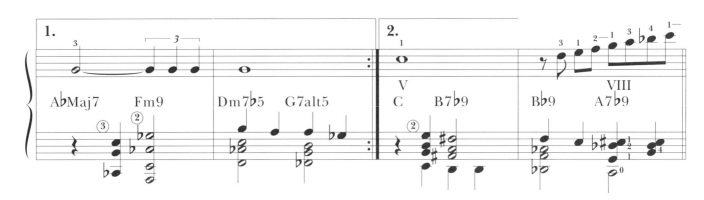

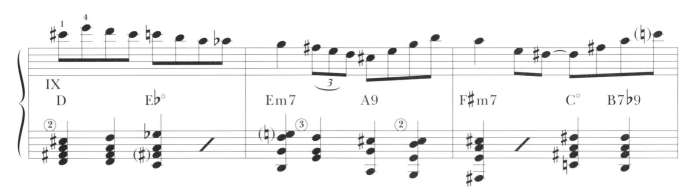

Five-Note Arpeggios
Dominant 7 (aug 9) Chords
Chord Spelling

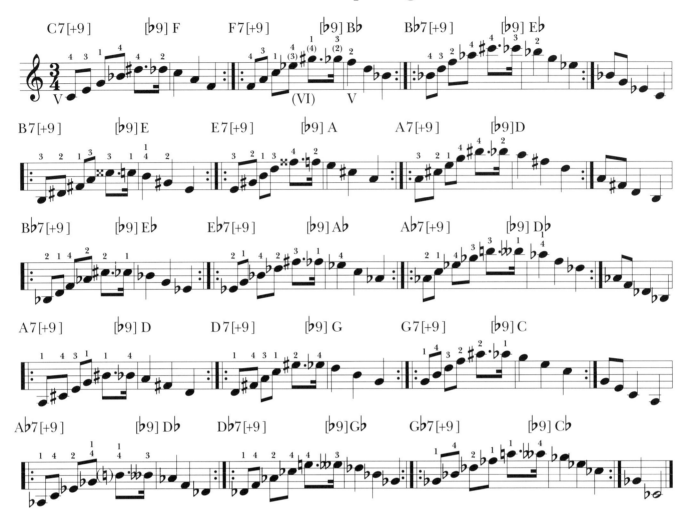

Harmonizing a Melody—From a Lead Sheet with Chords Indicated

Think of the melody as being written an octave higher. Add the most important chord tones under it that are physically available.

To attempt to play a chord for every melody note is impractical, and it denies you one of the most striking effects of guitar chord-melody playing—that of a moving melody over sustained chord tones.

E♭ Major Scale (Twelve Positions)

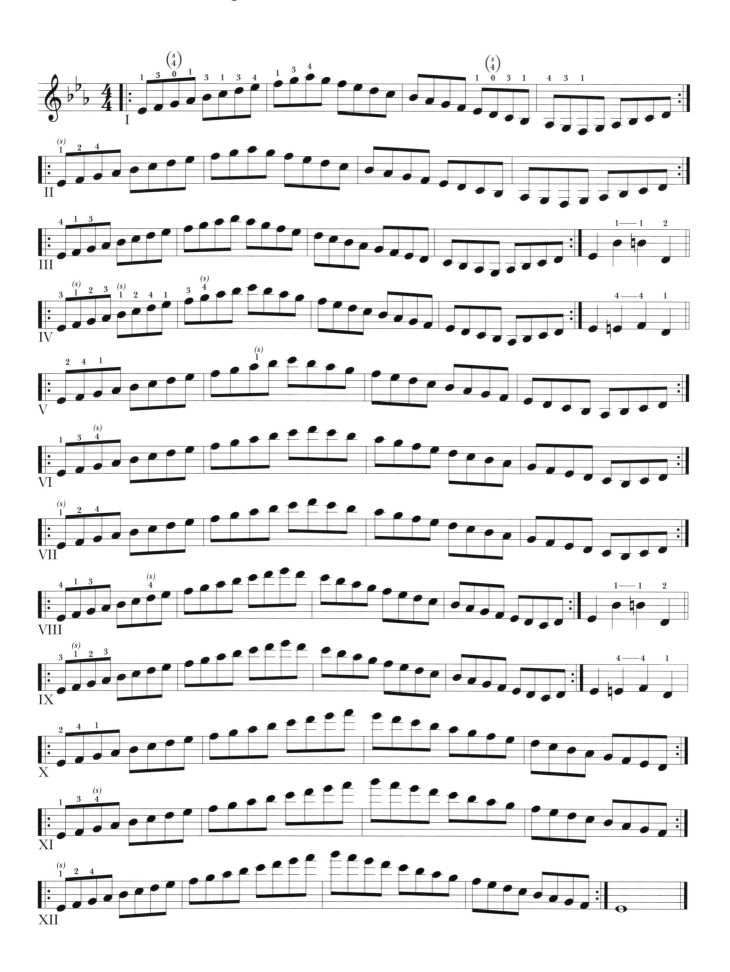

C Harmonic Minor (Nine Positions)

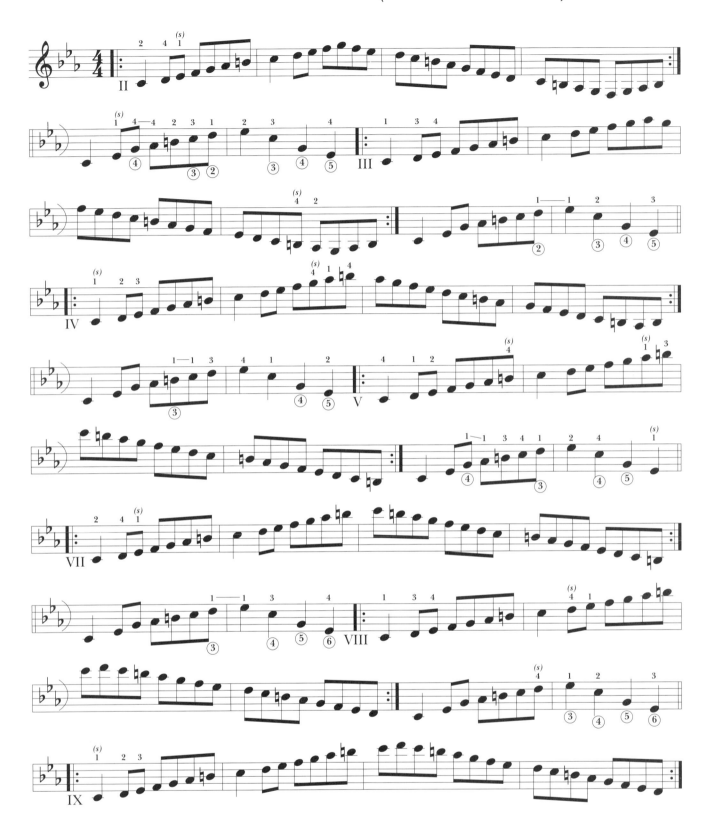

Track 29

Etude in C Minor (solo)

Chord-Scale Relationships

For improvisation.

Remember: Look ahead to the next chord to analyze a progression. Look back to the preceding chord to determine the related scale.

Major Chords

Major chords with scale tone roots (except IV) represent a tonic sound. Scale = major from chord name.

The IV chord and all major structures with non-scale tone roots represent the subdominant sound. Scale= Major from 5th degree of chord.

All major chords will accept being melodized as IV chords. But realize that the +11 is being forced on those that normally represent the tonic sound.

Also be advised that very occasionally, a nondiatonic major chord with a scale tone root represents a modal sound. That is, the writer wants only the major triad harmonically, but the melodic tones are to be the same as those used with a dominant 7 structure of the same letter name.

Minor 7 Chords

All minor 7 chords represent the subdominant sound of IIm7 (for IV), except IIIm7, VIm7, and VIIm7, which represent tonic sounds. IIIm7 and VIm7 are diatonic substitutions for I. VIIm7 = IIIm7 for I (key of the dominant).

IIm7	Major scale from ♭7 of chord
IIIm7 and VIm7 (for I)	Major scale from name of tonic chord being replaced
VIIm7 (as IIIm7 for I)	Major scale from name of tonic chord being replaced

A comparison of minor 7 chords with their related major 6 chords (containing the same notes) will reveal some second choice VIm7-for-I relationships. Scale = Major from name of related major 6 chord.

Note: All second choice scale relationships must be handled with care.

Chords—Three-Note Voicings
Minor-Major 7 and 6 Chords—Close and Open Voicings

MAJOR 7TH AND 6TH IN THE LEAD

5TH IN THE LEAD   **♭3RD IN THE LEAD**

MAJOR 7TH AND 6TH COMBINED IN SAME VOICING

MAJOR 7TH AND 6TH IN LEAD   **6TH AND 5TH IN LEAD**

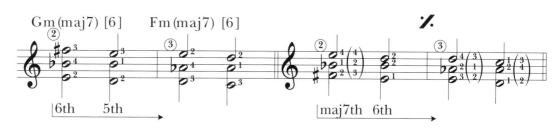

Minor 6, Minor-Major 7 Chords—Open Voicings, All Inversions

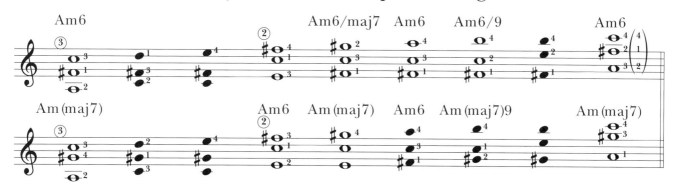

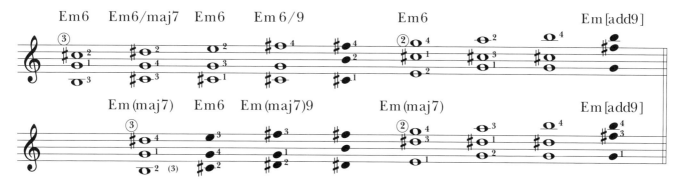

131

Five-Note Arpeggios
Dominant 7 (+5, +9), Dominant 9 (+5), and Dominant 7 (+5, ♭9) Chords
Chord Spelling

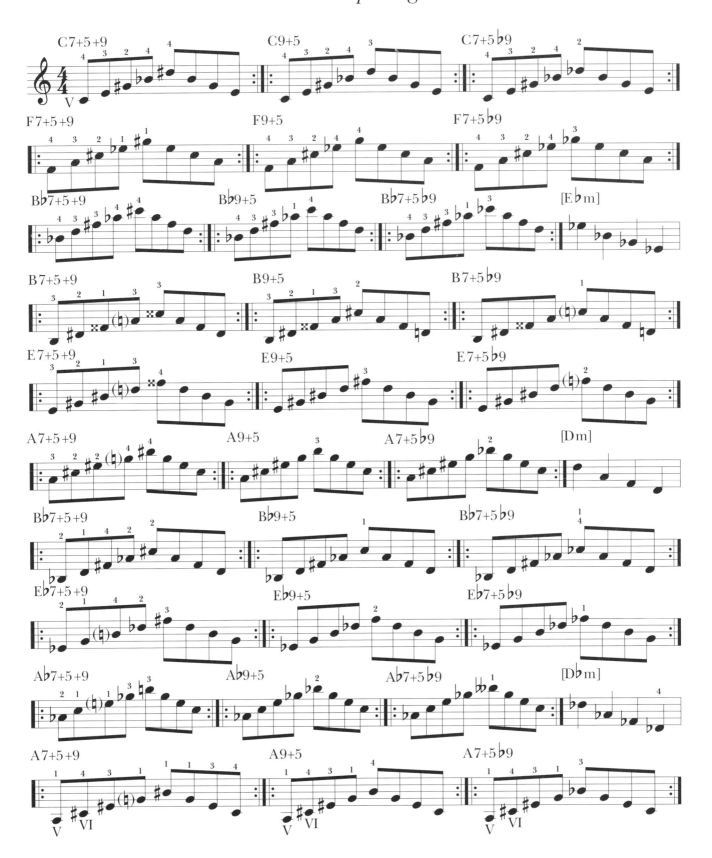

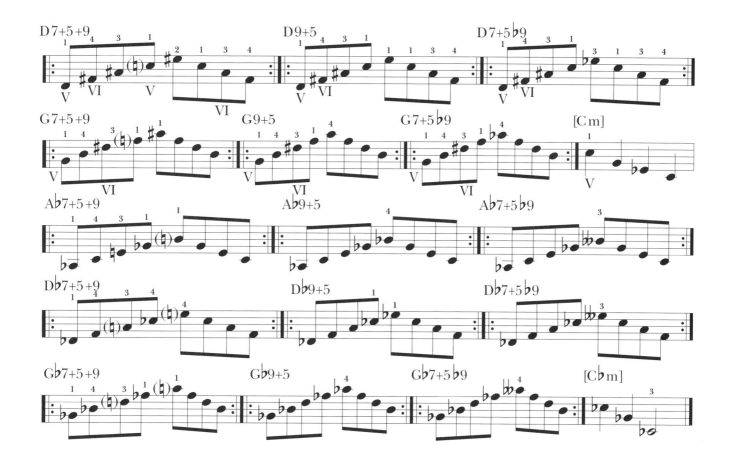

Chords—Three-Note Voicings
Melodization of I Minor Chords with Harmonic Minor Scale

Melodic degrees: Harmonic minor scale from chord name

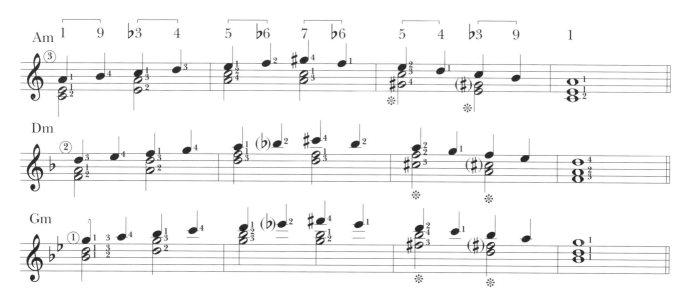

✳ Major 7 necessary as an undervoice

Melodization of IIm7(♭5) Chords with Harmonic Minor Scale

Melodic degrees: Harmonic minor scale from ♭7 of chord

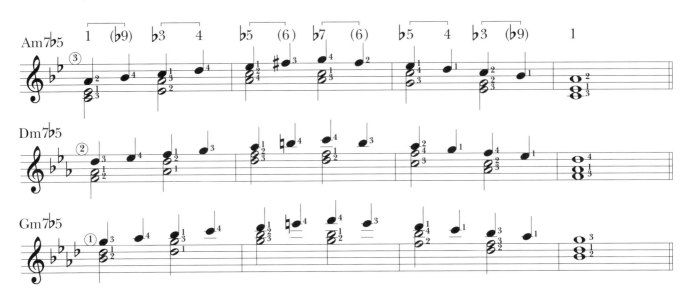

Melodization of Dominant 7 Chords with Harmonic Minor Scale

Melodic degrees: Harmonic minor scale from intended tonic

$\circledast$ = ♭9 for undervoice

135

Teeah-Wanna
Optional Duet with Rhythm Guitar

The notes contained in the bottom staves of the following study represent the chord-scale relation-ships. They are to be played with the rhythm guitar part (not the melody) to further acquaint the ear with these related sounds.

Moderate 4
Latin

To aid in the analysis of the preceding chord-scale relationships, observe the following numerical breakdown.

I	/	/	/	VII7	/	/	/	I	/	/	/	III7	/	/	/
VI9	/	/	/	**1.** II7	/	V7	/	IIIm7	/	♭III7	/	IIm7	/	V7♭9	/ :‖
2. II7	/	V7	/	I	/	/	/	I7	/	/	/	‖ IV7	/	/	/
IV7	/	/	/	I	/	IIm7	/	I	/	IIIm7	♯I°	II7	/	/	/
II7	/	/	/	IIm7	/	/	/	V9+5	/	/	/	‖ I	/	/	/
VII7	/	/	/	I	/	/	/	III7	/	/	/	VI9	/	/	/
II7	/	V7	/	I	/	♭VII7	/	I	/	/	⁀	‖			

137

Rhythm Guitar—The Right Hand

Moderately fast
Paso Doble 1

Moderately fast
Paso Doble 2

Chord Study—Minor 7 with ♭5 (Chromatic Approach) in the Bass

Five-Note Arpeggios
Minor (maj 7, 9) and Dominant 7(♭5, ♭9) Chords
Chord Spelling

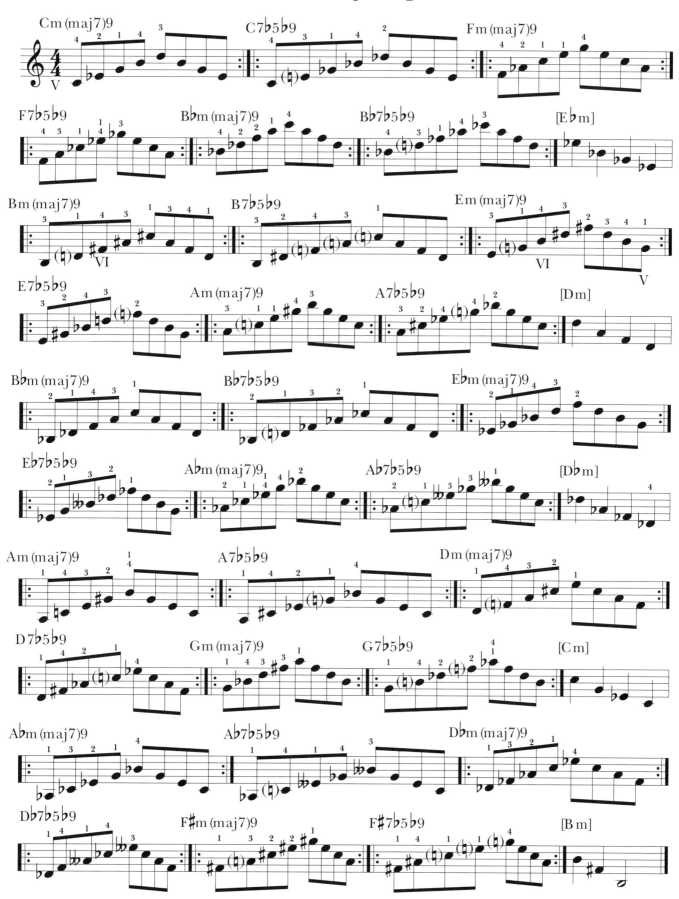

Chord-Scale Relationships

For improvisation.

Minor 6 Chords

All minor 6 chords can be considered as representing the subdominant or tonic minor sound. Scale = Real melodic minor from chord name. (However, IIm6, Vm6, and VIm6 will sound slightly forced. See next relationship.)

IIm6, Vm6, VIm6 are best treated as representing the dominant sound of IIm6 for V9. Scale = major from a whole step below the minor 6 chord.

A comparison of other minor 6 chords with their related dominant 9 chords (containing the same notes) will reveal that IIIm6, #IVm6, VIIm6, and #Im6 can also be treated as IIm6 for V9. But the scale for this harmonic situation is real melodic minor from a whole step below the minor 6 chord.

Minor 7(♭5) Chords

Minor 7(♭5) chords most frequently represent the dominant sound of VIIm7(♭5) for V7. IIIm7(♭5), #IVm7(♭5), VIIm7(♭5) = Major scale from half step above chord.

All other minor 7(♭5) chords represent the subdominant or tonic minor sounds of IIm7(♭5) (for IVm6) or VIm7(♭5) (for Im6) = Real melodic minor from ♭3 of chord.

A comparison of minor 7(♭5) chords with non-scale tone roots (except #IV) with their related dominant 9 structures will reveal some second choice chord-scale relationships. Scale = Real melodic minor from half step above min 7(♭5).

(Ex: #Im7(♭5) = VI9, #IIm7(♭5) = VII9, #Vm7(♭5) = III9, #VIm7(♭5) = #IV9)

Also a minor 7(♭5) chord represents the II chord in a minor key. It is often treated as a "package deal" with the V7 of that minor key when it is the next chord. Example: Bm7(♭5) to E7 = The harmonic (or natural) minor scale for both chords. (It is always the option of the player to treat the chords in this situation as one unit or independently.)

A Major Scale (Twelve Positions)

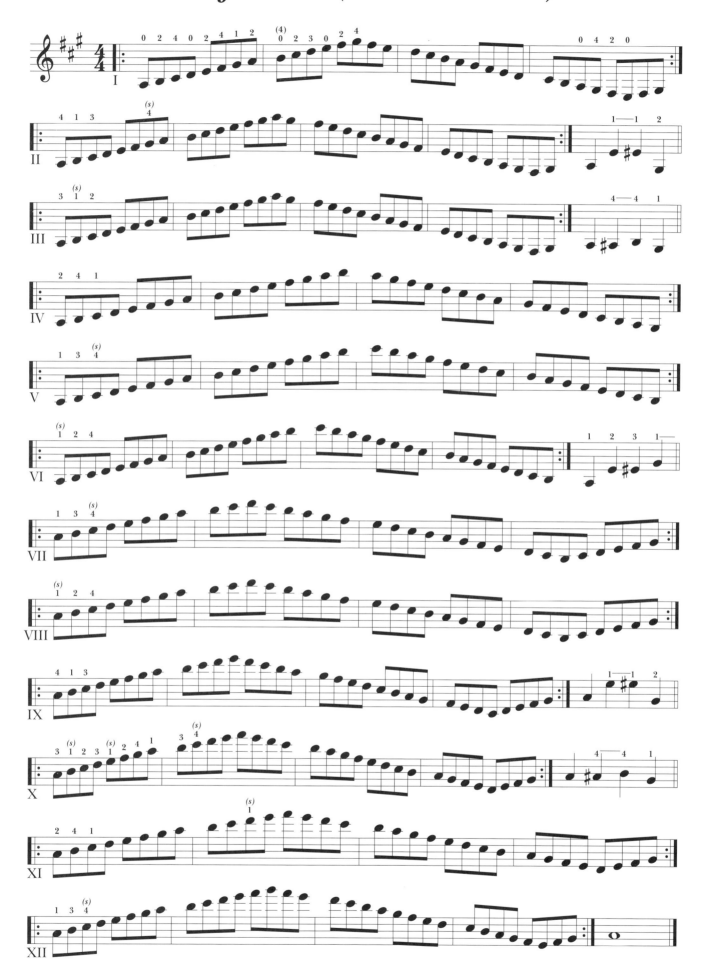

141

F# Harmonic Minor (Nine Positions)

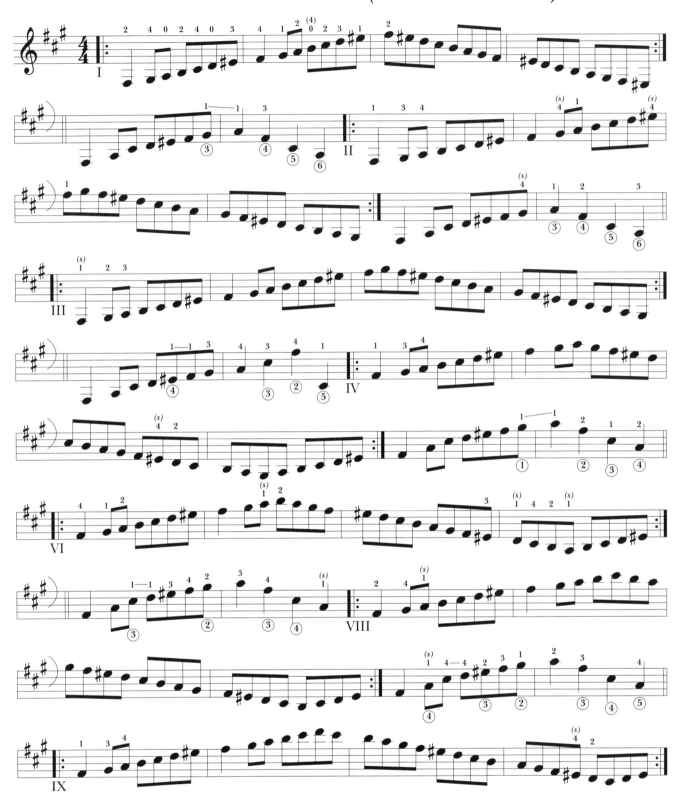

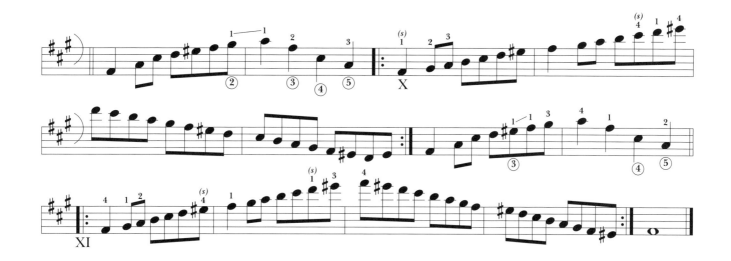

Track 35

F# Minor Etude (solo)

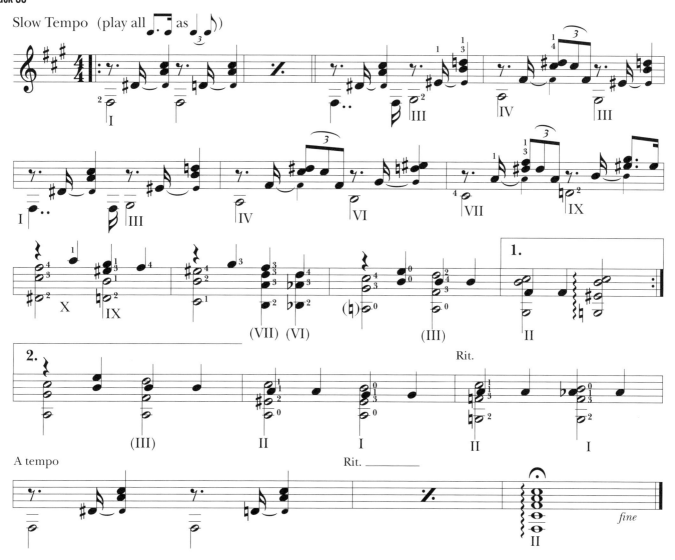

143

Five-Note Arpeggios
Dominant 7(♭9)sus4 and Dominant 9(♭5)
Chord Spelling

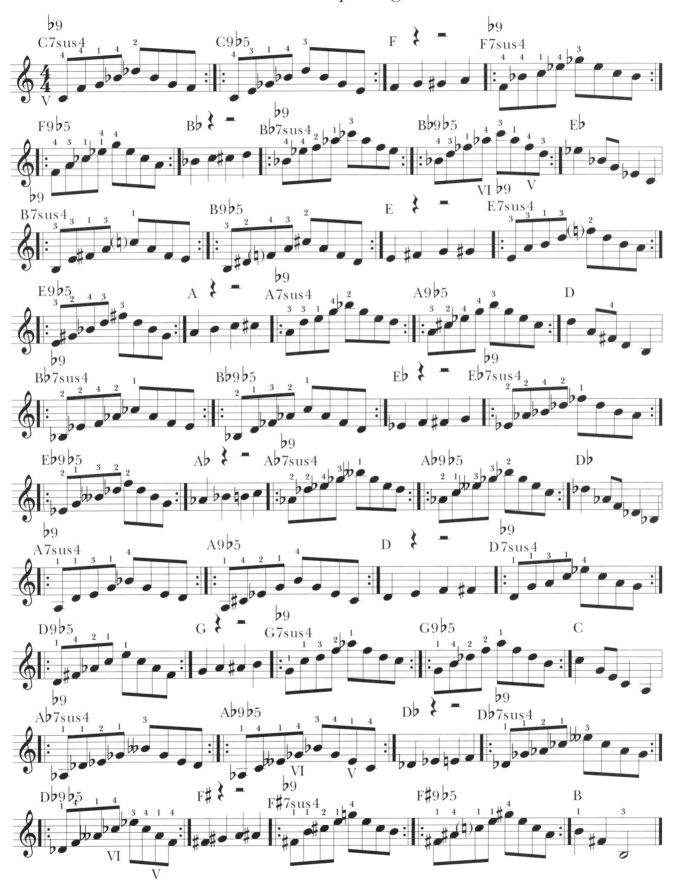

144

Chords—Three-Note Voicings
Study in F Major

Study in F Harmonic Minor

Five-Note Arpeggios
Dominant 7(+9)sus4 and Dominant 7(♭5, +9) Chords
Chord Spelling

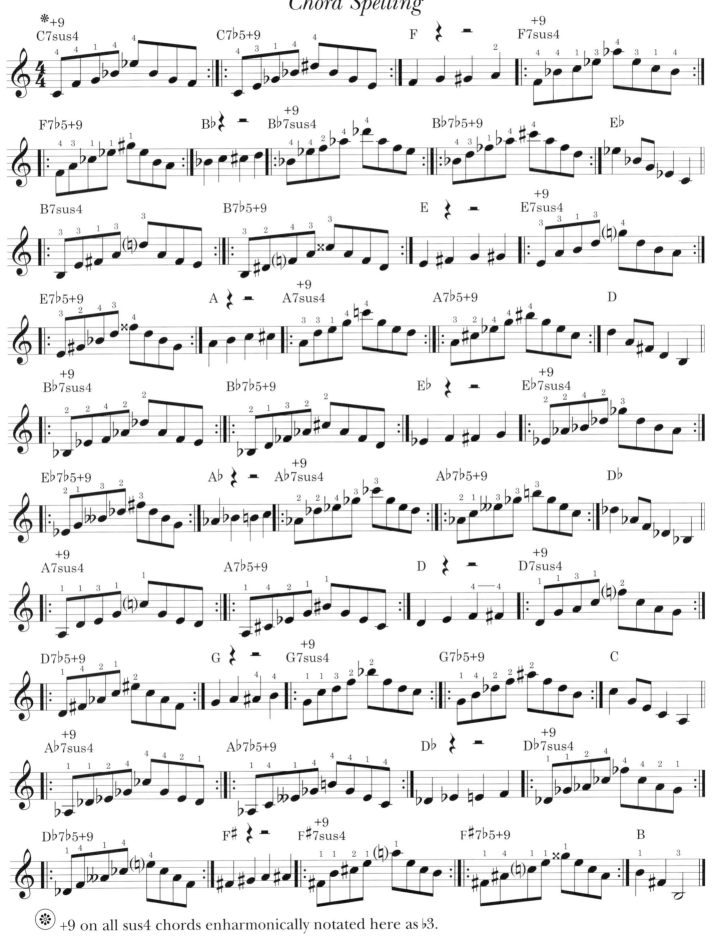

✳ +9 on all sus4 chords enharmonically notated here as ♭3.

Additional Fingerings for Minor Scales

These fingerings are less practical for general use, as they will not accommodate as many interval combinations as those presented earlier.

The principal fingerings shown are a result of the alterations on the major scale fingering type from which the minor scale is derived.

The optional fingerings (shown in parentheses) suggest some of the combinations possible when fingering types are mixed. When all fingerings have been mastered by thorough and precise study, you can and will do this without conscious effort.

Real Melodic Minor

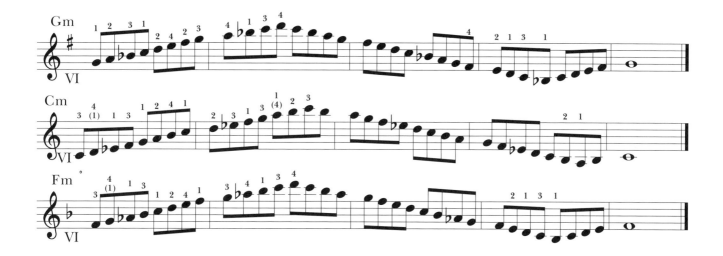

Harmonic Minor

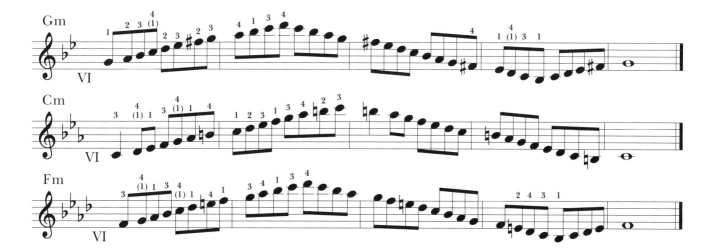

Chord-Scale Relationships

For improvisation.

Diminished 7 Chords

▌ All diminished 7 chords will accept a diminished scale from any chord tone. (In most cases, these are not perfect relationships.)

▌ Be advised that diminished 7 chord names are frequently misleading, in that most of the time they indicate only part of a larger harmonic structure. (The related scale remains hidden until the name of the complete chord is realized.)

▌ The following will help in the proper treatment of diminished 7 chords.

▌ Any diminished 7 chord that can be analyzed as:

#I° almost always = VI7(♭9)   (Occasionally #I° = I7(♭9))

II° almost always = III7(♭9)   (Occasionally II° = V7(♭9))

I° is usually a true diminished 7,   (Occasionally I° = II7(♭9))
but is more musical when
melodically treated as VII7(♭9).

▌ Also note: As all dominant 7(♭9) chords contain a diminished 7 built on 3, 5, ♭7, and ♭9 of the dominant 7, they will accept melodization with diminished scales from these notes. This chord-scale relationship is imperfect, but the uniformity of sound makes it work.

Augmented Triads

▌ Augmented triads are primarily melodized with the whole tone scale from any chord tone (including 9).

▌ As I and IV are the only scale degrees on which augmented structures could occur as strict triads, note the following relationships:

- I+ can be melodized with a harmonic or real melodic minor scale from a minor 3rd below the chord name. You may also use the real melodic minor from the intended tonic.

- IV+ can be melodized with the real melodic minor from a minor 3rd below.

▌ Be advised that an augmented triad on anything other than I or IV is an incompletely named chord. Include the 7th in your analysis of these structures to determine the related scale.

Preparation of Four-Part Open Voicings
Adding the 5th Degree to Three-Part Open Voicings

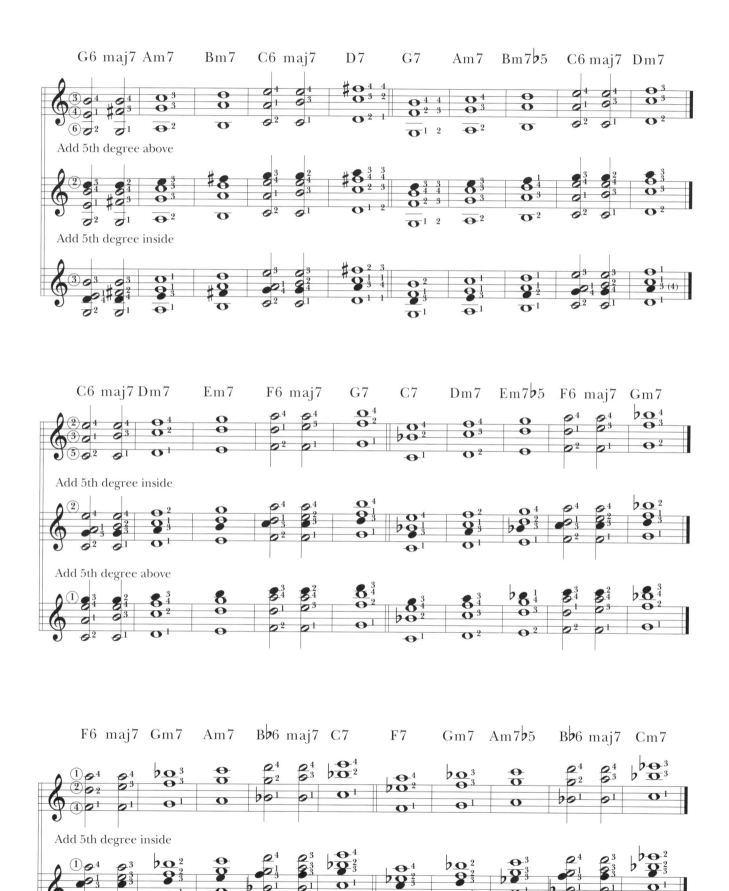

Preparation of Four-Part Open Voicings
Adding the Root to Three-Part Open Voicings

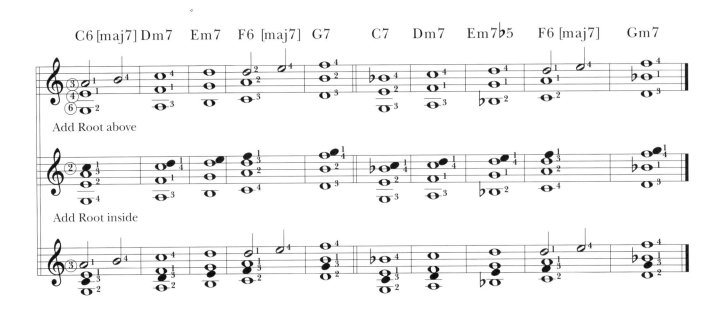

Add Root above

Add Root inside

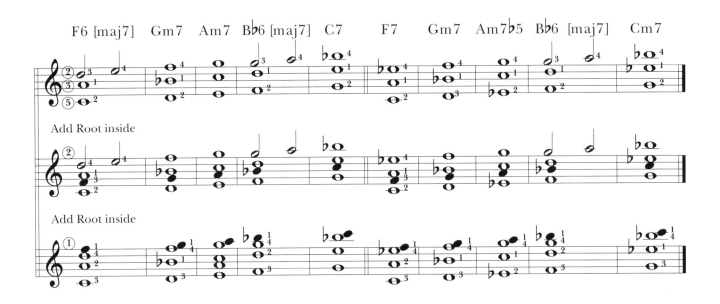

Add Root inside

Add Root inside

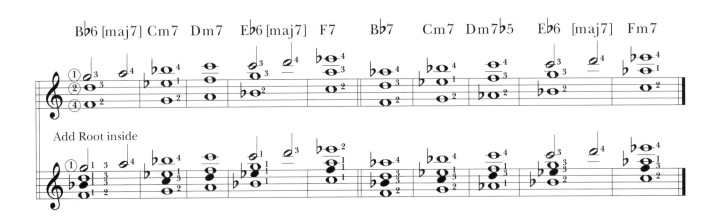

Add Root inside

Five-Note Arpeggios
Minor 9(♭5) Chords
Chord Spelling

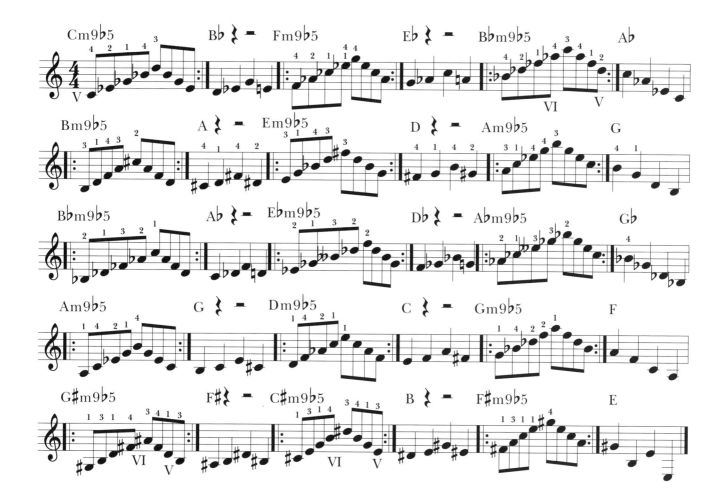

About Improvisation

Chord-scale relationships provide you with all the raw material (both melodic and harmonic) for any chord structure in any situation, but they will not make music for you.

In the final analysis, consideration must be given to each chord, for they contain a variety of sounds, such as the "warm" notes (3 and ♭7), the "bland" ones (1 and 5), and the various tensions and altered degrees that add the "sparkle" and/or the "buzz." Variety is certainly a factor in interesting music.

Also, very important are the "lines" that exist in a chord progression. These lines, resulting from the chromatic and scalewise movement of the inner voices of chords, form a solid basis for the creation of secondary melodies (especially valuable in comping.) Look for the chromatic motion that occurs between chords. Look for the tension and resolve possibilities available on each structure, for these are the pretty notes on which to build melodic ideas.

It's Late

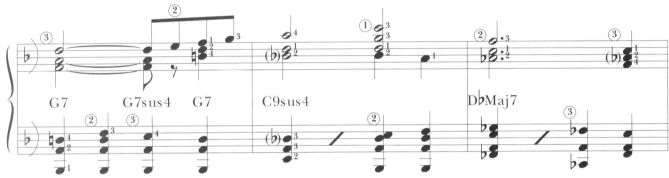

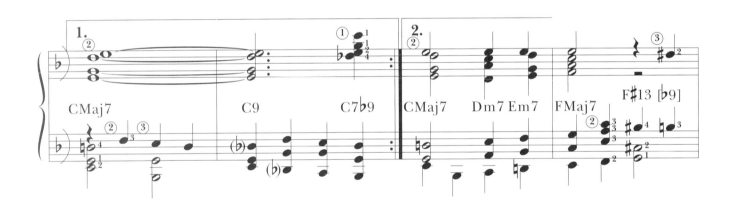

Preparation of Four-Part Open Voicings
Adding the 3rd Degree to (Very Incomplete) Open Voicings

Because these voicings have the 7th (or 6th) degree as the bottom note, tonality must be established before using them.

No 3rd degree present—use with discretion:

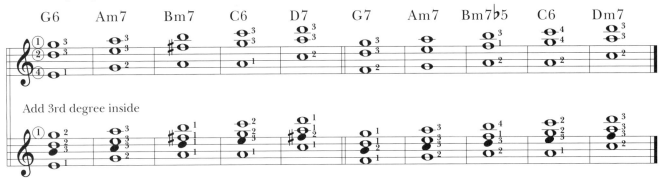

No 3rd degree present—use with discretion:

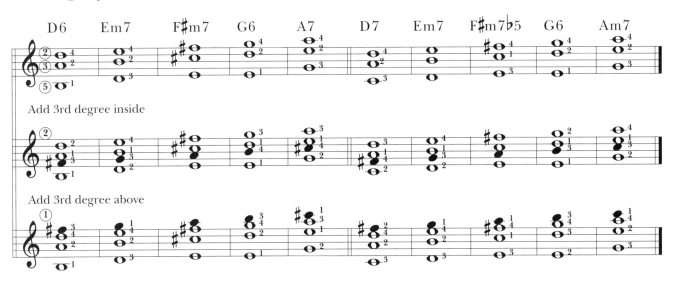

No 3rd degree present—use with discretion:

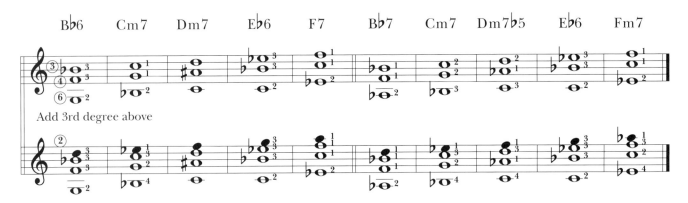

Be especially careful of these 7ths (or 6ths) on the bottom in the low register. Observe rules for use.
(See *Vol. II,* pg. 100.)

Preparation of Four-Part Open Voicings
Adding the 7th Degree to Three-Part Open Voicings

No 7th degrees present:

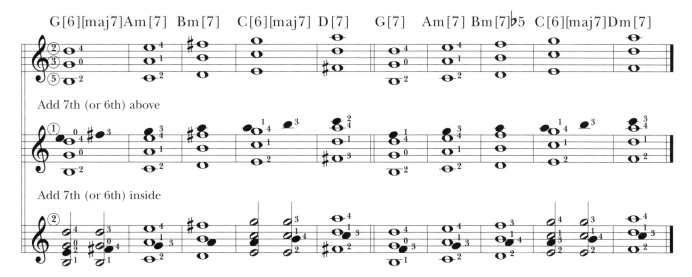

No 7th degrees present:

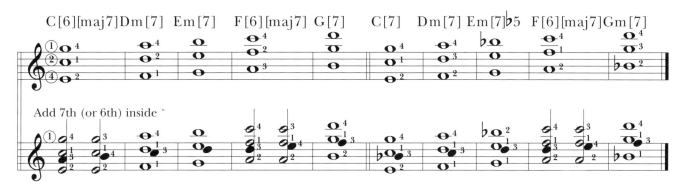

Scale-Chord Relationships
Major Scales

1. All diatonic structures in a major key.

2. All nondiatonic major chords with scale tone roots except IV, use the scale from chord name.

3. IV and all major chords with non-scale tone roots, use the scale from the 5th degree of the chord. (Note: This also includes all major chords with indicated +11 and is a second choice for the above-mentioned major chords with scale tone roots.)

4. All nondiatonic minor 7 chords (except VIIm7) usually function as IIm7. Use the scale from the ♭7 of the chord. (Note: VIIm7 is IIIm7 for I. Also note: A comparison of nondiatonic minor 7 structures with their related major 6 chords will reveal some second choice VIm7-for-I relationships.)

5. I7, II7, and all 13th chords with scale tone roots, except IV7, use the scale from the intended tonic.

6. III7, VI7(♭9), VII7 (second choice), use the scale from a major 3rd below the chord name. This can also be considered a natural minor scale from the intended tonic. (Note: The scale does not include the 3rd degree of the chord, and some melodic patterns may require the addition of this note.)

Harmonic Minor Scales

1. All diatonic structures in a minor key.

2. III7, VII7, VI7(♭9) (in a major key), use the scale from the intended tonic.

3. Diminished 7 chords that can be analyzed as I°, treat as VII7.
   Diminished 7 chords that can be analyzed as ♯I°, treat as VI7(♭9).
   Diminished 7 chords that can be analyzed as II°, treat as III7.

4. All dominant 7 chords with altered 9 and ♭13 (or ♯5 considered as ♭13), use the scale from the intended tonic.

5. I aug (I+) triad (second choice), use the scale from a minor 3rd below.

Real Melodic Minor Scales

1. IVm6 and Im6, use the scale from chord name.

2. IIm7(♭5) (occurring in a major tonality) treat as IVm6.

3. IV7 and all dominant 7 chords with non-scale tone roots, use the scale from the chord 5th. (Note: This is also a second-choice relationship for all dominant 7 chords, except IV7, with scale tone roots.)

4. All dominant 9 chords with specified +11 and 13, also I7(+11), II7(+11), V7(+11) (or ♭5 considered +11), scale from chord 5th.

5. All dominant 9ths with ♭13 (or ♯5 considered as ♭13), use the scale from the intended tonic. (Note: This includes VI7, III9, and VII9, each of which has a built-in ♭13.)

6. All completely altered dominant 7 chords (this means alt 9 and 5), use the scale from the ♭9 of the chord. This includes III7 (alt 5) and VII7 (alt 5), as they have a built-in altered 9. (Note: This can be a second choice of scale relationship for III7, VI7(♭9), and VII7 without the indicated alt 5 because of the built-in alterations of 9 and/or 13, and the fact that ♭13 can sometimes be treated as ♯5, or in this case, alt 5. However, the relationship is imperfect, so handle with care.)

7. I7(♭9), II7(♭9), V7(♭9), and all dominant 13(♭9) (or alt 9) chords with scale tone roots (except IV7), use the scale from the ♭7 of the chord. (Note: Scale does not contain the 3rd degree of the chord. Some melodic patterns may require the addition of this note.)

8. These do not occur very often. Use very cautiously:
Diminished 7 chords that can be analyzed as I°: treat as II7(♭9).
Diminished 7 chords that can be analyzed as ♯I°: treat as I7(♭9).
Diminished 7 chords that can be analyzed as II°: treat as V7(♭9).

9. I+ and IV+: Triads (second choice), use the scale from a minor 3rd below. I+ triad (second choice), use the scale from the intended tonic.

Whole Tone Scales

All major and dominant 7(♯5) (or alt 5), use the scale from any chord tone. (Note: The 9th must be unaltered in these structures. Whole tone scales are especially necessary for augmented dominant 7 chords with non-scale tone roots.

Diminished Scales

1. Diminished chords that can be analyzed as I°, use the scale from chord tones. (Note: This is theoretically more perfect than the previously mentioned treatment as VII7, but less musical.)

2. Diminished 7 chords that can be analyzed as ♯I° and II°, use the scale from chord tones. (Note: These are less perfect than the VI7(♭9) and III7 treatment, and less musical.)

3. IV7(♭9) and all dominant 7(♭9) chords with non-scale tone roots, use the scale from 3, 5, ♭7, ♭9 of chord. (Note: All dominant 7(♭9) chords may be treated in this manner with varying degrees of imperfection, however the consistent intervals of the scale will hold things together.)

4. All augmented 11(♭9) (or alt 9) chords, use the scale from 3, 5, ♭7, ♭9 of chord.

Remember: Look ahead to the next chord to analyze a progression.
Look back to the preceding chord to determine the related scale.

Index

SCALES

SOLOS

SPEED STUDIES

THEORY

More Fine Publications

GUITAR

BEBOP GUITAR SOLOS
by Michael Kaplan
00121703 Book $16.99

BLUES GUITAR TECHNIQUE
by Michael Williams
50449623 Book/Online Audio........... $27.99

BERKLEE GUITAR CHORD DICTIONARY
by Rick Peckham
50449546 Jazz – Book..........................$14.99
50449596 Rock – Book........................$12.99

BERKLEE GUITAR STYLE STUDIES
by Jim Kelly
00200377 Book/Online Media...........$24.99

CLASSICAL TECHNIQUE FOR THE MODERN GUITARIST
by Kim Perlak
00148781 Book/Online Audio..............$19.99

CONTEMPORARY JAZZ GUITAR SOLOS
by Michael Kaplan
00143596 Book..$16.99

CREATIVE CHORDAL HARMONY FOR GUITAR
by Mick Goodrick and Tim Miller
50449613 Book/Online Audio............$22.99

FUNK/R&B GUITAR
by Thaddeus Hogarth
50449569 Book/Online Audio............$19.99

GUITAR SWEEP PICKING
by Joe Stump
00151223 Book/Online Audio $19.99

INTRODUCTION TO JAZZ GUITAR
by Jane Miller
00125041 Book/Online Audio.............$22.99

JAZZ GUITAR FRETBOARD NAVIGATION
by Mark White
00154107 Book/Online Audio.............$22.99

JAZZ SWING GUITAR
by Jon Wheatley
00139935 Book/Online Audio............$24.99

METAL GUITAR CHOP SHOP
by Joe Stump
50449601 Book/Online Audio $19.99

A MODERN METHOD FOR GUITAR – VOLUMES 1-3 COMPLETE*
by William Leavitt
00292990 Book/Online Media $49.99
Individual volumes, media options, and supporting songbooks available.

A MODERN METHOD FOR GUITAR SCALES
by Larry Baione
00199318 Book..$14.99

READING STUDIES FOR GUITAR
by William Leavitt
50449490 Book.. $17.99

Berklee Press publications feature material developed at Berklee College of Music.
To browse the complete Berklee Press Catalog, go to
www.borklooprocs.com

BASS

BERKLEE JAZZ BASS
by Rich Appleman, Whit Browne & Bruce Gertz
50449636 Book/Online Audio........... $22.99

CHORD STUDIES FOR ELECTRIC BASS
by Rich Appleman & Joseph Viola
50449750 Book.. $17.99

FINGERSTYLE FUNK BASS LINES
by Joe Santerre
50449542 Book/Online Audio............$19.99

FUNK BASS FILLS
by Anthony Vitti
50449608 Book/Online Audio $22.99

INSTANT BASS
by Danny Morris
50449502 Book/CD................................ $9.99

METAL BASS LINES
by David Marvuglio
00122465 Book/Online Audio.............$19.99

READING CONTEMPORARY ELECTRIC BASS
by Rich Appleman
50449770 Book.......................................$22.99

ROCK BASS LINES
by Joe Santerre
50449478 Book/Online Audio........... $22.99

PIANO/KEYBOARD

BERKLEE JAZZ KEYBOARD HARMONY
by Suzanna Sifter
00138874 Book/Online Audio............$29.99

BERKLEE JAZZ PIANO
by Ray Santisi
50448047 Book/Online Audio $22.99

BERKLEE JAZZ STANDARDS FOR SOLO PIANO
arr. Robert Christopherson, Hey Rim Jeon, Ross Ramsay, Tim Ray
00160482 Book/Online Audio $19.99

CHORD-SCALE IMPROVISATION FOR KEYBOARD
by Ross Ramsay
50449597 Book/CD $19.99

CONTEMPORARY PIANO TECHNIQUE
by Stephany Tiernan
50449545 Book/DVD...........................$29.99

HAMMOND ORGAN COMPLETE
by Dave Limina
00237801 Book/Online Audio............$24.99

JAZZ PIANO COMPING
by Suzanne Davis
50449614 Book/Online Audio............$22.99

LATIN JAZZ PIANO IMPROVISATION
by Rebecca Cline
50449649 Book/Online Audio $29.99

PIANO ESSENTIALS
by Ross Ramsay
50448046 Book/Online Audio $24.99

SOLO JAZZ PIANO
by Neil Olmstead
50449641 Book/Online Audio...........$42.99

DRUMS

BEGINNING DJEMBE
by Michael Markus & Joe Galeota
00148210 Book/Online Video..............$16.99

BERKLEE JAZZ DRUMS
by Casey Scheuerell
50449612 Book/Online Audio............$24.99

DRUM SET WARM-UPS
by Rod Morgenstein
50449465 Book..$14.99

A MANUAL FOR THE MODERN DRUMMER
by Alan Dawson & Don DeMichael
50449560 Book..$14.99

MASTERING THE ART OF BRUSHES
by Jon Hazilla
50449459 Book/Online Audio............$19.99

PHRASING
by Russ Gold
00120209 Book/Online Media $19.99

WORLD JAZZ DRUMMING
by Mark Walker
50449568 Book/CD...............................$22.99

BERKLEE PRACTICE METHOD

GET YOUR BAND TOGETHER
With additional volumes for other instruments, plus a teacher's guide.
Bass
by Rich Appleman, John Repucci and the Berklee Faculty
50449427 Book/CD $24.99
Drum Set
by Ron Savage, Casey Scheuerell and the Berklee Faculty
50449429 Book/CD $17.99
Guitar
by Larry Baione and the Berklee Faculty
50449426 Book/CD................................$19.99
Keyboard
by Russell Hoffmann, Paul Schmeling and the Berklee Faculty
50449428 Book/Online Audio............$19.99

VOICE

BELTING
by Jeannie Gagné
00124984 Book/Online Media...........$22.99

THE CONTEMPORARY SINGER
by Anne Peckham
50449595 Book/Online Audio........... $27.99

JAZZ VOCAL IMPROVISATION
by Mili Bermejo
00159290 Book/Online Audio.............$19.99

TIPS FOR SINGERS
by Carolyn Wilkins
50449557 Book/CD $19.95

VOCAL WORKOUTS FOR THE CONTEMPORARY SINGER
by Anne Peckham
50448044 Book/Online Audio $24.99

YOUR SINGING VOICE
by Jeannie Gagné
50449619 Book/Online Audio...........$29.99

WOODWINDS & BRASS

TRUMPET SOUND EFFECTS
by Craig Pederson & Ueli Dörig
00121626 Book/Online Audio............$14.99

SAXOPHONE SOUND EFFECTS
by Ueli Dörig
50449628 Book/Online Audio..........$15.99

THE TECHNIQUE OF THE FLUTE
by Joseph Viola
00214012 Book.................................$19.99

STRINGS/ROOTS MUSIC

BERKLEE HARP
by Felice Pomeranz
00144263 Book/Online Audio..........$24.99

BEYOND BLUEGRASS BANJO
by Dave Hollander and Matt Glaser
50449610 Book/CD.............................$19.99

BEYOND BLUEGRASS MANDOLIN
by John McGann and Matt Glaser
50449609 Book/CD $19.99

BLUEGRASS FIDDLE & BEYOND
by Matt Glaser
50449602 Book/CD.............................$19.99

CONTEMPORARY CELLO ETUDES
by Mike Block
00159292 Book/Online Audio............$19.99

EXPLORING CLASSICAL MANDOLIN
by August Watters
00125040 Book/Online Media..........$24.99

THE IRISH CELLO BOOK
by Liz Davis Maxfield
50449652 Book/Online Audio.......... $27.99

JAZZ UKULELE
by Abe Lagrimas, Jr.
00121624 Book/Online Audio............$22.99

WELLNESS

**MANAGE YOUR STRESS AND PAIN
THROUGH MUSIC**
*by Dr. Suzanne B. Hanser and
Dr. Susan E. Mandel*
50449592 Book/CD $34.99

MUSICIAN'S YOGA
by Mia Olson
50449587 Book $19.99

NEW MUSIC THERAPIST'S HANDBOOK
by Dr. Suzanne B. Hanser
00279325 Book..................................$29.99

MUSIC PRODUCTION & ENGINEERING

AUDIO MASTERING
by Jonathan Wyner
50449581 Book/CD $29.99

AUDIO POST PRODUCTION
by Mark Cross
50449627 Book $19.99

CREATING COMMERCIAL MUSIC
by Peter Bell
00278535 Book/Online Media $19.99

**THE SINGER-SONGWRITER'S GUIDE
TO RECORDING IN THE HOME STUDIO**
by Shane Adams
00148211 Book...................................$19.99

UNDERSTANDING AUDIO
by Daniel M. Thompson
00148197 Book...................................$42.99

MUSIC BUSINESS

CROWDFUNDING FOR MUSICIANS
by Laser Malena-Webber
00285092 Book..................................... $17.99

ENGAGING THE CONCERT AUDIENCE
by David Wallace
00244532 Book/Online Media...........$16.99

**HOW TO GET A JOB IN THE MUSIC
INDUSTRY**
by Keith Hatschek with Breanne Beseda
00130699 Book..................................... $27.99

MAKING MUSIC MAKE MONEY
by Eric Beall
00355740 Book $29.99

MUSIC INDUSTRY FORMS
by Jonathan Feist
00121814 Book $16.99

MUSIC LAW IN THE DIGITAL AGE
by Allen Bargfrede
00366048 Book $24.99

MUSIC MARKETING
by Mike King
50449588 Book $24.99

**PROJECT MANAGEMENT FOR
MUSICIANS**
by Jonathan Feist
50449659 Book $34.99

THE SELF-PROMOTING MUSICIAN
by Peter Spellman
00119607 Book....................................$29.99

CONDUCTING

CONDUCTING MUSIC TODAY
by Bruce Hangen
00237719 Book/Online Media...........$24.99

MUSIC THEORY & EAR TRAINING

BEGINNING EAR TRAINING
by Gilson Schachnik
50449548 Book/Online Audio........... $17.99

**BERKLEE CONTEMPORARY MUSIC
NOTATION**
by Jonathan Feist
00202547 Book $24.99

BERKLEE MUSIC THEORY
by Paul Schmeling
50449615 Book 1/Online Audio.......$24.99
50449616 Book 2/Online Audio.......$24.99

CONTEMPORARY COUNTERPOINT
by Beth Denisch
00147050 Book/Online Audio..........$24.99

MUSIC NOTATION
by Mark McGrain
50449399 Book...................................$24.99
by Matthew Nicholl & Richard Grudzinski
50449540 Book...................................$24.99

REHARMONIZATION TECHNIQUES
by Randy Felts
50449496 Book...................................$29.99

SONGWRITING/COMPOSING

BEGINNING SONGWRITING
by Andrea Stolpe with Jan Stolpe
00138503 Book/Online Audio..........$22.99

COMPLETE GUIDE TO FILM SCORING
by Richard Davis
50449607 Book....................................$34.99

THE CRAFT OF SONGWRITING
by Scarlet Keys
00159283 Book/Online Audio..........$22.99

**CREATIVE STRATEGIES IN
FILM SCORING**
by Ben Newhouse
00242911 Book/Online Media.......... $27.99

JAZZ COMPOSITION
by Ted Pease
50448000 Book/Online Audio $39.99

MELODY IN SONGWRITING
by Jack Perricone
50449419 Book...................................$24.99

**MUSIC COMPOSITION FOR
FILM AND TELEVISION**
by Lalo Schifrin
50449604 Book...................................$39.99

POPULAR LYRIC WRITING
by Andrea Stolpe
50449553 Book $16.99

THE SONGWRITER'S WORKSHOP
by Jimmy Kachulis
Harmony
50449519 Book/Online Audio $29.99
Melody
50449518 Book/Online Audio $24.99

SONGWRITING: ESSENTIAL GUIDE
by Pat Pattison
Lyric Form and Structure
50481582 Book....................................$19.99
Rhyming
00124366 Book....................................$22.99

SONGWRITING IN PRACTICE
by Mark Simos
00244545 Book...................................$16.99

SONGWRITING STRATEGIES
by Mark Simos
50449621 Book $24.99

ARRANGING & IMPROVISATION

ARRANGING FOR HORNS
by Jerry Gates
00121625 Book/Online Audio............$22.99

BERKLEE BOOK OF JAZZ HARMONY
by Joe Mulholland & Tom Hojnacki
00113755 Book/Online Audio $29.99

**IMPROVISATION FOR
CLASSICAL MUSICIANS**
by Eugene Friesen with Wendy M. Friesen
50449637 Book/CD $24.99

MODERN JAZZ VOICINGS
by Ted Pease and Ken Pullig
50449485 Book/Online Audio..........$24.99

AUTOBIOGRAPHY

**LEARNING TO LISTEN: THE JAZZ
JOURNEY OF GARY BURTON**
by Gary Burton
00117798 Book.....................................$34.99

Berklee Online

Study Music Online with Berklee

Gain the skills and credentials to advance your music career with Berklee Online's award-winning courses, certificates, bachelor's, and master's degree programs.

Study Areas Include:

- Music Production
- Songwriting
- Music Business
- Performance
- Music Theory
  And more!

online.berklee.edu | 1-866-BERKLEE |